INDIGENOUS TORONTO

STORIES THAT CARRY
THIS PLACE

EDITED BY
DENISE BOLDUC
MNAWAATE GORDON-CORBIERE
REBEKA TABOBONDUNG
BRIAN WRIGHT-MCLEOD

COACH HOUSE BOOKS, TORONTO

first edition

Published with the generous assistance of the Canada Council for the Arts and the Ontario Arts Council. Coach House Books also acknowledges the support of the Government of Canada through the Canada Book Fund and the Government of Ontario through the Ontario Book Publishing Tax Credit.

LIBRARY AND ARCHIVES CANADA CATALOGUING IN PUBLICATION

Title: Indigenous Toronto : stories that carry this place / edited by Denise Bolduc, Mnawaate Gordon-Corbiere, Rebeka Tabobondung, Brian Wright-McLeod.
Names: Bolduc, Denise, editor. | Gordon-Corbiere, Mnawaate, editor. | Tabobondung, Rebeka, editor. | Wright-McLeod, Brian, editor.
Identifiers: Canadiana (print) 20210125640 | Canadiana (ebook) 20210125705 | ISBN 9781552454152 (softcover) | ISBN 9781770566453 (EPUB) | ISBN 9781770566460 (PDF)
Subjects: LCSH: Indigenous peoples—Ontario—Toronto—History. | LCSH: Indigenous peoples—Ontario—Toronto—Social life and customs. | LCSH: Indigenous peoples—Ontario—Toronto—Intellectual life. | LCSH: Toronto (Ont.)—History. | LCSH: Toronto (Ont.)—Social life and customs. | LCSH: Toronto (Ont.)—Intellectual life. | LCSH: Toronto (Ont.)—Civilization.
Classification: LCC E78.O5 I53 2021 | DDC 971.3/54100497—dc23

Indigenous Toronto: Stories that Carry This Place is available as an ebook: ISBN 978 1 77056 645 3 (EPUB); ISBN 978 1 77056 646 0 (PDF)

Purchase of the print version of this book entitles you to a free digital copy. To claim your ebook of this title, please email sales@chbooks.com with proof of purchase. (Coach House Books reserves the right to terminate the free digital download offer at any time.)

Dedicated to the trailblazers, ancestors, language speakers, lands, waterways, animals, nations, contributors, and generations yet to come, as well as those, past and present, whose stories are not included in this book.

In memory of Gregory George Younging, 1961–2019.

TABLE OF CONTENTS

RISING LIKE A CLOUD: NEW HISTORIES OF 'OLD' TORONTO

HAYDEN KING

Every year for the past few, my family and some close friends have travelled a few hours east of Toronto to Presqu'ile Provincial Park. Amid the Explorer RVs, CanRock from competing portable speakers, and smog from dozens of campsites burning green wood, we listen to the waves of Lake Ontario and watch our kids run and laugh and grow together.

The first of these trips included a visit to the lighthouse at Presqu'ile, where we also found a small historical archive of the peninsula, which is famous for its treacherous waters and shipwrecks. There is a plaque here, too, recognizing the HMS *Speedy*, lost in a snowstorm in 1804. The ship was transporting the accused Anishinaabe murderer Ogetonicut and his prosecutors from York (Toronto) to Newcastle (Brighton).

This incident was a devastating blow to a young colony, as members of York's ruling class (a justice and lawyers, a royal surveyor, the first solicitor-general of Upper Canada), plus six handwritten constitutions of Upper Canada, were lost.

I've since spent a lot of time thinking about this plaque, sitting with the uneasy reality of colonial expansion into our territories, to places like Presqu'ile and beyond. Toronto is unique in that sense. It is the heart of empire in Anishinaabe Aki, source of the flood of colonialism that moved through time and across space, bringing a physical infrastructure with it, but also a narrative of radiating 'progress.' What we find in historical plaques and texts is a Toronto – and a Canada – void of Indigenous people, except as criminals or ghosts, doomed like Ogetonicut in the darkness.

But what if Ogetonicut had lived, swimming to the familiar shore his captors could not see?

In the basement of my mother-in-law's Mississauga home is a small archive. Carol would not call herself a historian, but she understands more about Toronto's history than anyone else I know. When I was asked to write a chapter for this book, my first thought was of that archive: dozens of books on the history of Toronto that I had been keen for so long to crack and hate-read. Over a few weeks in the late summer of 2020, I did just that, sharing frustration with my sympathetic Torontophile mother-in-law.

I got familiar with Henry Scadding and John Ross Robertson, Edith Grace Firth and Eric Arthur, Mike Filey and Allan Levine – the noted Toronto historians across the eras, among many others. Despite works spanning 150 years, remarkably similar themes reoccurred in their telling of Toronto's early history. I am most interested in these early years, the genesis of Toronto, because that story frames all that follows. And, by and large, it is the only era of Toronto's history where Indigenous people appear.

The story proceeds along these lines: 1) there were probably some Indians in the Toronto area at one time, but with limited presence; 2) the actual discovery of Toronto was by Étienne Brûlé, aided by some Indians, and ostensibly on behalf of the French during their limited possession; 3) finally, the Englishman John Graves Simcoe arrived with his wife and son to carve Toronto out of the lakeshore as the Indians watched.

Between the lines, the corresponding themes revolve around the land being 'empty' and free for the taking; if any Indigenous people were here, they were of little consequence; and the Indians were childlike in the shadow of greatness. Taken together, this narrative serves a purpose: obscuring Indigenous presence, agency, language, and, perhaps most importantly, a contemporary existence (which reinforces all that comes before) to justify a settler colonial Toronto. This is the cycle and nature of erasure.

'OLD TORONTO'

The grandfathers of Toronto historians are undoubtedly Henry Scadding and John Ross Robertson. Both call their reflections on early history 'Old Toronto,' as if the 'pre'-Toronto history is somehow still possessed by the city. Interestingly, works by both men have been reproduced and/or edited into distilled volumes repeatedly, with mentions of Indigenous people or communities largely removed. Perhaps this editing was for the sake of more sensitive modern readers who might take offence at the language of 'savages.'

That being said, later writers differed little in their treatment of Indigeneity. In 1971, G. P. deT. Glazebrook wrote that the story of Toronto is the story of a 'town dropped by the hand of government into the midst of a virgin forest. For the site chosen no record exists of earlier habitation although small groups of Indians may have at one time lived not far from it.' Meanwhile, YA author Claire Mackay in 1991 wrote that 'this is the story of a city and how it grew: from an unknown and unpeopled place …'

Journalist Allan Levine's 2001 take is slightly more sympathetic, if general and with an enduring ethnocentrism. '[T]he Great Lakes region was home to nomadic hunters whose lives were governed by the seasons and supply of animals,' he wrote. 'Though these hunting and gathering societies were primitive, they had developed their own traditions, culture, and spiritual beliefs …'

This theme of *terra nullius* – where Indigenous people may have called what became Toronto home, but only during the Stone Age – is expanded as the history goes on.

BRÛLÉ'S BABY

The hero of 'Old Toronto' in the consensus history of Toronto is Étienne Brûlé.

Evidence for that heroism is bolstered by stereotypes. Levine explains that as 'Brûlé continued his explorations … he was captured by the Seneca. They tortured him, a sign of respect from the Iroquois' point of view. He managed to win his release by convincing them that a thunderstorm was a symbol of a higher power watching over him; or perhaps the Senecas hoped that he would help them make peace with the French …'

Levine doesn't cite his source for this childlike gullibility of the Seneca, nor their supposed respect for Brûlé. Nonetheless, the fable infantilizes the Seneca so they can be instrumentalized to venerate Brûlé.

Levine is not alone in this. Architect Eric Arthur is perhaps the most romantic of the Toronto historians. 'We can stand where Étienne Brûlé stood on a September morning in 1615,' he wrote in *Toronto: No Mean City*.

'To the south he would look on the great lake, its waves sparkling in the autumn sunshine, its farther shore remote and invisible. To that lonely traveller, the first of his race to set eyes on Lake Ontario, the sight must have been no less awe-inspiring than that which, under poetic license, Cortez saw from his peak ...'

The link to Cortez here is an obvious celebration and ode to the rightness of colonization. But this is all permissible because Arthur also peddled the empty-land narrative. After sparing one whole paragraph for the lives and humanity of those non-white people, nomadic fishermen and women, another paragraph is spent on the conflicts that 'emptied' Southern Ontario, allowing for the guilt-free exploration by Brûlé and later settlement by Simcoe, et al.

But alas, poor Brûlé, 'after some years among the Indians of Toronto, was murdered and likely eaten by them,' speculated the politician-pundit William Kilbourn in 1984.

SIMCOE STREET

John Graves Simcoe was a Cortez-like figure himself. The man was responsible for claiming land and erasing dozens – maybe hundreds – of Indigenous place names in much of the Toronto region and replacing them with the names of English men, many of which persist to this day. Notably, Simcoe's renaming of Toronto as 'York' was one that didn't stick.

Even without the embellishment of historians, Simcoe was a deeply colonial figure: he sailed on a schooner named the *Mississauga*[1] and slept in Captain James Cook's tent, E. C. Kyte notes in the 1954 edited version of Robertson's *Landmarks*. How it was retrieved after Cook's death while attempting to invade Kanaka Maoli territory, I do not know.

But like Brûlé, Simcoe gets the 'founder' treatment. The narrative of the ceremonial naming of the city is so similar in the Toronto history canon that multiple distinct authors appear virtually indistinguishable:

'When John Graves Simcoe landed on the marshy shore of Toronto Harbour in 1763, there were only a few just-finished huts marking the rude beginnings of the new capital of Upper Canada' (Bailey, 1984). But 'amid the beat of drums and crash of falling trees' (Innes, 2007) and 'in front of a small audience that included Mrs. Simcoe, ready as ever to support her husband (and) their young son Francis held in the arms of an old Indian delighted with the loud noise (Glazebrook, 1971), 'Simcoe christened his town site York. This was after the Duke of York, later Commander in Chief of the Army' (Firth, 1962).

In this version of the story, the 'old Indian' is to Simcoe what the Seneca were to Brûlé: passive elements of the scenery, their silence implying a sanction of 'civilization.'

RETURN OF THE RISING CLOUD

An accurate spelling of 'Ogetonicut' is Okaanakwad. The translation is 'Rising Cloud' or 'Rising Cloud Man.' It is unclear if colonial record-keepers knew the pronunciation and translation of Okaanakwad or if they cared. Considering that he was simply a prop in the colonial story of Toronto, like so many others, it is not surprising that his life was treated with disrespect.

After all, he was merely a criminal, though one whom the 'progressive' historians at least acknowledge was avenging a wrong: the murder of his kin by a white trader, John Sharp. Colonial officials had promised Okaanakwad – in the presence of Pontiac, among others – that the trader would be prosecuted. But when delays made prosecution unlikely, Okaanakwad sought out Sharpe himself, according to legal historian Brendan O'Brien in his 1992 account of the case. Soon after the confrontation, Okaanakwad was arrested in Toronto, charged, and bound in the hull of the *Speedy* to face trial in Newcastle.

As books on the history of Toronto move out of the early 'discovery' years and toward settlement, the mentions of Indigenous people thin. Exceptions are cases like these, where Indigenous people are noted as criminals who must be brought to heel. This is actually common in colonial settings. Australian historian Lisa Ford, in her 2010 study *Settler Sovereignty*, argued that colonial authority in New South Wales (Australia) and Georgia (United States) became formalized by criminalizing Indigenous people and installing 'law and order' in the colonies. It appears that was the case in Toronto, too, and it is reflected in historical narratives.

In that sense, the Toronto historians are complicit. The harms of colonization occur in many registers but include discourses of disappearance and the rightness of foreign rule at the expense of Indigenous life, repeated and reprinted in volumes of self-serving text. While alternative histories are emerging in the work of Victoria Freeman and Jennifer Bonnell, among others, it has to be acknowledged that the histories of

Toronto are typically histories (and historians) of violence.

We endure nonetheless. This book is a reflection of that endurance and a helpful corrective to settler fantasies. It tells a more balanced account of Anishinaabe, Haudenosaunee, and Wendat communities, then and now. It offers the space for us to reclaim our ancestors' language and legacy, rewriting ourselves back into a landscape from which non-Indigenous historians have worked hard to erase us.

But we are there in the skyline and throughout the Greater Toronto Area (GTA), along the coast and in all directions. I'll be back at Presqu'ile again soon, too, sitting with friends and trying to calm our wild children so we can share a new story of Okaanakwad, one about how we swam to shore.

(Thanks are owed to Carol Hepburn, Susan Blight, Angie King, Jeff Monague, and Vanessa Watts for their support, advice, and insight on this chapter.)

A NOTE ON SPELLING

Regarding terms or phrases in Anishinaabemowin, Kanien'kehá:ka, or any other Indigenous language that appears in these pages, there may be variations in spelling and grammar. This diversity is common among Indigenous authors and attributable to regional dialects or simply the result of translating orality to text. While there are standardized writing systems for most Indigenous languages, the editors have chosen to defer to the authors' preferred spelling and grammar.

AGREEMENTS, NAMING, AND PLACES

REMEMBER LIKE WE DO

ANGE LOFT

The following essay includes excerpts from 'Indigenous Context and Concepts,' which was prepared for the Toronto Biennial of Art in 2019. This non-authoritative conceptual document was geared toward the curatorial staff and international artists' cohort. Amidst overarching themes of collectivity and connectivity to the waterfront, I drafted a vision of the city through the lens of Indigenous alliances, governance, symbolism, and mnemonic devices.

I drew heavily on the research from the Talking Treaties project, an art-based research initiative to share and reflect Indigenous presence and knowledge in Toronto, initiated in 2015 with Jumblies Theatre and Arts. The excerpts are interrupted by ongoing thoughts, prompts for more research, and reflective activities from Talking Treaties' forthcoming illustrated workbook, A Treaty Guide for Torontonians. *Though certainly not exhaustive, these excerpts speak to the capacity of Indigenous ways of remembering in relating the agreements between our nations.*

Authority around Toronto's Indigenous narratives is a complex subject, as layered as the settlement history of the city. This was, historically, a place of bounty. It was a seasonal meeting place, a place for trade and ongoing council. It's been a place where Indigenous Nations have come together to remember and relate going back thousands of years. Toronto did a lot of forgetting to become what it is today. All rivers were renamed, 'requickened,' first in French and then again in the English image. Maps were updated, stripping away thousands of years of land-based knowledge. Though the name 'York' tried, the Indigenous title 'Toronto' won.

There's one theatre workshop I facilitate where I begin by placing a map and a small stuffed beaver on a table. It's an old map, drafted by the French for this area, from the time period when the Seneca had Teiaiagon and Ganatsekwyagon. It will show the Carrying Place leading up to Lake Simcoe,

Map of the Toronto Carrying Place, 1619–1793, C.W. Jefferys.

where it says 'Lac De Taronto.' Why is the word *Toronto* based on a Mohawk word for a Wendat/Neutral fishing practice, taken from the time when there were predominantly Seneca settlements in the area? Go back to why the French marked those weirs on their maps, and to why the English sat right on top of those spots later. There was a lot to be gained here. We start there with access to beavers and the need for keeping up alliances.

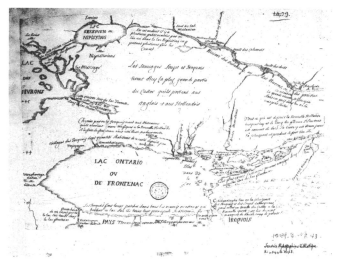

'Carte des Grands Lacs,' 1680, Abbé Claude Bernou.

THE KNOT THAT BINDS US

To the Haudenosaunee, the term used for the Covenant Chain had a meaning associated with clasped arms. There is an arm gesture, which involved grasping the forearms, which was commonly used to mean binding friendship. To show this union at an early pact for peace on the St. Lawrence, a French priest described a Haudenosaunee diplomat who: *Took hold of the Frenchman, placed his arms within his, and with his other arm, clasped that of the Algonquin, calling it the knot that binds us.*[1]

The linkage between the Haudenosaunee and the English was originally described as hands bound together with rope. This metaphor changed over time, because the bond could break. The concept was strengthened, imagined as a chain cast in iron, but that chain would rust with time and was too common. The Covenant Chain was cast in silver. To prevent it from tarnishing, it would have to be polished. The rhetorical interpretation of the connection between them changed over time.

Canada, made up of two European nations, has some big commitments it is avoiding. Does the federal government remember the Indigenous alliances made with the French? The name carried on for the French representative is Onontio, Mohawk for 'great mountain.' Onontio promised to mediate quarrels and provide supplies, too. What about the agreements made with the English crown? Do they know about the roles the English took up from the Dutch?

CORLAER REQUICKENED

Chiefs were often namesakes of others, carrying forward the legacy of the previous line of name holders. The fifty Chiefs of the Haudenosaunee have each their own name and insignia upheld since their confederation. The continuity of title is related to the condoling and naming practice of *Requickening*. The title of *Corlaer* was the name of the original negotiator on the Dutch side of the Two Row Wampum agreement with the Mohawk in 1613. The name continued to be used by Haudenosaunee and Anishinaabe even after the English took New York and assumed the Dutch role in alliance. This act allows the name of the deceased to be passed on along to a successor, with the roles and responsibilities of the prior name holder.

Does Canada know the duties of the names it picked up along the way? Does anyone there have time to learn? Who are their knowledge keepers? We know that the power is going to change hands, and decision makers will forget, on both our side and on the federal government's side. When we are in conflict with Canada, we are continually pointing to the symbols that bind us. We hold up our flags and adorn our bodies with reminders of our governance structures. In enacting unity between our nations and protecting each other, we show them that we remember our part of the story and that they are in the act of ignoring us.

ACTIVITY

Draw a rough outline of Lake Ontario in the centre of the page.

Start from as far back in time as you can imagine, origin stories welcome.

Plot the 'Ancestral Homelands' of the Neutral, the Wendat, the Seneca, Haudenosaunee, Mississaugas of the Credit, Anishnawbe, and any other nations you may be aware of having called this territory home.

Use the internet to research archaeological settlement sites, shifts of populations around Toronto, and forced relocations of each Nation. Plot the current locations of each Nation. Use symbols and gestural drawing to get across the spirit of the movement.

Add diamond shapes to indicate places of council and meeting.

Copy it on a fresh page without Lake Ontario present, zooming in or out to fit the shape to the page. Look at the resulting network as though it were an abstract artwork. Title it.

TKARONTO

Toronto/Tkaronto/Aterón:to/Tsi Tkarón:to roughly translates from Mohawk to *over there is the place of the submerged tree or trees in the water.* The word has been variously translated to *abundance* or *a place of plenty* in Wendat, then attributed to mean the meeting place. A French cartographer in 1680 wrote, *Lac Taronto at Lake Simcoe, north of the city.* Mnjikaning, *the place of the fish fence,* refers to the narrows between Lake Simcoe and Lake Couchiching, where remnants of a 4,500-year-old weir still stand. Other early French maps show variations of *Toronto* written along a few rivers leading through the current city into Lake Ontario, clearly indicating the frequency of weir fishing in and around the city, a factor in the founding of the French and English trade forts in the region. Hundreds of fishing camps have been located along flats of Toronto's rivers.

The name of the city has been highly disputed. For a long time, it was believed to mean *abundance* or *a place of plenty* in Wendat, then attributed to mean the meeting place. Every nation that lived here knew about the weirs. This would have been a place where the rules of the Dish with One Spoon would have applied, I imagine. The French took note of these places to hang nets and spear fish with ease.

I learn a lot about Indigenous Toronto through social media. Layers of contemporary voices have contributed to a more rounded understanding of the city's name and all the political complexity it carries. I picked up the Mohawk word *Tsi Tkarón:to,* 'over there is the place of the submerged tree,' from a social media post. The Seneca villages were right along the lakefront, and many of the old Wendat sites are upriver, north of Davenport Road, so 'over there' would make sense. This also indicated the presence of Mohawk people at the predominantly Seneca sites. It is clear to me that I will never fully grasp these descriptors without investing in my language.

When I started the research phase for Talking Treaties in 2015, I thought I'd be able to draw a clear picture for myself around the Indigenous agreement-making narratives in the city. Years later, I'm still digging my way through documents and oral narratives with more questions than answers. How much original source material must I carry with me? I know these written documents cannot be trusted alone. I worry about getting stuck on mistranslations. I can only get answers by having language speakers, knowledge keepers, anthropologists, and geo-mythologists all in one room. What essential understandings do I need first, before picking up these words? Can the Eurocentric scribe's choices ever represent the Indigenous spirit of intent? How can anyone be so confident in their assertions of text over context? What am I doing with all this information?

AND SO BE ONE

In 1700, the Haudenosaunee were at a trade meeting in Albany, New York, where they let the English know of the Anishinaabe call for peace, and to be united under the Dish with One Spoon.

We have come to acquaint you that we are settled on Ye North side of Cadarachqui Lake near Tchojachiage [Teiaiagon] where we plant a tree of peace and open a path for all people, quite to Corlaer's house [Schenectady], and desire to be united in Ye Covenant Chain, our hunting places to be one, and to boil in one kettle, eat out of one spoon, and so be one; and because the path to Corlaer's house may be open and clear, doe give a drest elke skin to cover Ye path to walke upon.

The Haudenosaunee answered:

We are glad to see you in our country, and do accept of you to be our friends and allies, and do give you a Belt of Wampum as a token thereof, that there may be a perpetual peace and friendship between us and our young Indians to hunt together in all love and amity.[2]

I spoke at an action blocking the train tracks for #ShutDownCanada in February 2020. I never speak publicly at those actions, but I went ahead and talked about the application of the teaching in the Dish with One Spoon to our personal relationship to resource extraction. The agreement is a gesture of regional genius born of the fact that this is a very rich territory. Everyone has the right to eat and sustain their lives, but there are some rules. I wondered, aloud, if it was too far-flung to apply the teachings of the Dish to the role and duty of the federal government in relation to environmental policy. The Eurocentric preoccupation with individual choice would be overridden by the dictates of the land.

GREAT PEACE

In 1701, the kettle was shared at the Great Peace of Montreal, orchestrated by the French. Thirty-six Indigenous nations sent representatives to negotiate a halt in fighting, including the Mississaugas. The beaver supplies had dramatically decreased due to overhunting and tensions between nations would often result in disputes in the common hunting grounds. Together, these nations confirmed an agreement: they would not kill each other if they met in common space.

At this meeting, the Mississaugas of the Toronto area were represented by Onanguice, Chief of the Potawatomi. He asked the Haudenosaunee to eat from the same kettle when they met on the hunt. Their relationship, now, when in common space, would be of trust and equality; they would look to each other as relatives. They had a shared common interest, that of the security and preservation of their way of life. The French presented a large dish of meat to the gathered chiefs. At this meeting, no specific territory was defined or rules laid out, but a common understanding was reached to share use of the hunting grounds.

And what of the French legacy of alliance with regional Indigenous Nations? Addressing the French king as Father implied a duty to protect and provide. As the English moved into the old French forts in Toronto, they also took up the task of continuing to provide gifts to Indigenous partners. With the Treaty of Paris, forged so far from Toronto, the King of England assumed the role of the dad, soon providing new rules for land cessions and trade.

The ideas in the Dish with One Spoon have been held up to bring us together in the face of European thought dominance. Odawa Chief Pontiac activated the Dish to unite Indigenous Nations against the incursion of English rules around the time of the Royal Proclamation in 1763. Seeking to solidify Indigenous alliances, English representative Sir William

Johnson must have been aware of the Dish as he designed the symbolism used in 1764's Treaty of Niagara, the wampum-based translation of the Royal Proclamation delivered from the English.

Although it's unclear if Johnson's Mohawk partner, clan mother Molly Brant, was involved in devising the acts of political theatre that made Niagara successful, the speeches and embodied acts of alliance-making were drenched in Indigenous metaphorical language. Was the shared vision of the Dish used to strengthen the words delivered at Niagara? How did the English understand the Indigenous conception of shared hunting territory at this time? It is still unclear to me whether the English ever saw themselves as partners in the Dish. Did we see them this way?

The Dish with One Spoon might be referenced on the 1764 Niagara belt. There is a theory that those Dish-shaped hexagons on the belt are places the English intended to 'polish the chain' that binds us, to return to talk. The hexagons might be representations of significant British forts at the time, one being the house of Molly Brant and William Johnson. There was a commitment made at Niagara to continue talking, to remember past agreements on a regular basis, and for the Crown to protect its Indigenous allies against frauds and abuses on their lands.

As Canada picked up the crown, did it also keep hold of these promises of protection? Could I discuss the Covenant Chain and the 1764 Treaty of Niagara in the context of the train blockades of 2020? I watched a press conference about Wet'suwet'en solidarity actions by the Band Council Mohawk Chiefs, and they remembered the agreement at Niagara. They mentioned the 1764 belt right off the top.

ACTIVITY – CO-CREATED WITH JILL CARTER

The Dish with One Spoon wampum is an agreement to take only what is required and to make sure that all living things are able to sustain their lives. This includes caring for the waters and their ecosystems – the soil, the rocks, the vegetation, the mammals, and the birds. The Dish with One Spoon is wide-reaching and covers much of the Great Lakes region, the north shore of the St. Lawrence River, and parts of New York and Michigan.

Some contemporary readings of the Dish with One Spoon bring up three key teachings that mediate how we should conduct ourselves in shared or contentious spaces. These teachings can be summarized as:

take only what you need, keep it clean, and leave some for the future. These can be viewed as ways to govern sharing with others, but also as self-regulating mechanisms for guiding our daily choices.

Take two blank sheets of paper.

Divide one page into four long columns.

Label the headings of each column: Shared Stuff, Take Only What You Need, Keep It Clean, and Leave Some for the Future.

Fill column 1 with Shared Stuff: words and/or symbols representing goods in life that sustain us, including common spaces and resources.

Here are some examples of Shared Stuff: rare books, bike shares, wild berries, public parks, precious metals, seafood, office kitchens, an Elder's time, a campground, waterfront access, intergenerational wealth, food-bank food.

Think up ways to apply each of the three teachings (the headings for columns 2, 3, and 4) to each item in the Shared Stuff column. Explore these concepts as though you were making policies to regulate physical and conceptual commodities. Make notes in text or symbols for each subject. Repeat for the rest of the Shared Stuff you have listed.

Configure the second page into three sections in any way you wish. Each of these sections corresponds to one of the three teachings: take only what you need, keep it clean, and leave some for the future.

Choose one item from the Shared Stuff column to focus on.

Rearticulate the item's management plan through symbols and illustrations, creating a step-by-step how-to visual guide for the sharing. Title it. Put it somewhere you will notice it.

The first page is your working document, your source for subsequent rearticulations. Keep this for the future. Repeat as many times as you like, addressing each of your Shared Stuff items.

A DIFFERENT KIND OF FOOD

The question of whether Europeans had ever formally entered into the Dish treaty remains. The Seven Nations of Canada, a group of Indigenous Christian-allied communities, including some Haudenosaunee, Wendat, and Anishinawbe, delivered a speech to the English around their understanding of sharing the Dish in 1794:

> When the King of France set foot on our ground he did not conquer us, he came as a Father who wishes to protect his Children. We communicated to him a parable of the Dish and the Spoon, he approved of it and encouraged

us to continue in our way of acting. He did not tell us children, 'I want to share in your Dish and have the best bit in it.' When our Father the King of England drove away the King of France, we were so earnest in nothing as communicating to him this Parable, He did more than the King of France for he had the goodness to prop up the Dish telling us that he did not wish that we should make use of Knives to eat our Meal, lest they should hurt us as a proof of it we preserve his word. He did not tell us that he wished to eat with us, being accustomed to a different kind of food.[3]

The mnemonic object requires lifetimes of passed-on references and hidden codes to interpret. We continue to mention that 'there will be no knives.' I wonder if this offer to share in our vision of the land went over the kings' heads. Did they think we were only talking about food? How many times must something be repeated to preserve the words? What are we not talking about enough? What symbols need to be on the ground, in Toronto, to remind us to keep talking these ideas through with others? What metaphors of authority are needed to back up our act?

Because I don't want to be a person of authority.

What business do I have in relating treaty stories here? I'm not Mississauga. Ojibwe Methodist missionary Peter Jones took notes for a reading of the Yellowhead Belt where my community is mentioned, stating that we had already emptied the Dish. Did we take more than we needed? Probably. I'll need to do more research about my community's relationship to the Dish. What old grudges are affecting how we talk about this place? How do we keep learning from each other, layering new findings, knowing they don't negate old knowledges? I imagine us locked together, hand to forearm, propping each other up, strong enough to keep the bowl from being emptied again.

SEPARATE AND UNCONNECTED

An Indian agent was put in place at York with the duty to prevent the Mississaugas and Haudenosaunee negotiator Joseph Brant from working together to gain better prices for the lands they were being pressed to sell. The Indian Agent was given the following instruction:

The primary duty of the new appointee is fomenting the jealousy which subsists between them and the Six Nations, and of preventing, as far as possible, any junction or good understanding taking place between those two tribes. It appears to me that the best and safest line of Policy to be pursued in the Indian Department is to keep the Indians separate and uncon-nected with one another, as by this means they will be in proportion more dependent on the King's Government.[4]

What I understand to be power is that you're able to hold up a tree, literally, by holding hands with your neighbour. It's our duty to hold up the people next to us and to teach, if we can. I teach knowing that I don't know everything, and that I am one of many. I'm always so afraid to put things down in writing. We know how that can go wrong.

How many people do we need to hold up all this shared Indigenous history? Is Indigenous history also a shared resource? When we have conflict on shared territory in academia, social media forums, and cultural venues, can we look to the Dish for some rules for sharing? How do we take what we need from Indigenous histories, keep them clean, and keep them for the future?

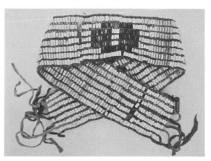

Dish with One Spoon wampum belt, 1701.

NO SHARP UTENSILS

The Dish with One Spoon Belt has a white background with a symbol of a rounded dish in the centre of the belt. The land is to be viewed as a dish/bowl or kettle from which all can eat together. The white wampum beads in the centre of the bowl represent a beaver's tail, a favourite dish of many nations around Ontario.

The Lords of the Confederacy shall eat together from one bowl the feast of cooked beaver's tail. While they are eating they are to use no sharp utensils for if they should they might accidentally cut one another and bloodshed would follow. All measures must be taken to prevent the spilling of blood in any way.[5]

I do a lot of the Talking Treaties performance work at Fort York, and I like to imagine its role as a place to keep the talk going, with dance, big puppets, and lots of people. If the federal government would like to host an annual 'Polishing the Chain' event there, I'm sure it could be arranged. I'll bring the giant beaver costume.

Who on the government's side can play the 'Corlaer'? Who takes this role if the federal government will not? Will the old Crown come to clear up their perspective? Who are their knowledge keepers? What responsibilities did Canada agree to take on? Will displaying our symbols of governance be enough to remind them? What foundational understandings will they need to have to be able to come to the table with us?

LOCKING THEIR HANDS AND ARMS TOGETHER

In 1840, Mississauga historian Peter Jones wrote of the 1701 renewal at the Credit River Grand Council meeting:

A treaty of peace and friendship was then made with the Nahdoways residing on the south side of Lake Ontario, and both nations solemnly covenanted, by going through the usual forms of burying the tomahawk, smoking the pipe of peace, and locking their hands and arms together to call each other Brothers ... [T]he treaty of peace mentioned has from time to time been renewed at general councils.

With the origin of Toronto's name being made ambiguous over the years, what did it make easier to forget? What federal and provincial bodies have a stake in maintaining a minimal narrative for this place? Who put trees in the water? They weren't around Toronto at the time the French made the maps. That made it easier to set up shop along these rivers, staking claim to territory that was seemingly unowned. The simplification of the hundreds of years of relationship between the nations here to three large movements of people does a disservice to the kin maintenance and peacemaking initiatives between us.

There are webs of alliances here, understandings which unite us and keep us stronger together. As we pick up more and more Indigenous history in Toronto, who will we task with remembering? As political representatives change, who needs to keep conversations about shared space going? How many people do you have to involve for it to make meaning? Imagine the federal government, coming to the table and enacting all the relationships and responsibilities of the Corlaer and Onontio.

Imagine if they wanted to remember as much as we do.

WILLIAMS TREATIES

WANDA NANIBUSH

What is it to surrender? Have we, the Anishinaabe, ever surrendered our lands? The verb to *give up* puts the onus on the one who acted, so we can wholeheartedly say, 'No.' *Surrender* as a noun in law started circulating in the fifteenth century, at the beginning of imperial and colonial incursions into North and South America. It's not an accident that this was also the moment when the notion of a legal surrender, a giving up of land, came into existence. A surrender was impossible on many levels, because it would have meant the end of the Anishinaabe way of life and being. It's not just the land; it's the food, the relationships, the heart, the love, the ceremonies, the language, and the freedom of us all.

I am Anishinaabe-kwe (Chippewa) from Beausoleil First Nation on Chimnissing (Christian Island) in Georgian Bay. The second (of three) Williams Treaty was signed on Christian Island on November 3, 1923. The signatories of the Beausoleil First Nation were Henry Jackson, Frank Copegog, Albert Monague, John S. Hawk, Edward W. King, Robert Marsden, Jerry D. Monague, Walter Simons, and William P. Assance. Our people, along with the Michi Saagig (Mississauga) of Rice Lake, Mud Lake, Scugog Lake, and Alderville, as well as other Chippewa of Georgina Island and Rama, signed three Williams Treaties in 1923. In September 2018, these nations concluded the fight for compensation for the impact of the wrongful interpretation of those treaties on our communities, our livelihoods, our families, and our bodies. What we signed this time is also an injustice, but I will speak to that later. We are always signing agreements with the government when we are backed into the corner of mere survival, without the strength to hold out for real justice.

The Williams Treaties had a 'basket clause' embedded in the text, whereby a surrender of huge amounts of land – a total of 12,944,400 acres minus some reservations lands – was agreed to. This clause was contested by every person from every First Nations community who was either directly involved in the signing or who holds the oral history of the event.

We did not surrender.

Our lands (covered in the Williams Treaties) were bounded by rivers and lakes – from the northern shore of Lake Ontario between the Trent and Etobicoke Rivers (including Toronto); from north of Lake Simcoe to Nipissing; and finally, between the Ottawa River and Lake Huron. In exchange, the Mississauga and Chippewa nations received a one-time payment of $25 for each band member, as well as a one-time lump sum of $466,800.

The Elders in our communities did not think they had given up their rights. This is why, according to Elder Doug Williams, '[t]hey continued to hunt and trap and fish as they had always done after the treaty was signed. It was not until the game wardens showed up and began harassing them that there was a problem.'[1] There had been a push to move Anishinaabe onto reservations, but it was understood that this was to clear the way for settlers, not an end to treaty rights. As Williams notes, 'They would never have given up their right to feed themselves.'[2]

The effect of losing access to our 'country' food had a direct impact on our health. According to Mr. Charles Big Canoe of Georgina Island, the increase in diabetes began with the introduction of government rations of white flour and sugar.[3] As we became increasingly reliant on the government for food because we could not legally access our lands, our diets began to kill us. Elders in my community speak about the fact that the theft of lands and the loss of hunting and fishing rights that were not supposed to be part of the Williams Treaties was due to the lack of translation and the inability of the signatories to read and write English.[4] In most countries, a legal agreement would be null and void if the signatories did not know exactly what they were signing. Instead, we hold on to the oral history of what was promised and continue to assert that what has become the written document is not the truth of what had been agreed to.

Our people starved because of the intentional misinterpretation of the Williams Treaties; the advent of harsh colonial measures under the Indian Acts of 1876 onward, which included the creation of reservations and the institution of Indian agents to control movements and commerce; and the establishment of residential schools for assimilation. Any action that looks like surrender was really about survival. It is also about resistance within the context of an extreme lack of freedom and power. Many of the Elders interviewed for the most recent Williams Treaty settlement claim speak about the ways they avoided or outwitted the game wardens – for example, by fishing at night. Many were caught and charged in direct violation of their treaty rights. In 1981, Doug Williams and a Mr. Taylor decided to take his charge to the Supreme Court. This case would be referenced and the judgment cited in subsequent case law protecting Aboriginal and treaty rights.

The late Associate Chief Justice MacKinnon wrote the opinion in R. v. Taylor and Williams (1981), 34 O.R. (2d) 360. He argued that First Nations history and traditions, as well as the perceived effect of a treaty at the time of its execution, needed to factor into fishing and hunting rights cases. Justice MacKinnon pointed out that the Crown needs to consider its relationship of trust with First Nations and therefore the Crown must act fairly.

'The principles to be applied to the interpretation of Indian treaties have been much canvassed over the years,' Justice MacKinnon wrote. 'In approaching the terms of a treaty quite apart from the other considerations already noted, the honour of the Crown is always involved and no appearance of "sharp dealing" should be sanctioned.'[5]

This means the government cannot be seen to be acting out of self-interest to the detriment of First Nations. In interpreting treaties, this argument shifts the emphasis onto First Nations interpretations, because the alternatives have meant starvation and poverty.[6] The current situation, whereby First Nations own less than .02 per cent of their lands and have high rates of poverty, represents a break in the trust relationship between

Rebecca Belmore, X. Performance on June 17, 2010. Wall of the Price Chopper, 181 Brock Street, Peterborough, ON. Performance for Mapping Resistances exhibition curated by Wanda Nanibush as part of the Ode'Min Giizis Festival, June 17–18, 2010, Peterborough, ON.

First Nations and the Crown. It also blatantly proves that treaty interpretation and government dealings around land have been shady, to the detriment of our people's survival.

It is an important fact that resistance in terms of taking the government to court was consistently attempted by many First Nations across the country but was made difficult by Section 141 of the Indian Act. This section made it illegal for First Nations to hire lawyers, obtain legal counsel, or raise funds for legal defence. The draconian nature of Canada's desire to shut down our dissent went so far as to institute pass systems to leave the reserve to sell goods, and to make it illegal to gather in large groups. It still amazes me, and fills my soul with pride, that our people persisted through this oppression and still keep fighting for their rights today.

When Williams and Taylor[7] fought the charge of poaching based on an interpretation of the Williams Treaties that maintained their hunting and fishing rights, the country was in discussions about repatriating the Constitution and ending colonial status with Britain. First Nations leader George Manuel, who was president of the National Indian Brotherhood[8] and was then president of the UBCIC,[9] chartered the train that would carry First Nations community members from Vancouver to Ottawa in a campaign called 'the Constitution Express.' The Constitution Express hoped to delay the repatriation of the Constitution and protest the exclusion of First Nations from the discussion. First Nations worried that their rights would be trampled and more land stolen without reparations, because that was how the Canadian governments had treated First Nations, Inuit, and Métis peoples until that point.

First Nations were not brought to the table, but a clause was added to the Constitution that has become one of the many sources of protections of rights used in courts today. Section 35 reads as follows:

> 35. (1) The existing aboriginal and treaty rights of the aboriginal peoples of Canada are hereby recognized and affirmed.
> Definition of 'aboriginal peoples of Canada'
> (2) In this Act, 'aboriginal peoples of Canada' includes the Indian, Inuit and Métis peoples of Canada.

The ensuing decades have witnessed a struggle in interpreting the term 'existing.' Again, the issue of surrender raises its ugly head. First Nations understand that their inherent right to their lands is an 'existing' right. The main reason is the desire to survive.

In 1992, after five hundred years of colonization, the Williams Treaties First Nations took the government to court, arguing that it did not act honourably and that harvesting rights were 'unjustly' denied. In November 2018, the federal and Ontario governments apologized for the impacts of the Williams Treaties and the notion of surrender implied by the 'basket clause.'

Crown-Indigenous relations minister Carolyn Bennett stated, 'We are sorry that, in not recognizing your rights to harvest in your pre-Confederation treaty areas, your communities faced hardship and hunger, with the bounties of the land being replaced by biscuits and tins of government meat. We are sorry that your people were not able to pursue traditional activities with pride and dignity, but instead were persecuted for exercising their rights. And we are sorry that your grandmothers and grandfathers, mothers and fathers, and aunts and uncles were constrained in their ability to do what their ancestors had always done – to teach younger generations about your communities' traditional lands and waters and pass along Anishinaabe culture and practices.'

The settlement came with financial compensation nowhere near what the land is worth today, as well as the right to purchase 11,000 acres to use for hunting and harvesting. One of the main wins in the settlement is an acknowledgement of harvesting rights as a treaty right under Section 35 of the Constitution.

An apology doesn't mark the end of the trauma caused by the Williams Treaties. This is not just the cognitive dissonance between pens and paper versus oral history. It is not resolved with the simplicity of land acknowledgements. This episode is still a life-and-death fight, and one that has had lasting impacts on our bodies, our cultures, our children. As Doug Williams courageously wrote, 'I witnessed the trauma and the fear that was put on my people that were trying to live on the land. They lived daily watching over their backs and trying to maintain their lifestyle as Michi Saagig Nishnaabeg.'[10]

I have travelled to many communities, listening to people describe the pain caused by development on their lands and by the destruction of their ways of life. I have heard through tears and anger the way their children now don't remember the time when the land and water was clean and bountiful. This sadness settles in our DNA and gets passed on; it is expressed in all the ways we try to numb the shame and loss, generation after generation. I have also heard the multiple exciting ways in which communities are reinstituting traditional governance that includes

Rebecca Belmore, X. Performance on June 17, 2010. Wall of the Price Chopper, 181 Brock Street, Peterborough, Ontario.

women and Elders. I have heard of folks moving back out onto their lands and practising the stewardship and relations with the Earth and her kin that a genocide has attempted to break.

This work remains illegal; we still do not have access to our lands, but we never surrender. We never surrender despite broken treaties, residential schools, Indian Acts, child welfare, and jails – all the institutions that have taken over where draconian laws have ended.

At the heart of the Williams Treaties is the issue of being able to present an Anishinaabe perspective, because colonialism still lives on today. The courts still treat our Elders' testimony as hearsay because it is known through someone living to whom it was passed down. The people who signed the treaty are not alive to be cross-examined. If the Crown stopped seeing itself as an adversary to First Nations' claims, our Elders' understandings could be honoured.

Ultimately, it will mean Canadians who have made their wealth at our expense will need to shift some resources back to us so we can also

Performance for Mapping Resistances exhibition curated by Wanda Nanibush as part of the Ode'Min Giizis Festival June 17–18, 2010, Peterborough, ON.

thrive. It will also mean accepting as equally valid our ways of thinking, being, and doing. Currently, when we step into the arena of the street, the courtroom, and the boardroom, we are stepping into someone else's world view, just like the original treaty signatories did. Until this inequity is acknowledged, we will always lose land at the negotiating table.

The reason we harp on land rights is for our physical survival, but also for our spiritual survival. As long as the land and water remain clean and bountiful, our cultures will exist. The millennia of knowledge were built up through observing and working with the lands that are here, so we could regain that knowledge through careful, thoughtful, guided observation and experimentation for many generations to come. Many Elders speak of the speed at which settlers have polluted the land and water, making the exercise of treaty rights almost impossible.

As Charles Warren of Georgina Island said, 'The local people didn't know anything about the treaty [with] the non-Native people. Wild rice and wild cranberries grew southeast of the island. Last time when I was twelve – I remember wild rice and wild cranberries. There's no native fish in here anymore – the lake is polluted and the fish are horrible.'[11]

While treaty recognition is a very important step in the right direction, the Anishinaabe notions of land stewardship and communal relations with non-human beings need to come back to the forefront of the discussion of land. We speak in ownership terms because that is what is understood in the white world we inhabit. But if we could – as Anishinaabe writer Gerald Vizenor has asked – unwind ourselves from the white words we have become,[12] the idea that all lands are there to sustain life in a collective stewardship model doesn't seem so idealistic.

A STORY ABOUT THE TORONTO PURCHASE

MARGARET SAULT

Even though this event occurred over two centuries ago, in 1787, it still inspires fascination, as there are so many documents, letters, and reports on what happened.

When the Mississaugas of the Credit First Nation negotiating team met with representatives from the Justice Department in 1996, the head lawyer made a comment that remains in my mind. 'I cannot believe there is so much written on this subject,' he said, referring to the Toronto Purchase. The records and documentation are so abundant, and all that was needed was to find them. So this is a story about the Toronto Purchase.

Let's start in 1787. The Crown felt it needed a secure military communication route from Lake Ontario to Lake Huron that did not utilize the current one, along the lakefront. They wanted a route that would take them out of harm's way. The colonialists explored some routes and determined they had to make purchases with the Mississaugas and the Chippewas.

Sir John Johnson, then the head of the Indian Department, called a meeting of the Mississaugas and other First Nations to distribute 'annual presents' for the military alliance during the American Revolution. At the time of this gathering, Johnson talked to the Mississaugas about land he wanted to purchase from them, along the north shore of Lake Ontario, as well as the 'carrying place' from Toronto to Lake Simcoe. This was the route the British wanted to be safe from their enemies.

What actually transpired is that Johnson thought the British had a treaty with the Mississaugas for the passage and the land known as the Toronto Purchase. As it turned out, discussions leading to a potential treaty, and the annual presents given, settled on the amount that was said to be paid to the Mississaugas of the Credit for the land.

Life went on, and the Crown thought it had secured the land. Some years later, a law clerk was going through the files and came upon the so-called treaty, finding instead a blank deed with no land description, but with the marks, probably dodems of three Mississaugas chiefs, wafered onto the document.

However, the Crown was already selling the land and building the capital there. When the law clerk made the higher-ups aware of the situation, their initial response was to withhold from the Mississaugas that there was no treaty. The correspondence went back and forth, and the Crown decided it would be best to tell the Mississaugas in order to avoid an uprising if they were to find out later on. This was a very delicate time, as one of the Credit River chiefs, Wabakinine, along with his wife, were murdered by the Queen's Rangers. The Credit Indians wanted to retaliate, but Joseph Brant talked them out of it.

In 1798, Johnson, when asked what lands he purchased from the Mississaugas in 1787, wrote: 'I think it was a ten-mile square at Toronto, with two to four miles on each side of the carrying place to Lake Simcoe, where the same ten-mile square was at the end of the trail.' It is strange that Johnson's recollection of the land was only for the ten-mile square with two to four miles on each side of the 'carrying place' up to Lake Simcoe. In its wisdom, the Crown decided to treaty again with the Mississaugas for the lands. They had no choice – without a treaty, they did not own the lands they were already using, selling, and building as the Town of York.

The boundaries of the purchase were the next difficult issue. In 1788, Alexander Aitkin, Upper Canada's surveyor general, was given instructions to survey the lands purchased from the Mississaugas. He encountered some tense moments when he was surveying the eastern boundary to the end of Ashbridge's Bay. The Mississaugas of the Credit said they had only given lands to the Don River in the original treaty. The same problem occurred at the western boundary, where the Mississaugas protested the boundaries, saying the agreement extended only to the Humber River, and not to the Etobicoke River.

The discontent was so severe that Aitkin feared for his life. The Butler's Rangers were brought in to watch that nothing happened, and Aitkin went ahead and surveyed west to the Etobicoke River. He had only surveyed about three miles when the Rangers left. He stopped his work and left, too, as he did not want to encounter the wrath of the Mississaugas again.

With all the discrepancies over the boundaries, only a partial survey was completed. With an incomplete survey and no description of the

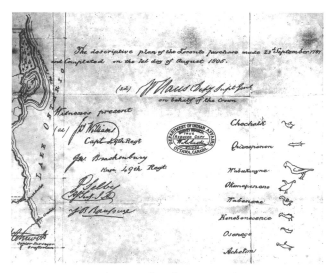

Signatures of parties ratifying the Toronto Purchase (1805).

land, what would be the next step? The Crown believed a second treaty had to be negotiated with the Mississaugas, and in 1805, the next negotiation took place. But there were more problems around resolving the land issue.

Johnson wanted a ten-mile square with two to four miles on each side of the carrying place. But the Mississauga chiefs who had been at the 1787 meeting and the 1788 survey attempt were now dead. The Crown had waited until 1805, as another large land surrender was being considered to the west of the Toronto Purchase, known as the Mississauga Tract, extending west to the Brant Tract. The Crown needed to get the land survey straightened out so it could proceed with the Mississauga Tract treaty.

In preparation for a meeting with the Mississaugas, the Crown created four maps: two of the Mississauga Tract and two of the 1787 Toronto Purchase. Something we did not find in our research was any evidence showing how the Crown determined the northern boundary of the Toronto Purchase. One map shows the western frontage to Ashbridge's Bay and the eastern frontage to the Etobicoke River, while the other details the boundaries of what the Mississaugas told Aitkin in 1788 – east only to the Don River and west no further than the Humber River, and not including the Toronto Islands. The two versions of the Mississauga tracts would extend either from the Etobicoke River or the Humber River. The Crown's only interest was to secure title to the capital, York, as well as to the rest of the Mississaugas' land along Lake Ontario.

When the meeting took place, on July 31, between William Claus, the Crown's Indian Department agent, and the Mississaugas, Claus asked the Chiefs what the boundaries of the 1787 treaty were. Chief Quinepenon stated: '[A]ll the Chiefs who sold the land are dead and gone. We cannot absolutely tell what our old people did before us, except by what we see on the plan and what we remember ourselves and have been told.'

Claus only showed the Mississaugas the map with the broader boundaries, from Ashbridge's Bay to the Etobicoke River, with the northern boundary being twenty-eight miles inland and fourteen miles across. The total area spanned 250,880 acres (101,527 hectares).

In other words, the so-called 1805 treaty went far beyond the acreage of the ten-by-ten-mile square that Sir John Johnson had talked about in 1787.

LAND CLAIMS POLICIES

Prior to 1990, First Nations were not able to submit pre-Confederation land claims. This made it difficult to find resolutions, as most if not all of the treaties were signed prior to 1867, when Upper and Lower Canada joined to form a confederation. The only option was to take the federal government to court.

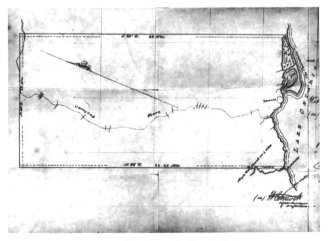

A map of the Toronto Purchase (1860).

That kind of legal action rarely happened, as First Nations did not and still today do not have the abundance of money needed to hire lawyers and pursue court challenges. It was not until 1972 that the federal government began to fund the First Nations to conduct research into land claims. In order to flow money for such research, First Nations set up 'political territorial organizations' known as the Association of Iroquois and Allied Indians (AIAI) and the Union of Ontario Indians, Treaty #3 and Treaty #9.

In 1982, with the new Constitution Act, the federal government began to rework the land-claims policy. Specific claims involved the federal government's failure to honour the treaties, agreements, and legal obligations. But the onus was on the First Nations to prove that the federal government had 'a lawful obligation.'

First Nations had to fit their claims into four boxes:

- The non-fulfillment of a treaty or agreement between Indians and the Crown.
- A breach of an obligation arising out of the Indian Act or other statutory obligation.
- The mishandling of Indian funds or assets by government administrations.
- An illegal disposition of Indian land.

The policy also recognized claims considered to be 'beyond lawful obligation,' based on the following criteria:

- Failure to compensate a band for reserve land taken or damaged under government authority. (The example given is paying less than market value or nothing for land taken by the government in a legal surrender.)
- Fraud by federal employees in connection with the purchase or sale of Indian land.

Specific claims are for monetary compensation only. The federal policy 'Outstanding Business' clearly states that land will not be given back and third parties will not be displaced.

THE JOURNEY OF THE MISSISSAUGAS OF THE CREDIT FIRST NATION

In 1985, the Mississauga Nation (Mississaugas of the Credit, Alderville, Scugog, Curve Lake, and Hiawatha First Nations) came together to meet about their land claims and the treaties made in the past. The following

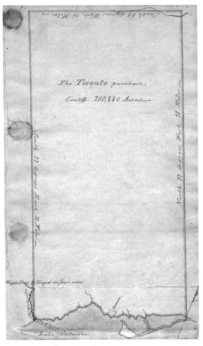

Toronto Purchase (1787).

year, the Mississauga Tribal Claims Council submitted the Toronto Purchase to the federal government's Specific Claims Tribunal.

Canada rejected the claim in 1993 due to inaction by the MTCC. But the Oka Crisis had occurred during that time, resulting in the formation of the Indian Claims Commission. It could conduct an inquiry into a rejected claim and make a recommendation to the federal government to negotiate a land claim. Yet this body lacked the authority to compel the federal government to take action.

Until then, First Nations had to take their land claims to court, which is a costly process. The Mississaugas of the Credit were able to submit claims, as they were not signatories to the 1923 Williams Treaties. First Nations had grown tired of hearing 'take it or leave it' from federal negotiators. In February 1998, the Mississaugas of the Credit requested an independent inquiry into the Toronto Purchase. This process included the First Nation, the Department of Justice, and the ICC as facilitator. After three planning sessions, Canada agreed to review the claim.

On March 8, 1999, the Mississaugas of the Credit submitted a new legal opinion, including a position on the Toronto Islands. The claim was accepted on the basis of the fact that the 1805 treaty was valid, meaning the Toronto Islands were included. It was a difficult task trying to fit a square into a circle in order to keep the claim moving.

The Justice Department raised the question of beneficiaries. Were the Mississaugas the sole beneficiaries of the Toronto Purchase? The Mississaugas of the Credit submitted a paper on September 9, 1999, to address this issue (i.e., identifying the rightful First Nation to make this claim), which the federal government accepted. The Mississaugas of the Credit were declared the sole beneficiaries of the Toronto Purchase, but the door was left open for other Mississauga First Nations to advance claims.

The next challenge concerned the compensation received in 1787. The government said the Mississaugas of the Credit had received annual presents and were trying to price them. The annual presents had been provided by the British for a military alliance, not a land sale. A position paper making this argument was submitted on October 18, 1999, and accepted by the federal government. On that basis, the ICC recommended that the federal government negotiate the Mississaugas' claim over the Toronto Purchase, and the federal government accepted the recommendation to begin negotiations on July 23, 2002.

Throughout this process, a lot of political lobbying and meetings had taken place. One of the points the planning committee agreed on early in the process was to keep the same teams on the government's side and the First Nation's side, as far as possible. This was accomplished, and the two groups worked well together.

On June 17, 2003, a joint media briefing was held to announce that the negotiations were finally underway. These negotiations moved quickly to the question of compensation, as most of the arguments had been discussed and resolved during the inquiry phase.

Between August 2002 and March 31, 2007, David Walker served as the chief negotiator for the federal government. Then, on September 26, 2007, the government – with input from the First Nation – named former Toronto mayor David Crombie to replace Walker.

One of the first points agreed upon by the two parties was to conduct joint research on the interest rates from 1805 to 1900. The federal government argued that Canada had no banking system in 1805. The study was done by an independent consultant, who found that Canada did have a banking system, and paid 6 per cent interest through the years.

All the work done through the years by all parties finally came to fruition on January 25, 2010, with a joint announcement that the federal government would make an offer of $145 million, which included compensation for the Brant Tract Treaty (1797) that covered 3,450 acres between what is now Hamilton and Burlington.

The First Nation had their work cut out for them now. Meetings with the membership had been taking place during the whole process to keep them up-to-date on the progress of the claim. A trust agreement and then a settlement agreement had to be drafted, based on input from the membership.

The trust agreement included a per capita distribution, a Community Wellness Policy, and an Estate Policy. On May 29, 2010, the Mississaugas of the Credit voted in favour of the Toronto Purchase Settlement Agreement.

Reflecting back over the years of this journey, from start to finish, was not an easy task. A lot of hard work and sometimes difficult choices had to be made by the First Nation. I believe that the Mississaugas of the Credit made a decision that was to their members' benefit. If the First Nation had sued the federal government over this claim, we probably would still be in court, or would have had to withdraw for lack of funds. Many of our elderly members would have passed away during the process, without seeing the end or any benefit, and the only ones getting rich would have been litigation lawyers. I have nothing against lawyers, but that is the truth. The Mississaugas of the Credit would not have benefited at all.

Today, instead, the membership benefits every year, thanks to the settlement of the Toronto Purchase.

ON THE BACK OF THE TURTLE: ANCIENT LIFE AND DEATH IN THE CITY

RON WILLIAMSON AND LOUIS LESAGE

Most of what has happened in Toronto occurred well before there was any kind of written history. There are almost two hundred places around the city where tangible fragments of Indigenous lives have survived for thousands of years.

The earliest of those traces dates to about 13,000 years ago, when people came to live along glacial shorelines like the Davenport Ridge. It had formed a thousand years earlier during the retreat of a continental glacier that had stretched across most of Canada and the northern United States. People used these ridges for their sightlines to track caribou, mastodon, mammoth, and other game in what was then an open spruce forest much like the environment found today in the subarctic region of Canada.

At this time, early Lake Ontario was about one hundred metres below its present level and had receded to a distance of several kilometres south of its present shoreline. The resulting expansion of the land provided a productive habitat for plants and animals, and this complex landscape now lies hidden at the bottom of Lake Ontario, along with, perhaps, evidence of the lives of these early peoples.

There is not much to find at their camps since their populations were small and few of their belongings have survived the millennia. Sometimes the wear patterns and organic residues on their

Figure 1: 13,000-year-old miniature projectile point.

stone tools offer clues to how they were used. Traces of mastodon or mammoth blood were recently found along the edges of a stone tool discovered on a site of this period located in Hamilton. Evidence of dog blood was also found on tools from that site, including on an imitation projectile point the size of a thumbnail (Figure 1). The association of miniature points and butchered dog has been found previously in the Plains area of the U.S. on sites of this age, but this is one of the earliest signs of dog ceremony in the Great Lakes region.

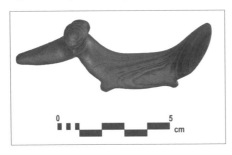

Figure 2: Banded Slate Birdstone.

By nine thousand years ago, Southern Ontario had warmed, with the result that new species migrated and colonized the region. Humans had to adapt to changing environmental conditions by shifting their hunting strategies and developing new implements, like drives, traps, and nets. With time, populations increased, and people began to interact and exchange ideas and goods with others across vast distances. By four to five thousand years ago, populations in Ontario shared elaborate mortuary ceremonies with distant groups throughout northeastern North America. The group that constructed a cemetery on the west side of Grenadier Pond south of Bloor Street four thousand years ago, for example, identified with a larger Great Lakes–wide religious belief system that originated in the Mississippi Valley.

People at this time also created artifacts made of banded slate that were carved and ground to resemble animals. While these artifacts may have had day-to-day uses, such as weights for spear-throwing devices, they also had a sacred meaning, since they were included in burials. Regardless of the context in which they were used or found, they rival any of the art produced anywhere in the world at that time (Figure 2).

The introduction of corn to Indigenous populations in Southern Ontario about 1,600 years ago profoundly changed their lives. Producing food through agriculture meant abandoning the mobility that had characterized Indigenous life for millennia. Instead, people established base settlements and transformed their environments by clearing land around them for crops, while sending out hunting, fishing, and gathering parties to harvest other natural resources.

The first agriculturalists of southern Ontario were the ancestors of the Neutral, Huron-Wendat, and Tionontaté (Petun). The Haudenosaunee or League of the Iroquois to the south of Lake Ontario, in what is now central New York State, consisted of the Seneca, Cayuga, Onondaga, Oneida, and Mohawk nations, with the Tuscarora joining as the sixth nation in 1722.

Base settlements around which corn was initially grown are discovered and excavated regularly; one dating to around 1,300 years ago was found recently near the mouth of the Rouge River. In Toronto, these settlements can be attributed to the ancestors of the Huron-Wendat. Within a few centuries, these places evolved into villages, which were several hectares in size and surrounded by hundreds of hectares of cornfields. A village was only moved once its cornfields lost fertility and firewood in the vicinity became scarce.

Moving an ancestral Wendat village meant creating a new ossuary over which a Feast of the Dead was held. All those who had died during the fifteen to twenty years the village was occupied were taken out of their primary graves and brought to a large pit, where they were mixed together to create a new community of the dead. Toronto is home to a dozen known Wendat villages and four ossuaries that date from 700 and 450 years ago. There would have been far more villages and ossuaries, but land development in the twentieth century destroyed them. Anishinaabeg also held Feasts of the Dead in the seventeenth century, but only the Wendat created ossuaries filled with the commingled remains of ancestors.

The Moatfield village and its associated ossuary were found in 1997, during construction for upgrades to a community soccer field just south of the Leslie–Highway 401 interchange. Six Nations Council of Ohsweken, the closest Iroquoian-speaking First Nation, directed that the ossuary be moved since a lamppost had not only pierced actual ancestors' remains, but the soul of the community of the dead. In their judgment, the souls could not rest in that location. The ossuary was completely excavated and the remains of eighty-seven ancestors were reinterred in another location nearby, never to be disturbed again.

Villages and ossuaries are found regularly throughout south-central Ontario, but any decisions regarding their investigation and protection are now governed by the Huron-Wendat Council at Wendake, Quebec.

THE MOATFIELD VILLAGE AND OSSUARY

Situated on a small tributary of the Don River about twelve kilometres from Lake Ontario, just south of Highway 401, the Moatfield village would have involved planning and a great deal of hard work during its construction. The villagers had to clear the one-hectare settlement area and its surrounding hardwood forest, dominated by maple and beech, for a distance of about eight hundred metres to establish agricultural fields. They then used thousands of the felled saplings to construct their houses, covering them with elm and cedar bark. Smoke holes would have been placed in their roofs to encourage some of the smoke to escape from the winter heating and cooking hearths. Later descriptions of these houses by European settlers all depict a four-foot smoke ceiling, making standing up for any longer than a few seconds impossible.

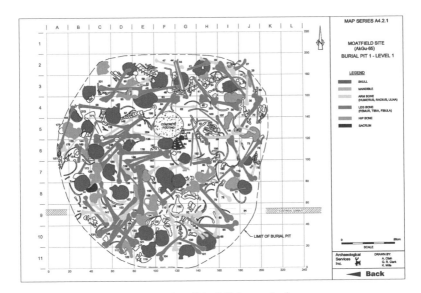

Figure 3: Map of Moatfield Ossuary, Level 1.

A portion of a longhouse was found along with the remains of thirty-two ceramic cooking vessels, all of them consistent with forms and designs used seven hundred years ago. The ossuary was situated on the edge of the village, perhaps adjacent to the palisade.

As the ancestors had been mixed together when the ossuary was created, they were removed bone by bone. Examination of each allowed for a determination of the age, gender, and health of the ancestors. Diets were scrutinized using a single molar per person for carbon isotopic analysis, which produces a measure of the amount of corn consumed versus other naturally occurring local plants. Permission to examine each bone and to retain one tooth for each individual was granted by Six Nations Council at the time of the excavation.

The ancestors had been placed in the ossuary pit after varying amounts of decomposition had occurred in their primary burials. Body parts as complete as entire torsos were sometimes included. An absence of weathering on the surface of the bones suggests that ancestors were initially buried quickly, then years later interred in the ossuary in small groupings, perhaps families, and then covered quickly (Figure 3).

A thick layer of soil between two large concentrations of bone pointed to its creation in at least two separate episodes. There were no bones from the same individual found across this boundary and there was evidence that the top level contained the remains of the more recent deaths from the community.

Most of the skeletal remains had likely been removed from any wrappings prior to their deposition. Some of the bones had been manually arranged – in particular crania. Almost 30 per cent of the crania were placed near the top of the ossuary, many in groups of two to four skulls. There was no age- or sex-based patterning of the position of the crania or any of the other bones.

To refine the age of the site that had initially been estimated on the basis of artifact styles, a series of accurate radiocarbon dates was obtained on corn remains from the village and on bone fragments from within the ossuary. These indicate that the village and the ossuary are contemporary and date to around seven hundred years ago. This is the earliest ancestral Huron-Wendat community ossuary in southern Ontario. It is also the most thoroughly investigated ossuary.

Eighty-seven ancestors were removed from the ossuary, including six infants (under one year), seventeen young children (one to five years), one juvenile, five adolescents, and fifty-eight adults. This is the estimated number of people who would normally die over a fifteen-year period for a community of two hundred to four hundred people at that time.

While all the ancestors seemed similar in what would have been their appearance and general health, inherited traits such as various foramen (small nerve holes) or bony projections or grooves in the crania of women were less alike than in Huron-Wendat ossuaries established a few centuries later. This may be because some Southern Ontario communities like Moatfield were not yet fully 'matrilocal,' a custom where men regularly went to live with a woman's family. Because the traits are so variable in this case, it seems women had moved to join their new marriage families rather than men.

In 2013, the Huron-Wendat Nation established a protocol to approve genetic investigation of ancient ancestors' teeth, which was later extended to include ones from Moatfield. Wendat oral tradition, recorded as long ago as the 1630s, tells of an origin for the Wendat peoples by the sea and from a cave north of Quebec City. Analyses conducted at the University of Huddersfield in the UK, under the supervision of Dr. Maria Pala, a molecular biologist, have now revealed that two Huron-Wendat women from Moatfield and a number of Beothuk individuals from Newfoundland, along with some other ancient Ontarians, share ancestry through a common ancestral gene pool that seeded mitochondrial lineages across eastern North America thousands of years ago.

It is interesting, although not necessarily related, that the Beothuk language shared words with the Iroquoian groups living along the St. Lawrence River in the sixteenth century, many of whose descendants went to live with the Wendat. These tantalizing hints at connections demonstrate how modern science and Indigenous oral tradition might be able to yield details of stories of the distant past that neither alone divulges.

ELDERS AND ADULTS

While the population profile of this community is more accurate than most because of the way the ossuary was excavated, one observation is at odds with previous investigations – there were just more aged elders.

Patterns of tooth wear, decay and loss, and jaws with less bone supporting teeth were common. There was evidence of deteriorative diseases among the adults, including at least one case of probable cancer, a form associated normally with post-reproductive age.

Among adults more generally, respiratory infections were common, resulting from life in smoke-filled longhouses, as well as dental decay because of a corn-dominated diet. In ossuaries a century or two later, these conditions were even worse because of increased crowding in villages and exposure to new pathogens from more distant Indigenous communities. The higher proportion of old adults at Moatfield is perhaps a result of better living conditions compared to their descendants.

The climate of Southern Ontario necessitated people spending the winter months indoors, where smoky air from wood fires, with age, irritated their facial sinuses. Sixty per cent of adults showed chronic sinusitis. Four showed changes to bones of the spine consistent with long-standing tuberculosis. Since modern clinical evidence indicates that bone is rarely involved in this disease, four cases means there was a relatively high proportion of infected people. Three adults showed lesions to the inner surfaces of the ribs, which is seen accompanying pulmonary tuberculosis, although these also occur with pneumonia or a collapsed lung.

There were also various infected wounds, including a dramatically altered femur (upper leg bone) that had been placed near the centre and top of the ossuary. The individual likely had a systemic infection throughout their body, but it did not result in their death, as the femur was completely remodelled. Similar inflammatory responses in two tibiae (larger lower leg bones) and a fused left foot could all be linked. A chronic infection of a bacterium like staphylococcus would be typical after a serious trauma to a leg.

On the other hand, there were relatively few healed fractures. With the exception of one healed femoral fracture, the breaks were not very debilitating (ribs, fingers, toes), indicating the ancestors suffered only from occasional accidents.

The larger proportion of elders in the community ossuary than seen in subsequent Huron-Wendat villages is also consistent with the absence of interpersonal violence. Political instability, crowding, and feuding, which can have strong negative effects on life expectancy, were also perhaps absent. Two sawed halves of a human cranium found together in the village, however, were being fashioned into a rattle; dozens of such artifacts – ground on their edges, polished, and featuring a series of drilled holes for fastening the two halves together – have been found on Iroquoian sites throughout Southern Ontario and are thought to have been made from the skulls of prisoners of war.

CHILDREN

Some of the community's children were physically stressed. About half of the leg and arm bones that were radiographed showed growth arrest lines, and over half of the crania showed signs of anemia. The bone growth was not maintaining the expected pace. This and other evidence suggest these children may have needed care during prolonged bouts of ill health, and while it's not possible to determine causes of death, the episodes appear to have been more often chronic than acute. The healed adult leg fracture, like this evidence from the children, attests to the long-term care available to a person who had a long period of illness.

DIET

The soil samples collected from within one of the community longhouses yielded corn, together with a diverse range of gathered wild plants, such as raspberry, strawberry, elderberry, and several types of greens and grains that likely flourished along the margins of the settlement and its field clearings. It was corn, however, that formed the most significant portion of the diet of the ancestors, as confirmed by analysis of their teeth. Isotopic analyses of teeth from the site indicate that corn comprised at least half, if not more, of the diet. Such horticultural dependency was a necessary response to the food needs of a larger population living together year-round. Because the corn was prepared as a sticky gruel, it did cause dental cavities and periodontal disease, problems faced by all Indigenous peoples with diets dominated by corn.

In addition to agricultural crops, the community relied on the natural resources afforded by their rich local environment, including deer, small mammals, and fish. Although it is clear that a number of habitats were exploited, waterfowl, turtles, and fish productivity would have been highest in the estuary and coastal marshes of the lower Don River. One group of fish in particular, comprising American eel, Atlantic salmon, lake whitefish, and lake trout, played a significant role in the diet of the site inhabitants. Together with pickerel, these species, which consume primarily smaller fish, resulted in a signature of high levels of nitrogen isotope in the teeth and bones of the ancestors. They did, however, also fish opportunistically for bow fin, sucker, brown bullhead, rock bass, smallmouth bass, yellow perch, and sunfish in the warm season in the lower reaches and estuaries of the streams and shallow inlets along the north Lake Ontario shoreline.

REBURIAL

The Moatfield remains were reinterred shortly after the conclusion of the excavation. Six Nations hereditary faith keeper Barry Longboat offici-ated at the ceremony. It was not the first time such a ceremony had taken place in Toronto. The skeletal remains from the ancestral Wendat Tabor Hill ossuary in east Toronto were reinterred in October 1956. That ceremony was presided over by Hereditary Chief David Thomas, father of legendary Cayuga Chief Jacob Thomas, and attended by many other hereditary chiefs; there was national media attention.

Perhaps reflecting the Huron-Wendat creation story and the origin of life on Turtle Island, the placement on the floor of the Moatfield ossuary of a complete turtle effigy ceramic pipe is consistent metaphorically with the community resting on the 'back' of the turtle. It was at the very bottom and centre of the ossuary, sitting adjacent to the oldest male skull, and placed at the reburial ceremony in exactly the same place with the same skull. As they had in life, the Moatfield community members continue their jour-neys on the back of the turtle (Figure 4).

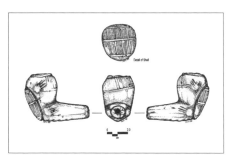

Figure 4: Complete Turtle Effigy Pipe from bottom of Moatfield Ossuary.

By about AD 1610, all of the ancestral Wendat communities along the north shore of Lake Ontario had moved northward, joining with other groups in present-day Simcoe County (between Lake Simcoe and Georgian Bay) to complete the formation of the Huron-Wendat confederacy (two nations had already joined in the fifteenth century). Some villages in the western GTA may have joined their brethren in the late sixteenth century to form the Tionontaté (Petun) confederacy, which was situated between the Nottawasaga River and Craigleith on Georgian Bay. While this movement of communities occurred over many generations, the final impetus was conflict with the Haudenosaunee (Five Nations Iroquois) of neighbouring New York State. Inter-tribal warfare with the Haudenosaunee during the first half of the seventeenth century, worsened by the intrusion of Europeans (and their diseases), ultimately resulted in the collapse and displacement of the Ontario Iroquoian-speaking confederacies and their Algonquian allies. In the 1630s, the Huron-Wendat lost about two-thirds of their population due to European-introduced epidemics that swept through their villages and those of their neighbours.

By the 1660s, the Haudenosaunee had established villages along the north shore, including two in Toronto near the mouths of the Rouge and Humber Rivers. They were only occupied until the 1680s, when hostility between the Haudenosaunee and the Anishinaabeg (and Wyandot allies) ended with Anishinaabeg occupation of Southern Ontario. It was with the Anishinaabeg that the treaties were signed by the new British colonial government, treaties that to this day affirm inherent Aboriginal rights on the land.

AN INDIGENOUS ARCHAEOLOGIST AT THE ROUGE NATIONAL URBAN PARK

STACEY TAYLOR

It's difficult to imagine while driving on Highway 401 through Toronto that this was once a land of trees, rivers, and the ancestors. But if you look hard enough, you see the past landscape peeking through as you drive over the valleys of the Rouge, Don, Humber, and Credit Rivers. These rivers and their many tributaries were once our highways. If you head north, the urban sprawl soon gives way to the bucolic landscapes, including corn fields. These corn fields also hide the past, a time when they surrounded the palisaded village built by the ancestors.

Boozhoo. Stacey ndiszhinakaaz. Michi saagiig ndoonjibaa. Parks Canada ndoonjinakii. Emookdaang daasat.

I'm Stacey from the Michi saagiig (Mississauga), and I'm an archaeologist at Parks Canada, a federal agency mandated with ecological and cultural resource preservation and presentation. Archaeologists and Indigenous people have not always understood each other. Aandi wenjibaayan/So where do I belong? To me, archaeology is a way to walk with the ancestors, a way to connect with the past. A history that was taken from my family, but not forgotten.

In my almost twenty-year career with Parks Canada, I have had the opportunity to attend powwows, meetings with council members, and ceremonies held by Indigenous groups throughout Ontario. In my role as an Indigenous person who is also an archaeologist, I take these opportunities to share our history through a different lens: that of the artifact. Artifacts may only be remnants left behind by the people who went before us, but to me, holding an artifact is like shaking hands with the ancestors. They are teachers who have their own stories of how they were created, utilized, and, sometimes, discarded. I encourage other

Indigenous people who may have never seen a sherd of Indigenous ceramic or an intricately flaked projectile point to hold them and see the technical and artistic skills needed to create them. And to feel pride in knowing that our ancestors created these objects that have lasted thousands of years. Often, Elders and others attending these functions will teach me about the artifacts by sharing their own stories.

Parks Canada archaeologists photographing artifacts uncovered at the Rouge National Urban Park.

Even in the field, conducting archaeological work, I am being taught our history. Though Indigenous people walked lightly on the landscape, they left behind many ways for us to reconnect with them. Understanding how to read those clues is what archaeologists try to do. When standing at a potential archaeological site, we take note of the landscape. Are we on a high bluff, near water, in a valley? When excavating, we note the soils: are they well-drained, are they rocky, would I camp here? Reading the landscape and the soils offers us a more in-depth understanding of how people lived on the land. I have worked in all the national parks, national marine conservation areas, and many of the national historic sites within Ontario. These are all unique areas that protect archaeological sites that reflect how the Indigenous and later settler populations utilized the landscape and its many natural resources.

One of the parks where I have worked is the Rouge National Urban Park, on the east side of Toronto. This national park was established in 2011 to protect the watershed of the Rouge River, from its headwaters in the Oak Ridges Moraine down to its mouth at Lake Ontario. The park – created to protect the Carolinian ecosystem, meadow, and riverine habitat – is the first federal area in Canada to protect agricultural land. Once fully established, it will be the largest urban park in North America. The park also protects ten thousand years of human history.

There are approximately 326 registered archaeological sites, both Indigenous and settler, identified within the Rouge National Urban Park.

The Indigenous sites range from single, isolated finds to palisaded villages. They date from the Archaic period (7000 BC to 1000 BC) through to the Contact period (circa 1650), and well into the twentieth century. The park also contains a national historic site: Bead Hill, a seventeenth-century Seneca village. The settler sites include mills, blacksmith shops, designated heritage houses, cemeteries, and even the foundations of a post office known as the Mongolia site.

Many of these sites were registered during archaeological surveys conducted in advance of urban expansion prior to the establishment of the Rouge National Urban Park. The Toronto and Region Conservation Authority (TRCA), set up after Hurricane Hazel's destructive 1954 flooding, recorded many archaeological sites during its conservation work within the Rouge watershed. An extensive archaeological survey also took place in the 1970s, when large tracts of land were expropriated for the creation of an airport in Pickering. Though the airport was never built, that survey registered a large number of sites and confirmed the importance of the Rouge River to both Indigenous and settler histories.

The Rouge connects with other large rivers, such as the Holland, to provide access to Lake Simcoe, the Trent-Severn Waterway, and Georgian Bay on Lake Huron. The Rouge and the Little Rouge Rivers, which join and separate along the valley, formed the eastern arm of a major trading-settlement area along the north shore of Lake Ontario. The Humber River formed the western arm of this area, now referred to as the Toronto Carrying Place Trail. These rivers, the highways of the past, transported goods and people for millennia before the landscape was dramatically changed by settlers. When settlers arrived in the late 1700s, they

Decorated rim from an Indigenous ceramic vessel uncovered at the Rouge National Urban Park.

began to clear forests and establish small villages that would eventually grow into the cities of Stouffville, Markham, Scarborough, and Pickering that now surround the Rouge National Urban Park.

Deforestation and other changes to the landscape altered the Rouge River, which was once navigable many kilometres farther upstream than it is currently. To combat these changes, the Rouge National Urban Park and the TRCA have jointly undertaken an extensive watershed rehabilitation program. This program, in co-operation with local farmers, includes riparian planting as well as the creation of new wetlands and fish-spawning habitats. During these initial years of establishing the park, visitor welcome areas, over twenty-five kilometres of trails, and the restoration of an existing campground are also planned. Parks Canada's archaeological team conducts archaeological assessments prior to the implementation of any of these projects.

In addition to this work, the archaeology team confirms the inventory of registered archaeological and cultural heritage sites, assessing their condition and investigating areas that have not had previous archaeological assessments. These assessments take many forms, depending on the type of site or the proposed impact to the area. Pedestrian, test pit, and ground-penetrating radar surveys, along with the photographic recording of heritage buildings and cemeteries, have been conducted. One of the results of all this work is the identification of new Indigenous and settler archaeological sites.

Parks Canada has a small archaeological team that focuses on the Rouge National Urban Park during these critical establishment years. I conducted archaeology in the park in 2015–16. To complete the enormous amount of work scheduled, our team relied on field liaisons from various First Nations communities that represented the ten Indigenous members of the Rouge National Urban Park First Nations Advisory Circle to help us conduct the fieldwork. The FNAC is comprised of ten First Nations communities, including the Mississaugas of the Credit, Six Nations of the Grand River, the Huron Wendat, and the Williams Treaty First Nations. The field liaisons not only assisted in conducting the fieldwork, but also shared their experiences working on other archaeological sites. Their experience and knowledge of artifacts greatly sped up our work. More importantly, we developed a mutually beneficial exchange of ideas, knowledge, and history. Many expressed their desire to uncover their history and connect with the ancestors, something archaeology can provide.

As Indigenous people, we are deeply connected to our history, our ancestors, and the land. Even though cities like Toronto cover and hide it, our past is still there. We just have to see. The ancestors walked before us, but they are still teaching us.

DON SONG
(2002)
REBEKA TABOBONDUNG

TEACHING #1: URBAN LANDSCAPE

I found a song along the Don River
just before you run into the tents and shacks
where the brown water picks up
you can easily climb down to the muddy shore
hardly anyone goes down that far
on the Discovery Trail
except for the fast bikers
and the people who live there
I'm told at one time
the River's mass used to glide across the entire valley
It has always been a highway
before cars were thought of
or White people
birch bark used to cut the water
passing songs along the shores

Did you know, for fifteen dollars you can buy a ticket to go on the Great Indian Bus Tour of Toronto? Your urban Indian guide will tell you that the waters of Lake Ontario once reached as far as Casa Loma. That whole damn City should be underwater!

They had been on her tongue her whole life
but after all the years of swallowing the numbing burn
It appeared too late
the ancient story had rolled off
to dry into the dampness of the dirt

Eventually turning hot and wet again
(The burn always stayed)
from the Island to the new city
a quick thinning of the blood
won't soften the concrete in either place
the biker didn't even notice
the song still muddy down there
waiting for a heavy dream

Off to the side of the spot where the Castle sits, a regularly frequented campsite was used by traders and travellers from different First Nations.

URBAN LANDSCAPE: TEACHING #2

The song floated shallow along the muddy water
underneath rainbows
It gelled with slick persistence
something crept from under it
suspended from the pillow
attached to the belly
and the stench
It appeared wasted and distilled by cables
always pumping
stealing the bright nothing
until even its shades and shadows had faded
so the vibrations would be gone
and the story forgotten
of the misty sun about to burst
letting go the Idea
blackness so bright Creation had slipped out

Your guide will share some stories too, like the one about Grand Chief Wabakine of the Mississaugas. He tried to stop Toronto's first murder from happening. Some Dominion soldiers were raping his sister. When he intervened they clubbed him over the head with a rock, then killed his entire family. The soldiers didn't receive so much as a slap on the wrist because the courts only understood English. That was in the late 1790s. The murder took place at what is now St. Lawrence Market.

She bled with moon and fell
hard against the dirty brick
steady with the rain
the cloud closed across her breasts
his hands too
gliding his mouth along soft edges of skin

(On The Great Indian Bus Tour of Toronto you won't find out how many
of us women have been raped.)

The brush moved through her
collecting small tales
she spit out
at certain moments
apple and strawberry
watched the tiny buds about to burst
those nights when the moon held her
and laughed
deep over the city
across the sidewalks, drunks and patios
caught her in its pale surface
suspended in firs
elusive to the climb and the reach
and gone again
taking rhythmic direction
into the expanse of bats and stars
the firs still trembling
for her small fingers
fumbling for the deliverance of the moon

*On The Great Indian Bus Tour of Toronto, your guide will tell you that contrary to
popular perception, Spadina Avenue is not derived from a European language but from
Ishpaadinna, the Anishinaabe word describing the area meaning 'going up the hill.'*

The moon had called again
through meshed blood
It hung across the landscape
teasing her onto the Island

away from artificial light
She told her cousin to park the van further down the street
so she could watch the red
dance beyond the concrete
letting its scars mark her skin
and go further
motioning at the dirty city
and its endless bodies of water
the main street and surf
the sterility found only in makers' hands
She only wanted living things
pressed her body into their beauty
and the endless sadness
attached to it
she felt confused and betrayed when the sadness stayed past mornings

Now buried under the concrete and buildings there used to run a creek. A rich salmon spawning ground fished by the Mississauga Nation. Today it's a path known as Philosopher's Walk located just behind the Royal Ontario Museum. Sometimes I use that path as a shortcut to get to class.

My father and brother
the stark emptiness of their absence
of unravelling, of soul transport
of ancient stone and youthful steps
My desperation for stone was beaten
by disfigured lips and sank
with secrets and mistakes
of a beautiful woman
offering her body to alcohol
holding her till morning
the vision has come in drunk and sober nights
she lied to both and still wanted the water stories
they couldn't give her
the dreams abstracted daylight
carried shadows of cedar
and suspended her into a film reel
black and white and subtitled

In Toronto there's a sweatlodge right in the downtown eastside. A guy named Tom runs them. Tom encourages any Nishnab to join him. If it gets too hot in there all you need to say is 'All My Relations' and you can get out. You don't have to be sober for four days before getting in. But he's sure to remind you how much you stink up the lodge.

URBAN ESCAPE: TEACHING #3

She wanted to know how high the water reached
in a daylight and through brick
she heard the Jingle dress
ice shattering
500 years of wailing, screaming
Their faces fanned with eagle feathers masked by their clan names
Mukwa, Ahmik, Maaiingan
come into them
Their bodies were momentarily suspended by the animal spirits

TEACHING #4

Her ancient leathery skin is still ALIVE under the sidewalk!

I don't expect you to understand this white man/Zhaagnaash
It penetrates your metres
I don't expect you to understand …
… from the bedroom window
the shock of electricity compounded
hit the air and willow with a slap
Bouncing hard on hearts
she walked again to the shore
tobacco offering
asked for medicine
she made a drum
A sharp light flashed along his temple
she guessed it had always been there
as the song slipped from his tongue
and fell into her
It blew softly on her chest
And slid back into the brown water

FOUR MURALS

PHILIP COTE, MFA

THE ANISHINAABE CREATION STORY

In the beginning there was a Great Black Void and in that void there was a spirit, the Great Mystery, who sent his thoughts out into the Universe. When no response happened, those thoughts were called back and the Great Mystery said, 'Create light in the Universe as you come back to me.' All the stars were born and from them the planets were formed. It is at that moment we had light and dark in the Universe. The Anishinaabe people believe we are all made of light and dark, the physical and the spirit.

– Miigwetch to Edward Benton-Banai

The mural I created for CentreCourt Condos, at Jarvis and Dundas, is entitled *The Original Family*. It depicts one of our oldest stories, 'The Anishinaabe Creation Story,' which was brought down through oral traditions and pictographic images drawn on birchbark scrolls. This mural is in my own contemporary style of Woodland painting and begins with the First Man and the First Woman and their sacred union, and the beginning of the Creation Story.

It is said that the First Man (Waynaboozhoo) came down from the sky and was lowered. The first thing he did was to travel across the land and begin naming everything – all the plants, all the trees, all the animals, all the insects, all the fish, and all the birds, etc. The Anishinaabe Elders say this is where our naming ceremony comes from, and also where our Anishinaabe language comes from. This is why all the animals have gathered around the First Man and the First Woman – as a reminder of how our story is closely connected to all life on Earth.

The next thing the First Man is asked to do by the Creator is travel to the Fire Keeper in the East and learn about the Sacred Fire and all its connections to the heart and the Universe. In doing so, he meets the Fire Keeper's Daughter, whom we now know as the Morning Star. It is their sacred union that marks the beginning of humanity here on Turtle Island.

In the West is the First Thunderbird, the Co-Creator and protector of the people, who helps them to remember that we all have gifts and we should always be humble and know those gifts came from our ancestors. The fish reminds us of our close connection to the Underworld/Spirit World, for the fish is the guardian or gatekeeper, and the otter is the helper who brought the teachings of the four directions and knowledge of what we know today as the Medicine Wheel Teachings.

The moose represents the hoofed beings and the teacher of the forest and the children. The birds are reminders of spiritual connections to our hearts (our Sacred Fire) and to the Universe. The rabbit is here to remember the trickster and that not everything can always go as planned. Last is the bear, a reminder that we are in changing times, which our prophets predicted as the Seven Fires Prophecy.

The Prophets also gave us teachings about the Eighth Fire, a time we are now in. It is said that in this time, our stories and ancient wisdom will come to the surface and be shared with the Western peoples, and a new beginning will happen, called the Eighth Fire. A new people will emerge, and this will be the beginning of the Golden Age.

The Original Family, Philip Cote, acrylic and latex on brick wall, 120' × 37', 2019. Location: Jarvis (and Dundas), southwest wall of CentreCourt condos.

There were ancient Ice Runners known as the 'Oh-kwa-ming-i-nini-wug' of Algonquin/Anishinaabe lineage that predate the current Indigenous population by some 100,000 years. They travelled across the icefields that came down to the present-day City of Toronto right up along Davenport Road. These 'Wisconsin glaciers' were two kilometres high and at the edge became hunting grounds for the Anishinaabe. On the Ice Runners' hunting grounds were woolly mammoths, short-faced bears, sabre-toothed cats, woolly rhinos, giant elk, two-metre-tall, 180-kilogram beavers, dire wolves, giant Mi-gi-zi' eagles with six-metre wingspans, giant sloths, American bison, stag moose, shrub-ox, and giant condors.

Resurge: First Timeline, *Philip Cote, lead artist, acrylic and spray paint on concrete, 16' × 30' each (ten pieces in total), 2017. Location: King's Mill Park, Toronto (under Old Mill Station).*

The beginning of the mural depicts an Eagle Dancer representing the ancient Ice Runners, also known as the 'Oh-kwa-ming-i-nini-wug' of Algonquin lineage, who were here in those early days looking toward the future. The Return of the Buffalo is represented here and is part of the story of this land, as there were once giant wood buffalo that roamed across this territory now called the City of Toronto.

The second Ice Runner is the man running behind the wolf, who is the First Brother of Man. The Black Thunderbird symbol in the Medicine Wheel Circle is the symbol of the Anishinaabeg nation, the first to inhabit this territory.

Then you will see the Tobacco Plant, an important sacred medicine offered up in our ceremonies. Tobacco is in the East on the Medicine Wheel. It is one of the four sacred medicines.

The Crane is part of the Anishinaabe clan system and governance. The Crane Clan shares power of Chieftainship with the Loon Clan. It takes care of the leadership of external relations, external negotiations, speaker of the community, leadership, and mediation, and expresses sentiments for the people, but the wishes of the group.

The next symbol, the Beaver, represents the Wendat people, the next in the order of inhabiting this territory.

Next you will see an Anishinaabe Moccasin, a message of the many trails Indigenous peoples travelled across the city over 13,500 years ago. The Moccasin is on Cedar, a medicine that is put down on the arbour of the Sundance. Cedar, in the South on the Medicine Wheel, is most often used as a tea and for bathing and cleansing in Cedar Baths.

The next symbol is the Star Symbol of the Cree peoples, who next came to the land to live here.

Then the mural depicts the Eagle, which can travel between the physical world and the spiritual world, and is thus closest to the Creator.

The eagle feather and eagle wings are sacred. They are used in Smudge Ceremonies, and the eagle feather is a symbol of truth, power, and freedom.

The Beaver is a symbol of advancement and industry/progress, since he is a builder.

Next is the Canoe and Sage. Sage, in the West on the Medicine Wheel, is another medicine used for smudging and cleansing. The Canoe is a symbol of all the paths the Indigenous people created that are still used to this day, like the Humber River trail, the Don River, etc.

The next Circle is the flag of the Haudenosaunee people. It represents the Hiawatha wampum belt.

Beside the Circle, we have the Raven (also known as the Trickster) and the Bear.

The Fish, a knowledge keeper, represents the intellect of the community.

The Bear is another Clan animal. Bears are settlement guardians: they patrol the local area. They also know medicinal plants and are healers, guardians of traditions. The Bear stands on a loop of braided Sweetgrass. This medicine is in the North, another one of the four sacred medicines used in smudging and ceremony. Sweetgrass is a symbol our Mother Earth's hair. We braid sweetgrass to show our respect for her and all she does for us every day.

The History of the Land, *Philip Cote, acrylic and latex on brick wall, 65' × 9', 2017.*
Location: Spadina and Dupont, northeast corner.

The Bear looks on toward the Giant Buffalo. There were once 60 million Buffalo in North America, only to be slaughtered by the settlers so they could take the land from the Indigenous peoples. The Buffalo was vital for the survival of Indigenous peoples of North America, who used all the parts of the animal: the furs for clothing and warmth, the meat for food, and the bones for tools. Nothing was wasted. Buffalo was a major food source and taken away due to the murder of the Buffalo by the colonists.

It is said that one day there will be a Return of the Buffalo to this land and territory, so they can roam free as they once did here. This is what we all look forward to.

'Nindinawemaaganidok' – 'All My Relations,' which means 'We Are All Related.'

(The mural was commissioned by Dupont by the Castle BIA and the City of Toronto.)

The title of this work is 'Ojibway Dreamer,' a tribute to Chanie Wenjack, who symbolizes the struggles of all Indigenous peoples across this country. We start with the Seven Fires Prophecy. It was told that seven prophets came from the water on the eastern shores of North America. At that time, this land was known to the Indigenous peoples as Turtle Island.

The Seven Fires each saw stages of future history through a vision of what was to come, and for wisdom keepers who remember to tell this story. It is now clear that what was predicted by the Seven Fires has come true. Chanie doesn't know this, but he was a part of the Eighth Fire. His role was to become part of the healing needed to help bring understanding about heart thinking, and how we all must leave a legacy for future generations. For Chanie Wenjack, it was to tell us his story, one among many losses due to the residential school system.

The Seven Fires Prophecy states that one day there will be a choice of two roads: the dark road or the light road. Each one of the Seven Fires represents a time period.

The **First Fire** is that the Anishinaabek Nation will go on a great migration across the land, following the Sacred Shell to seven sacred stopping places.

During the **Second Fire**, the nation will camp by a large body of water. In this time, the direction of the Sacred Shell will be lost. The Midewiwin (the faith keepers of the Anishinaabe) will diminish in strength. A Potawatomi boy will be born to point the path back to the traditional ways. He will show the direction to the stepping stones to the future of the Anishinaabe people.

During the **Third Fire**, the Anishinaabe will find the path to their chosen ground, a land in the west to which they must move their families. This will be the land where food grows upon the waters.

The **Fourth Fire** prophecy was delivered by a pair of prophets. The first said, 'You will know the future of our people by the face the light-skinned people wear. If they come wearing the face of brotherhood, there will come a time of wonderful change for generations to come. They will bring new knowledge and articles that can be joined with the knowledge of this country. In this way, two nations will join to make a mighty nation. This new nation will be joined by two more so that four will form the mightiest nation of all. You will know the face of the brotherhood if the light-skinned race comes carrying no weapons, if they come bearing only their knowledge and a handshake.'

In the time of the **Fifth Fire**, there will come a period of great struggle that will grip the lives of all Native people. At the waning of this Fire, there will come among the people one who holds a promise of great joy and salvation. If the people accept this promise of a new way and abandon the old teachings, the struggle of the Fifth Fire will be with the people for many generations. The promise that comes will prove to be a false promise. All those who accept this promise will cause the near destruction of the people.

In the time of the **Sixth Fire**, it will be evident that the promise of the Fifth Fire came in a false way. Those deceived by this promise will take their children away from the teachings of the Elders. Grandsons and grand-daughters will turn against the Elders. In this way, the Elders will lose their reason for living … they will lose their purpose in life. At this time, a new sickness will come among the people. The balance of many people will be disturbed. The cup of life will almost become the cup of grief.

In the time of the **Seventh Fire**, New People will emerge. They will retrace their steps to find what was left by the trail. Their steps will take them to the Elders, whom they will ask to guide them on their journey.

Ojibway Dreamer, *Philip Cote, canvas-wrapped panels, 17' × 6.5' (triptych), 2020.*
Location: Scotia Bank Legacy Space in partnership with the Gord Downie & Chanie Wenjack Fund,
Scotiabank branch at 392 Bay Street in Toronto.

But many of the Elders will have fallen asleep. They will awaken to this new time with nothing to offer. Some of the Elders will be silent because no one will ask anything of them. The New People will have to be careful in how they approach the Elders. The task of the New People will not be easy.

If the New People will remain strong in their quest, the Water Drum of the Midewiwin Lodge will again sound its voice. There will be a rebirth of the Anishinaabek Nation and a rekindling of old flames. The Sacred Fire will again be lit.

It is in this time that the light-skinned race will be given a choice between two roads. One road will be green, lush, and very inviting. The other road will be black and charred, and walking it will cut their feet. In the prophecy, the people decide to take neither road but instead to turn back, to remember and reclaim the wisdom of those who came before them. If they choose the right road, the Seventh Fire will light the Eighth and final Fire, an eternal fire of peace, love, brotherhood, and sisterhood. If the light-skinned race makes the wrong choice of roads, the destruction they brought with them in coming to this country will come back at them and cause much suffering and death to all the Earth's people.

As you can see, it is Chanie's story. Even though it's a sad one, his story tells us that we are going in the right direction, to a place where our ancestors lived somewhere deep in our hearts. Chanie would love to know his suffering wasn't in vain and his life is helping this generation to find where home is.

Special thanks to Edward Benton-Banai, Chief of the Grand Medicine Society of the Medewiwin for sharing his wisdom here.

The image (previous page) that shows this story is a combination of symbols representing the Seven Fires Prophecy. It is said that during this time of great change, a great white bear will show itself and come down from the north. I know some of you will think it's a polar bear, but, in fact, it will be a black bear that is white.

A boy representing Chanie Wenjack will be riding on the bear's back, dreaming about the future, and on the left will be a thunderbird. It's understood that the thunderbird is a Co-Creator and was given the power to create new life, just as the Creator did in making life on our Mother Earth. The thunderbird will have its wings stretched out, pointing in the direction the bear is travelling. The sky will be full of stars, with constellations named by our ancestors, showing the seasons and direction to travel during the night.

Symbolically, the thunderbird represents Chanie travelling in the spirit world. As Chanie and the bear travel, bear tracks are left behind. As the ancestors said, we would one day get lost and need to look for the bear to help us find our way back to the original teachings, and it would be the bear who would show us the way.

TRAILBLAZERS AND CHANGEMAKERS

TANNIS NIELSEN: THE SIMCOE STREET MURAL

INTERVIEW BY ERICA COMMANDA

Tannis Nielsen has been a part of the Toronto arts community for over twenty years. Her work includes research, teaching, and a range of visual arts (drawing, painting, new media installations, sculpture, and performances). She mainly focuses on anti-colonial theory, natural law/Indigenous governance, Indigenous arts activism(s), and the relative investigations of Indigenous science and Western quantum physics. She attended the University of Toronto, where she obtained an Art and Art History-Specialist Degree, and a Masters in Visual Studies (MVS). Nielsen also has a Diploma in Art and Art History from Sheridan College. Her most recent project is 'The Simcoe Underpass Mural,' which features two walls. The eastern wall, 'Gchi-twaa-wendan Nibi – Honour the Water,' is dedicated to the Water Walkers; the western wall, 'N' gekaajig kidowog – My Elders Said,' is dedicated to Elders who have lived/are living in Toronto.

Can you introduce yourself and explain what brought you to live and work in Toronto?

I am a mixed Métis, Anishinaabe, Danish multimedia artist and mother. My mother is Merle Monkman, who was born in Goldfields, Saskatchewan. My grandma told me they had to take a dogsled across the Athabasca to get to a hospital. My grandmother was born in a Métis village called St. Louis, in Saskatchewan. Her name is Kitty Boucher. My grandfather was Joe Monkman. He was born in Halcrow District, Saskatchewan, across the river from St. Louis. His family was originally from Peguis, Manitoba. In the 1880s it was known as St. Peter's. I haven't met any Monkman relatives from Manitoba, but I have maintained my familial connections to my granny's side in St. Louis. My dad, Paul Nielsen, was born in Aalborg, Denmark. I always try to be as specific as possible in providing my introductions to ancestry/territory while also ensuring the

Danish side is honoured. It's more than just protocol, as it's also a fun way to discover new cousins and community.

I came to Toronto in 1989, when I was nineteen. Before that, I lived in almost thirty different places across Canada. What brought me to live and work in Toronto was my daughter's father. I met him in Calgary, as he was about to get signed with the Toronto Argonauts, but then we separated. Because my daughter's mixed (with Jamaican ancestry), I didn't want to bring her back to redneck Alberta, where I came from. It was important that she also be connected to her dad's family. It takes two to parent, so we stayed here. Then I entered university in 1996. That's when I first met Rodney Bobiwash, the first person to welcome me to the Indigenous community. What an amazing person to first meet! I was at U of T for eight years.

Artist Tannis Nielsen painting portrait of Lee Maracle on the Simcoe Street Mural.

What inspired you to create the Lower Simcoe mural and what do you hope people take away from it?

I look at that mural like a land acknowledgement. Oftentimes, I'll be in a faculty meeting and I'll be asked to do the land acknowledgement. I'm like, 'No, you should do it.' I often put it on settlers to do that land acknowledgement. I painted the mural because I wanted pedestrians walking by to immediately gain the sense that this is Anishinaabe-Haudenosaunee territory. There are twenty portraits of Elders on the wall. There's also going to be quotes from each Elder. I'll have a quote from Art Solomon and a quote from Rodney Bobiwash, so pedestrians can also begin to understand a little bit of the natural laws, which is our governance and classification of this place.

Hopefully, they'll be inspired toward environmental sustainability by gaining some access to those teachings. That's what the water wall is about. To honour Grandmother Josephine Baa and the water. And also because the mural is so close to the water. It's really funny because the night we started the water wall, there was a huge flood. The Simcoe underpass got flooded out and cars got stuck in the water. My friends who live under the bridge, Mitch and Alex, said, 'Hey, as soon as you started, the water wall was flooded!' That was just the water reminding us that it's this force of nature. I hope that people gain an introduction to Indigenous territory, cosmology, and environmental sustainability. That's my inspiration for that.

The mural subjects are recognizable Indigenous leaders who have made an impact on the Indigenous community here in Toronto. Who did you select and why did you choose them?

They're recognizable to our community. They are not recognizable to mainstream society. I wanted to honour them on a platform, showing the mainstream who our teachers and leaders are. It was really hard to choose who to select. I went on Facebook and asked the Facebook community who they wanted me to paint, and they gave me eighty-something names, which is great because we have so many respected people in our community who others wanted to honour.

Marie Gaudet was my cultural advisor. She's an Anishinaabe Elder from Wiki. She's been one of my best friends for fifteen-plus years. We wanted to have a representation of the traditional caretakers of the land here. There are also some people on the mural who aren't from here, including Lee Maracle, who is Sto:loh. She's been living and working in our community as an Elder and teacher for decades.

In what ways has the Indigenous community, including artists, impacted Toronto?

Indigenous artist Nyle Johnston is from Cape Croker. He worked on the Simcoe Mural project with me. If you look at the work he did on the mural, it's very much of scroll painting, or petroglyphs painting – symbols and iconography. He refers to himself as a rock painter. I think we are continuing in the original use of the function of our form, which is to identify and to mark place and territory. The natural laws of place and territory are transcribed through our visual iconography. Western anthropologists say we never wrote our history down, but if you look at the Lakota winter counts, the petroglyphs, the symbols, geometry, and iconography that are woven into baskets and blankets – that's our written history and visual literacy. I think Indigenous artists are continuing in that original intention with our art.

There's a quote: 'All Indigenous art speaks either to, from, or about the land.' I forget who said that and have tried finding the quote many times, but I believe them. I had an Indigenous artist disagree with me once. And that's cool, we don't need to all agree, but I believe even if you paint someone wearing a ribbon shirt or skirt, the teaching of the ribbon skirt or shirt is from the land. Teachings of that fashion are of the land.

We visually transcribe our teachings. That's our literacy. That's our visual sovereignty. That also continues the land acknowledgement. You look at the work that Robert Houle has done throughout the city and the performances of Rebecca Belmore. Those artists are within the notion of place and they start with the land first – most of us work that way. Indigenous artmaking is also mapping Indigenous territory through our art.

How should the City of Toronto acknowledge and celebrate Indigenous presence in Toronto?

Simcoe Street Mural portrait of Anishinaabe activist Rodney Bobiwash.

Land back. They often ask an Anishinaabe person to do the land acknowledgement and give them an honorarium, but I sometimes wonder if they do that so they don't have to learn how to pronounce the nation's words. It goes beyond the land acknowledgement. It is a practice of token recognition. It's also just about the land, acknowledging the rivers that were paved over, the mounds, the sustenance we are given from living in this place and that we need to thank, honour, respect, and take care of the land.

The City of Toronto fundamentally is built from a capitalist economy. The crux of a capitalist economy is that it was built and sustained through racist ideology. Without treaties or doctrines of discovery, there wouldn't be that economy. It's built on the backs of attempted erasure of our sovereignty.

When the residential schools apology happened, I googled the true meaning of reconciliation. I

Simcoe Street Mural portrait of Anishinaabe writer and storyteller Basil Johnston.

found it under a Christian context – it's a physical act of sorrow. In the movie *Black Robe*, where the Jesuit priest is whipping himself with the reed – that's a physical act of sorrow. The priest was seeking penance. It's not that I want settler society to whip themselves with reeds, but they could make their reconciliation physical. If we look at truth and reconciliation under a Christian context, the truth is the removal of territory, family, ancestry, language, ceremony, the denial of our humanity and civility. The truth is the intentional spread of smallpox and other genocidal strategies. That's the truth. Knowing that everything they tried to take away is tied to land: culture, ancestry, cosmology, ideology. Where that all came from is from the land. If reconciliation is a physical act, it's an attempt to put *all of that* back. The way you put all that back is starting with the land. That's the foundation and where everything comes from.

Do you have any favourite stories or understandings about Toronto?

What I love most about Toronto is the Dish with One Spoon agreement and how normally contested nations came together and agreed to share the land and resources. We're continuing to do that today, but there's a problem today. It's like a knife is on the table today, whereas the Dish with One Spoon had no hard edge, no fighting.

But there is sure one hell of a fight under capitalism. Indigenous homelessness, suicide, oppression. If we can go back to that original agreement of the Dish with One Spoon and have every citizen in Toronto being in understanding of that, and build an economy around that, that would address things like the token land acknowledgement. If we could go back to that land-based economy and equal-access reciprocity, the Dish with One Spoon treaty would enable more sharing and less competition by recognizing the original economic structure and the original constitution/natural laws of place.

You often centre your work on Indigenous cosmological understanding. What inspired you to do so?

My Danish father once asked me, 'Why you always painting your mother's culture?' I told him that I'm on Turtle Island. One day, I got to go to Denmark to learn about Danish culture. I find that there's this reversal – you know, how people look at Native North America with this romantic stereotypical view and lack of knowledge. I'm guilty of doing that to Denmark. I romanticize and stereotype Denmark because I have very little knowledge. There's Hans Christian Andersen, there's castles, the national animal is a swan. How could you not romanticize it? (Joking.)

I think before Christianity, we all had land-based spirituality. I'd like to go to Denmark and see what that spirituality is like and if there are any remnants of that around still. When I try to google land-based spiritual practices in Denmark, I get taken to spiritual New Age sites. It just inherently doesn't feel right to me.

Learning and growing into a deeper understanding of an Indigenous/Anishinaabe cosmology helped ground me through a reconnection to land, place, and spirit. I was on my own at the age of twelve for a few months when I first quit school, never graduated high school, lived all over, and was nomadic. With the birth of my daughter Brittany, I thought I better get some grounding. Literally what was grounding was my grandmother, my grandfather, my mother, and gaining a greater awareness of who they were, where they were from, and entering into the community here.

I was a really angry kid growing up, so once I started learning about historical trauma, colonization, and its effect on our psyche, I started to redirect the anger from my family toward the system instead. That was healing for me to do.

That was what my thesis was about, too, because my grandma spoke Cree, Dene, Saulteaux, Anishinaabemowin, Michif, French, and English, but not with me. She only spoke the colonial languages to us. My thesis idea was about the undoing of that. She got Alzheimer's and started speaking in Cree to me. She started to let go of her colonial erasure. They say when you have Alzheimer's, you remember all of these things from childhood, but you can't remember two hours ago.

With my grandma's permission, I recorded her telling me all of the stories from her childhood, how her brothers would trap, how she would skin the furs and sell them. She'd tell me how she started making bison robe coats for the RCMP. She used to put the collars on the coats. The collar on the bison robe coat is the hardest to do because it comes from the gruff – under the neck of the bison – which is the longest hair. She started telling me all of these cultural physical actions in her life. It was incredible to gain access to it.

I was twelve when I first quit school and my parents divorced. That's when I went to my first powwow in Mission, BC, by a residential school. I thought it was a family reunion because my mom and everyone looked alike. I never grew up with specific cultural identifiers from either side of my family. After the divorce, my mom started bringing our culture into our home and started telling me stories. Unfortunately, I didn't care because I was twelve. When I was sixteen or seventeen, I was into partying, and then afterwards I was just trying to survive being nomadic and living all over Canada.

With the birth of Britanny, I began to ask, where am I located? What's my ancestry? What are my roots? I often tell people my cultural knowledge is only about twenty-eight years old, even though I'm fifty.

THE TWO LIVES OF DOCTOR O

MNAWAATE GORDON-CORBIERE

Oronhyatekha was born on August 10, 1841, on the Six Nations reserve and eventually became one of the most influential Indigenous people in nineteenth-century Canada. As he grew, he learned how to bring Kanien'kehá:ka culture and values into Western society. One of his greatest accomplishments was the turnaround of the Independent Order of Foresters under his leadership. A fraternal society that provided insurance benefits to its members, the IOF was in debt and membership was down, but thanks to Oronhyatekha, it became one of the leading fraternal benefit societies in North America, even expanding globally. He was able to achieve so much not just for himself but also for those around him due to his own ambitions, which grew bigger with each new achievement. His legacy lives on in all those across the world whom he helped.

His name, Oronhyatekha, meant Burning Cloud or Burning Sky in Kanien'keha (Mohawk), and he insisted he be called by this name throughout his life rather than by his baptismal name, Peter Martin. Throughout his adult life, he straddled two lives/spheres, one as a Kanien'kehá:ka man and another as a Victorian Canadian man. He was one of Toronto's first 'Urban Indians' – those who grew up on a reservation or in a small town and later decided to try out city life, often for educational or employment opportunities.

Growing up, it didn't seem as though he would end up in the city. His father was from Six Nations by Brantford and his mother from Tyendinaga, close to Belleville. He had many siblings and in his extended family were many chiefs and a clan mother. As a child, Oronhyatekha experienced the reduction of the Six Nations territory, with the Kanien'kehá:ka being displaced into a new area. He was raised with Kanien'keha language and culture, and learned English at Martin's Corner School until he was ten years old.

At that age, Oronhyatekha began attending the Mohawk Institute (then known as the Mechanics' Institute), the residential school in Brantford run by the Anglican Church of Canada. Many Haudenosaunee from Six Nations, as well as Mississaugas from Credit, were made to attend by Anglican missionaries and by their parents, who believed the education would benefit their children. The school taught basic subjects like English, math, geography, and history, while also maintaining a strong focus on the trades so students would leave to become labourers and tradesmen in Canadian society. It is believed that Oronhyatekha tried to run away from the school at least three times, but

In 1860, age 19.

was caught and forced to pledge to never leave again. He was not the only student of the institute to rebel. The school had to be rebuilt many times due to fires set by its students. In his fourth and final year at the school, Oronhyatekha focused on shoemaking. He emerged from the institute ready to begin his shoemaking career.

As a shoemaker, he drifted through life, drinking and making friends with shady characters. It didn't take him long to realize that a career in shoemaking wasn't for him – he wished to pursue more in life.

He attended the Wesleyan Academy in Massachusetts and in the summers would teach on the reserve at Martin's Corner School. He then enrolled at Kenyon College in Ohio, although funding was always a problem during his time there. Despite the financial problems, Oronhyatekha did well in his class and was involved in extracurriculars. In his second year, he participated in a protest with his fellow students, who refused to attend their 8:00 a.m. class due to a school event running long the previous night. The college insisted that all those who participated make up for the missed class or face expulsion. Oronhyatekha ended up pledging to make up for what he missed rather than risk his education.

Unfortunately, at the end of that year, Oronhyatekha requested an honourable dismissal due to lack of funding. He planned to complete his degree, but due to fate, he ended up elsewhere.

In 1860, Edward VII, then Prince of Wales, was to tour the United States and Canada, with a special visit to Six Nations. From the entire reservation, Oronhyatekha, then nineteen, was chosen by the Chiefs to give the welcoming address to the British prince. The Haudenosaunee still greatly valued their alliance to the British and remained loyal. Such a visit by a member of the royal family was a huge honour. It is believed Oronhyatekha was selected due to his extensive education and his command of the English language.

Oronhyatekha prepared a two-minute-long speech that mainly detailed the Haudenosaunee allegiance to Great Britain, hopeful that the visit would 'renew and strengthen the chain' between the two nations, write Keith Jamieson and Michelle Hamilton in their 2016 biography. His sisters diligently made his outfit for the address. The clothing was adorned with beadwork and Haudenosaunee floral designs while the accessories included a bandolier bag and a Plains-style headdress, which had become something of a fashion for Indigenous peoples across Canada to express their Indigeneity. The outfit became one of Oronhyatekha's most prized possessions.

The prince and his physician, Henry Acland, were much impressed by Oronhyatekha's address. Acland, the Regius Professor of Medicine at Oxford University, saw Oronhyatekha's potential and invited him to attend the university. From that moment on, Acland became a great influence in Oronhyatekha's life.

In 1862, Oronhyatekha arrived in England and enrolled at Oxford. With him he brought the outfit his sisters had made for him. As far as records show, he is the first Indigenous man to ever attend Oxford University. He began his studies in May 1862. A month later, he was heartbroken to find his funding revoked, thanks to Reverend Abraham Nelles.

Nelles had been Oronhyatekha's teacher at the Mohawk Institute and later his boss when Oronhyatekha taught on the reservation. Nelles used Oronhyatekha's Kenyon College protest as grounds for cutting his funding. The protest had actually been nearly erased from memory at Kenyon College, remembered only as a trivial incident of the past. Knowing his own guilt, Oronhyatekha could not defend himself and returned to Canada. Nelles's motivations are unknown, although his biographer, Keith Jamieson, suggests he may have been angry at no longer being a mentor to Oronhyatekha.

Rather than Six Nations, Oronhyatekha returned to his mother's reservation, Tyendinaga. It seems likely this decision was due both to the shame he felt over leaving Oxford and the accusations made against him.

He took up teaching again while there and in the summers apprenticed with Dr. John W. Fergusson. He hoped to become a doctor one day.

It was during this time that he met Deyorouseh, meaning Pretty One, with the baptismal name Ellen Hill. Like Oronhyatekha, she was also part of a prominent family – a descendant of legendary Kanien'kehá:ka war chiefs Joseph Brant and John Deseronto. She and Oronhyatekha fell in love and married in 1863.

In that same year, Oronhyatekha enrolled in the Toronto School of Medicine (now a part of the University of Toronto). This time, he used his own earnings and his shares of land to fund his education. Astonishingly, he wasn't the only Indigenous man enrolled in the school at the time. Kahkewaquonaby, a Mississauga of the Credit, was also studying there to earn an MD. Kahkewaquonaby, baptized as Peter Edmund Jones, was named for his father, a prominent Mississauga minister, chief, and historian. Unfortunately, little is known about their relationship. Kahkewaquonaby eventually transferred to Queen's College (now Queen's University) to complete his MD in 1866, a year before Oronhyatekha.

While at the Toronto School of Medicine, Oronhyatekha again immersed himself in extracurricular activities. He joined the University Rifles and became noted for his shooting skills. He served in the Fenian Raids of the late 1800s. He also began his foray into fraternal societies, joining the Independent Order of Good Templars, a temperance society, and King Solomon's Lodge, a masonic society. If Oronhyatekha wasn't busy enough, he and Deyorouseh began a family. In 1864, she gave birth to a girl, whom they named Karakwineh, which means Moving Sun. He earned his MB (Bachelor of Medicine) with honours in 1866 and enrolled in the Doctor of Medicine degree that fall, earning his MD in 1867.

A new chapter in Oronhyatekha's life began as he finally reached a long sought after and fought for goal.

Upon graduating, he searched for a place to set up his practice, eventually settling in Frankford, Ontario. He became established there and was elected the first secretary of the Hastings County Medical Association. In a few years, he moved his practice to Stratford, and then to London in 1875. It was in London where he became a Forester.

In February 1878, Doctor Oronhyatekha was made a charter member of the Court Dufferin in London. Up to then, the Independent Order of Foresters, a fraternal benefit society, had only admitted white men and even outlined this restriction in their constitution. Doctor O (as he was called) was adamant that he get in, and his admission was brought to the attention of the Order's High Chief Ranger. Oronhyatekha was well recommended by all who knew him and initiated into the order.

The membership of the Independent Order of Foresters was composed of white men who joined for the community and insurance benefits. At the time, employers offered few benefits to their workers, and insurance company rates were high. Fraternal societies like the IOF had low rates and provided life insurance and funeral funds, among other benefits. However, at the time of Oronhyatekha's entrance in the order, membership and funds were dwindling. In 1879, there was a secession in the IOF, with a large number of members leaving to create their own order, the Canadian Order of Foresters. It seemed likely that the IOF would soon cease to exist.

In 1881, Doctor O was elected the head – Supreme Chief Ranger – of the order and began drastic improvements that turned the organization around. He instituted age-graded assessments for entry, so it was easier for younger men to enter; membership for women, which helped grow membership numbers; medical examinations and checkups for all members; and a reserve fund. The IOF began to offer more expansive benefits, such as pensions, sick benefits, and disability insurance. The organization grew rapidly, thanks to Oronhyatekha's reorganization. Membership went from fewer than a thousand members when he stepped in as Supreme Chief Ranger to 250,000 within twenty years.

Oronhyatekha was so dedicated to the IOF that he stopped his medical practice to focus on the organization. He wholeheartedly believed in the cause, likely because, as a doctor, he had met many people in need of affordable insurance.

As he became a more prominent member of settler society, he faced controversy. When the Canadian Order of Foresters split from the IOF, they tried to discredit Oronhyatekha's position of Supreme Chief Ranger because of his Indigenous heritage. The COF wanted to claim property of the IOF as their own, and the IOF took them to court. The COF attempted to get the case thrown out by claiming Oronhyatekha was not a legitimate member. While the IOF's constitution explicitly stated that only white men could enter, Oronhyatekha offered a strong rebuttal:

'The Constitution which you have quoted was only intended to exclude applicants who belonged to a race which was considered to be inferior to the white race … [I was granted] admission because they recognized the fact that I belonged to a race which was superior to the white and therefore not under the ban of the laws of the Order.' ('History of the Independent Order of Foresters,' by Oronhyatekha, 1895)

Those who opposed the IOF and its success would criticize the organization for having an Indian leader. Oronhyatekha always remained proud of his heritage, though, as he stated to a *Globe* reporter on June 19, 1903: 'I told you the other night that it was not my fault that I came into the world a full-blooded Indian, but I say to you to-night that if I had my choice in the ordering of things I would come into the world a Mohawk Indian.'

The IOF's headquarters moved from London to Toronto in 1889 and so did Oronhyatekha. The IOF continued to expand under Oronhyatekha's leadership, and in the late 1890s, he decided to create a central headquarters for the IOF. The Temple Building, designed by George W. Gouinlock, stood at Bay and Richmond – at ten storeys in height, it was Toronto's first skyscraper. Equipped with offices and an assembly hall for use by the organization, the building was also decorated for special events, like the Canadian National Exhibition or royal visits. (The Temple Building was torn down in the 1970s.)

At the grand opening, Dr. Oronhyatekha was a guest of honour and was frequently thanked throughout the night in speeches from executive members of the order, who credited him with its current success. When speaking of the doctor, Supreme Vice Chief Ranger D. D. Aitken, in an 1897 interview with *The Evening Star*, said he was 'proud of the genius and of the courage to fashion aright a system that did absolute equity and justice to its membership.' The Temple Building became an important part of Toronto's landscape and helped

The Temple Building, Bay Street.

further establish the IOF. And as the IOF expanded, Oronhyatekha also became prominent within North American society.

Though he lived primarily in Toronto, in order to maintain business within the IOF, he also established an estate in Tyendinaga called the Pines. The land was owned by Ellen's family and acquired by the couple after marrying. His wife and family lived there and he tried to visit frequently. He stated that only the Kanien'keha language could be spoken there. At the Pines, he housed and displayed an impressive collection of Indigenous and European artifacts that was later donated to the early collections of the Royal Ontario Museum. His wife, Deyorouseh, much like Oronhyatekha, dedicated her time to helping others in her community and became an active member of their church. She passed away in May 1901 at the age of fifty-eight.

Not far from the Pines was an island Oronhyatekha acquired, which he named Forester's Island. On this island was another residence known as Sherwood's Castle, and in 1903 he established an orphanage there. He

Sherwood's Castle.

had wanted to provide a home for the children of IOF members who had passed away. He called the orphanage his 'crowning achievement,' according to a 1907 article on Dr. Oronhyatekha's life in the *Toronto Daily Star*. It was elaborately constructed with modern utilities; however, it took in very few children, though it could house up to 250. Unfortunately, due to its high cost to run for so few children, it had to close down not long after Oronhyatekha died.

Oronhyatekha spent his final years travelling the globe to establish new courts of the IOF and recruit more members. Branches were established in Europe, Australia, and even India, still a British colony at the time. In 1907, he made a trip to the southern U.S. in hopes of restoring his health. He stopped in Washington, D.C. on the way to pay a visit to President Theodore Roosevelt. Not long after he reached Savannah, Georgia, his health took a turn for the worse. In his final moments, he made arrangements for his own funeral and the future of the IOF. He sent for his son Acland, who sadly couldn't make it to his father's side in time. Acland accompanied his father's body on the journey back to Toronto for a procession and funeral.

Dr. Oronhyatekha's funeral truly demonstrated the impact he had had on the city. Tens of thousands turned out to be a part of the procession that went from Union Station to Massey Hall. Many were seen wearing black ribbons that read, 'In Memoriam, Our Chief.' The Temple Building was draped in black, though it was not just Foresters who mourned the passing. City council, members of the other fraternal societies he had joined, and citizens who knew him also came out to pay their respects. The procession was followed by a visitation in Massey Hall and then a memorial service.

Portrait of Dr. Oronhyatekha, taken by Lyons, Toronto, c. 1900.

Oronhyatekha was taken to Deseronto for his funeral and burial. There was a service held at the Pines, another at All Saints Church, and the final one at Deseronto Cemetery. Indigenous people from Tyendinaga and Six Nations attended, along with many executive members of the IOF. Dr. Oronhyatekha was laid to rest beside Ellen.

Throughout his life, Dr. Oronhyatekha always strived to do better for himself so he could help others. Though he became more immersed in Victorian culture in the latter half of his life, he held on to his heritage and maintained pride in it. He is remembered today with a mural and plaque at Miziwe Biik Employment Services as well as a street, Doctor O Lane, named for him and located near Carlton and Parliament Streets, not far from one of his homes in the city.

THE DANCE FROM CABBAGETOWN CONES TO SHIIBAASHKA'IGAN CONES

KAREN PHEASANT-NEGANIGWANE

The soothing Nokomis[1] sat with quiet resolve across the table from him, her shawl draped gracefully across her shoulders. The offerings of semaa[2] and other items let her know that consuming this steaming drink was more than sipping some tea for this young man.

Moses had been born in 1926 in Wiikwemikoong, on Manitoulin Island. He shared that he wanted to leave home, to find a better life, a place of mino bimaadiziwin.[3] Moses had a dream – to work the big ships of the Great Lakes, maybe even cross the large waters, but he was not sure. What he was sure of was he wanted to go and sit with ol' Mrs. Whiteloon, to have her tea and seek answers for his life. She had the gift to see, to know what was to be. The tea brought a stillness to him. He drank it in solemn reverence. With astute mindfulness, she waited for him to finish the tea. He returned the near-empty cup to her. The tea leaves at the bottom of the cup made for the most revealing moment of this visit. She ceremoniously took the cup from him and looked from all angles at the leaves – now it was his turn to wait in still eagerness to know what the tea leaves said to her.

He left her place with a confident air of the promise of a new life. The only person he knew who had gone down south was that visitor who came to their home camp when he was a child of about five or six. The old men were sitting around the makeshift cooking stove, drinking their tea and sharing stories. Watching the old men always brought warmth to the little boy. Their animated movement and descriptive narratives let him feel the excitement of their adventures. His favourite story was about that visitor who came to talk about the big city down south.

The visitor was different; he spoke so fast in his enthusiasm about what it was like in the city. The foreign language of English was hard to understand, and even harder to speak. As much as the little boy did not know much about this language, he was more interested in hearing about the houses that didn't need wood for heat. Somehow, this man had left the reserve without the permission of the Indian agent. The 'pass system' was not forcefully practised, as in the prairie provinces in my Mishomis'[4] time. He spoke about the turn of a switch to heat the homes or to get a stove going. The men were both awed and bewildered, but not as much as the little boy.

At twenty-five, the young man was called to seek mino bimaadiziwin.[5] It was 1951. His teacup visit told him that everything would be niizhen.[6] That federal legislation called the Indian Act had changed a little bit. No longer was there a gate on the reserve, blocking those who wanted to leave. He had learned enough of the foreign language at the Indian residential school to get by. He also learned some farming skills while there and spent time in the tailor shop to make small leather projects, such as gloves. He figured it was enough to find something to do in the city. Moses had loaded the Great Lakes ships when they came to Manitoulin with pulp wood. He knew enough of the foreign language to get by – he was good; he would find a job. Besides, his tea-leaf reading had said he would be working in a 'waanzh.'[7] The way that ol' Mrs. Whiteloon described it was that it looked like a long, dark tunnel. That was all Moses needed to hear – she was probably describing the inside of a ship.

The meandering bus trip from Manitoulin to Toronto took all day. He crossed the street from the Bay Street coach terminal and checked into a hotel. He decided to wait until early morning to ask for directions to the shipyards to find a job. On his first day in the big city, his heart was racing. As directed, Moses followed Dundas and watched for the Yonge Street sign. The clerk at the hotel's front desk had told him to follow Yonge to the waterfront, where there were shipyards on both sides. Moses could not help but notice the big hole as he approached Yonge Street. He leaned over the guardrail to see the sweating Black men digging and toiling in the deep ground. He yelled at them to ask what they were doing. They reciprocated his 'colour' reference and asked him, 'Hey, Chief, want a job…come back tomorrow with work clothes on.' Truth is, they were dark-skinned, and he was just about as dark as them. He knew he'd fit in.

Moses never made it to the shipyards at the bottom of Yonge Street. After working and building the Yonge Street subway line, he heard City Hall was hiring. He walked over and started working there shortly after.

He took care of the streets, collected the garbage, changed signs, repaired fire hydrants, and came to know every neighbourhood of the city. Different languages, different foods, and different homes. Vegetable gardens in front, clotheslines out back. The Beaches, Little Italy, Chinatown, Greektown, and then there was Cabbagetown. But he was missing something.

Moses went back home to Manitoulin and met Rosemary. Courtship involved trips back and forth to the Island, a small family gathering for the wedding, and the next part of a new life – mino bimaadiziwin. Rosemary started work up the road from City Hall and became a nurse at the Toronto General Hospital. Although she and Moses both worked, their joint incomes were meagre for the big-city life. They found an apartment flat a few blocks over, not far from their workplaces. The neighbourhood was Cabbagetown, on a street across from Allan Gardens. They knew it was skid row, but it was the start of a dream. It was home. That is where I was born.

I am the first-born of my parents. Our world at the time stretched from Spadina to Parliament, north to St. Clair and south to the waterfront. Dad's favourite Sunday-morning walks were over to Queen's Park, circling

the large trees while pushing the carriage proudly – living his dream. The walk generally included a stop for Mom and Dad at Fran's Restaurant, on College Street, for an ice cream cone. As our family grew, stopping at Fran's for an ice cream became a rare special treat. It wasn't until a recent recounting of this story by my mom that the vision of me crawling up onto the blue vinyl stools came to mind – reaching for my ice cream cone on those hot, humid summer days.

Rosemary Lavallee (Mishibinijima), Moses Lavallee (Wassegejig), and daughter Karen, December 1957.

My parents, but more so my mother, lived by the structured, strict, and righteous order that reflected a colonialist rule instilled by their Indian residential school experience. The 1950s and 1960s were not a safe time for Indians in a big city. Living in the slums, dealing with evictions, and being taken advantage of by landlords were unfortunate truths. By the time we were school age, my parents attained their first home from a little old Italian man who owned shops and other homes. Only after the second bombing of one of his buildings did my parents realize that an ongoing Mafia war included our mortgage holder. Our life had to change drastically, and it did.

By the time we were young teens, Mom knew we had to do other activities. Though we lived in the city, all our free time was spent going back home to the reserve. It's what we knew, it's what we did – to be with family on Manitoulin Island. As much as we went to white schools and lived in white neighbourhoods, we didn't know that life. Only friends and relatives from our reserve or other reserves came to our house. Rarely was English spoken when we had visitors. Mom did attempt to socialize us to the city: she had us go to the United Church for Girl Guides, but we didn't fit in. Then she sent us up the street on St. Clair Avenue to the Catholic church, but again we didn't fit in.

Just as the Jesuit order was a strong part of our Wiikwemikoong home, it was also a strong part of our Toronto life. Once, one of the brothers dropped in to visit. My mother shared her woes of not finding a place for us teenagers to fit in. He suggested the Indian Centre and said to call Millie Redmond. He told Mom, 'She's a kind, helpful lady and she will have something for your kids.' This set Mom on a mission to meet Millie Redmond and see what she had in mind for my sister and me. Millie responded that she didn't have any teen programs but would think of something. Not long after that, Millie suggested a powwow club with dancing and outfit making. I was fourteen and the only powwow I had seen was on my home reserve every civic holiday weekend. I didn't know anything about powwow dance or how to create powwow clothes. As much as I loved to dance, I was shy and had no clue what I would do at a powwow club.

Shortly afterwards, the Jesuit brother dropped by the house again and was glad to hear about the Indian Centre and the powwow club. He pulled my mom aside and warned her about those people who attend the club – those who sit and sing around the drum. He said, 'Be careful, those people can get militant and very political.'

Our home became a regular stopping place for newcomers and settled Torontonian Indians. It was nice when community members dropped by for tea. Overall, it was a very busy time in Toronto. Dad was a news junkie, both with the evening news on TV and the *Toronto Star*. One of the regular headline names and a visitor to our home was Jeannette Corbiere Lavell. She became a big dinnertime topic, as her Supreme Court case[8] and the atrocity of the Indian Act impacted her with a loss of Indian rights.

In the bigger picture, there were political stirrings across Canada and the United States. In 1969, the nineteen-month takeover of Alcatraz Island by the American Indian Movement (AIM) created an uproar in both countries. Not far down the road, across the border, the activism of the civil rights movement was happening. We in Canada were not far behind. Like my father, I followed in becoming a news junkie. It was 1972, and the Black Panther movement and Angela Davis were regular topics of discussion in our home.

Each Tuesday, I hurried home after school for dinner, did the dishes, then headed out to 210 Beverley Street to the Indian Centre. The weekly powwow club became a spiritually driven nurturing time for me. I learned the AIM song and listened to the stories of those who came from the U.S. or from out west. At the same time, I read *Bury My Heart at Wounded Knee*. This was my 'turn of the switch' moment. Dee Brown's book taught me about the hidden stories of colonialism and its impact on Native Americans – I WAS ANGRY! All the history classes I took in school had never taught me about the slaughter, the death, and the lies that governments inflicted on us Indian people. I was raging furious.

The phone rang late one evening. 'Rosemary, aren't you proud of your children … Rosemary … aren't you proud?'

My mom responded: 'What are you talking about?'

The caller on the other end of the line said, 'Didn't you see the news? Right now, they are on the news.'

My mother turned on the television to see me front and centre at the Queen's Park legislative buildings. A beaded headband adorned my glowing cinnamon face, and a strategically placed 'Indian and Proud' button adorned my jacket. We were hundreds of Indian rights activists, marching, protesting, and singing the AIM song … loud and proud. Mom hung up the phone, stormed up the stairs, woke me, and yelled, 'Were you at school? I saw you on television.'

I stayed silent; she was raging.

Fact is, I was a little too young to hang out with the AIM people. I continued with the weekly powwow dance program. It was my saving grace: being with Indians, learning songs, and dancing. Although I did not know it at the time, powwow dance became a healing salve for me. It felt safer, and my parents seemed okay with it. Structure, routine, and righteous order returned to our daily lives. A short while later, the Jesuit brother stopped by again to visit my mother. She had long calmed down after the AIM political protest. The brother suggested, 'Since powwow is going so good, you should go to a big powwow, like the one at Mount McKay in Thunder Bay this summer.'

My dad always had a curious nature about him and loved travelling on the backroads to see new terrain. When an adventure was suggested to visit Anemki-waucheau, known locally as Thunder Mountain (Mount McKay), both my parents' excitement grew. This was the summer that the spirit of Anemki-waucheau touched my dance spirit.

I had only seen powwow at our home community arena onstage or at staged powwow shows in Toronto. Gratefully, with my dad's adventurous nature and my mom's cautionary concerns for cultural practices for me, we packed up. It was the first powwow road trip and it lasted for decades. The long road trip to Anemki-waucheau remained in our memories and created a lifetime of dance memories. I had never been to a powwow camp, or a powwow dance arbour like the one in Thunder Bay. It was a magical moment to witness dancers move to the songs and the drums like I did at my Tuesday-night powwow club, and not for the tourists. It was here, also, that I witnessed for the first time a jingle dress dancer, a Shiibaashka'igan dancer. I was awed and bewildered. Just as my dad had a dream, the desire of mino bimaadiziwin, now I had that same desire.

As a young adult and still in pursuit of a dance, I studied with the late René Highway. He held community contemporary dance classes upstairs at the Native Canadian Centre, at 16 Spadina Road. I did the pliés, attempted *cou-de-pieds*, and stretched myself across the makeshift ballet barre. But I could not find my place within that space. What René did give me, however, was the confidence to chase my dream of dance. I left Toronto, first for Manitoulin, then off to the western prairie provinces to dance.

It was almost fifty years ago at Anemki-waucheau that I witnessed the Shiibaashka'igan Nookomisag dancing in Thunder Bay. Shiibaash-ka'igan were made with jingle cones, customarily with rolled tobacco lid. It was more commonly known as the jingle dress, which represents healing both literally and figuratively. It is understood that this dress came to the Anishinaabe to bring healing.

'Our objective is to continue until there is not a single Indian in Canada that has not been absorbed into the body politic and there is no Indian question, and no Indian Department,' said Duncan Campbell Scott, deputy superintendent of Indian Affairs in 1921. That was the intention of colonial policy, rule, and the sanctioning of Indian residential schools. Somehow, some way, within the muddled confidence of our people, my mom and my dad believed, had faith, and knew to pursue mino bimaadiziwin.

The journey has been long and dark, as like a waanzh, or tunnel. She knew it, that soothing Nokomis. It was in the tea leaves. She also said Dad would marry a twin. My mother is not a twin, but her dad is. Together, they twinned a life for our family between the big city down south and our home on Manitoulin. My dad had thought the tunnel was the ship, and then thought it was the Yonge Street subway line. They say there is light at the end of the tunnel.

When my mom shares the Queen's Park protest story, she glimmers with pride. It was okay that her children did not 'fit in.' Today, she could answer that phone call and say, 'YES! I'm proud.' There is light at the end of the waanzh.

REZ ROCKET ROMANCE

ELAINE BOMBERRY

I am a first-generation Indian residential school survivor and I want to share a unique modern-day Indigenous love story. It began in 1960, and it's the kind of story we rarely hear today – about how my parents found love on a Toronto streetcar and how that love grew into a family.

My late mom, Rita Bomberry (née McCue), was Anishinaabe, from Christian Island (now known as Chimnissing) in Georgian Bay. She was the middle sister of six siblings, three brothers (Wilmer, Bernard (Bev), Orval) and three sisters (Dorothy Crow, Delphine Williams, and Debbie Peltier); all are now deceased. Rita's family were staunch Roman Catholics. From age six to sixteen, my mom went to the Spanish Indian Residential School, on the north shore of Georgian Bay. Her parents were Flora and Merritt McCue.

My dad is Peter Bomberry, Cayuga from Six Nations of the Grand River Territory. He is the youngest of five siblings – four brothers (Leeman, Alfred, Norman, and Hilton) and one sister, Eva Greene, all now passed. Peter's family were traditional Longhouse people. He never had to go to residential school; rather, his parents – Margaret and Harry Bomberry – left Six Nations for Burlington, where his father got a job, and he was enrolled in school.

One evening in the spring of 1960, a handsome young Cayuga man, dressed in a dashing suit and collared shirt, was riding the College streetcar westbound on his way to the North American Indian Club Dance, organized by Patricia Turner from Six Nations. He sat in the middle of the car.

At a main intersection stop along the route, a beautiful young Anishinabe (Ojibway) woman got on the same streetcar. She was all dressed up to go to the dance. When she boarded, these two young people laid eyes on each other for the first time.

My dad's first thought when he saw her was that he could imagine her in a wedding dress. When reminiscing about seeing him for the first time, my mom told me, 'He was the handsomest Indian man I had ever seen.'

Unfortunately, my dad soon had to get off the streetcar as it approached his stop. My mom said she was disappointed to see him leave. Her stop was the next one. But she, too, was on her way to that dance.

Once in the dance hall, my mom sat with her girlfriends as she waited for her date to show up. She waited and waited, but he never appeared. She went to the bar to get herself a drink and saw that the handsome young man from the streetcar was bartending. He told her he was volunteering for the dance. They introduced themselves and continued talking. By the end of the evening, Peter had given Rita his phone number.

The North American Indian Club held dances for the young Indigenous people who were flocking to Toronto. These events gave people like my mom and dad an opportunity to meet one another socially. Many of these young people had been sent to Indian residential schools throughout Ontario. In the city, a large number enrolled in colleges. Rita went to a career college for secretarial and shorthand courses. Peter went to George Brown for welding.

After they'd dated for four months, Peter proposed to Rita on the same College streetcar where their eyes had first met. They planned to get married on Christian Island.

Although their love for one another was undeniable, their families were not happy about their impeding union. The two were from different Indigenous Nations, with very different cultures and religions. The Haudenosaunee and the Ojibway had been at war with each other in the 1700s, and this bitter history was still felt in 1960.

Both sets of parents did not want them to marry. My dad had been expected to marry a traditional Longhouse woman, and my mother was supposed to marry a good Catholic man. Throughout the world, it's like this with any couple who are in love and want to marry but come from different cultures and religions. Both families may get angry at first, but love rules, and the couple get married anyway. This is exactly what my parents did. My dad even went to Catholic catechism classes so he could marry my mom.

Both sets of parents came to accept that Peter and Rita were going to get married, and they made the effort to attend the wedding ceremony on Christian Island. My paternal grandparents, Margaret and Harry, rarely travelled; for them to leave Six Nations was a big trip.

One day in mid-June 1960, the small Catholic church had filled up with family and friends waiting for the ceremony to begin. Time passed, and everyone began to wonder where the priest was. A few people standing outside the church kept looking at the dock to see if he was coming over on a small boat in case he had missed the ferry. The families and friends waited and waited. My mom told me decades later what a gut-wrenching, sad experience it was, waiting for the priest to arrive on the island so he could perform the ceremony. In the end, the priest was a no-show.

Of course, my mom's tears flowed and flowed. How could this happen on their wedding day? There was no way to contact the priest and find out whether or not he was on his way. He travelled on Sundays, delivering sermons from rez to rez in the southern Georgian Bay area.

Three decades later, in the early 1990s, my mom ran into an old friend from her early Toronto days. The friend, who was from Cape Croker, now Chippewas of Nawash, told my mom that the priest who was going to marry them also delivered church services in Cape Croker.

In one of his sermons, he had bragged about 'saving a good Catholic girl from Christian Island from marrying a pagan savage.' My mom's eyes filled with tears. She couldn't believe what she was hearing: thirty years later, she had found out that that priest never had any intention of marrying them.

Back in the summer of 1960, however, Peter and Rita were not going to be thwarted by that priest. Two weeks after their ill-fated first attempt to get married, they wed in Toronto, at St. Peter's Church at Bathurst and Bloor Streets. My mom's bridesmaid was Marilyn Toulouse, one of her best girlfriends, and my dad's best man was Bev (Bernard) McCue, my mom's eldest brother. The four of them were the entire wedding party.

Peter and Rita Bomberry on their wedding day, July 2, 1960, Toronto, ON.

After the ceremony, my parents hopped into my dad's car and drove to my parental grandparents' log cabin in Six Nations, where they had a small celebration and cut their wedding cake.

It was obvious they would establish their life together in Toronto. My parents were both at the beginning of their careers. My dad worked for a

Elaine and her father.

large steel company as a welder, and my mom worked as a secretary in various departments for the Province of Ontario.

I was born during their first year of marriage, in 1961. I was an only child for two years before my brother Michael was born. Our family lived for many years on Christie Street, above a store across from Christie Pits. That park became our year-round playground. We went to Palmerston Street Public and were the only Indigenous children in the entire school of over a thousand students.

As school-age children, we were taught by our mom to be proud of who we were, and to not let anyone ever call us 'wagon burners' or that awful dreaded word 'sq___.' I can't even type it, it's so abhorrent! These are words I've had to deal with and address throughout my life.

During the winter months, my dad would play in snowsnake tournaments in Six Nations and on various rezzes in Upstate New York. He was quite the thrower back in the day and would come home with the U.S. dollars he had won.

It was just Michael and I for five years, and then my sisters Tracy and, two years later, Nancy were born. There we all were – two working parents and four rug rats within a nine-year span, eking out a somewhat middle-class life in downtown Toronto.

My mom's youngest sister, Debbie, came to live with us to attend school in Toronto from Grade 7 on through high school. Even though she was my aunt, we were more like sisters since we were only three years apart in age. Like my parents, she was a major influence in my life.

(L–R) Tracy Lynn, Michael Peter, Nancy Rita.

On weekends or holidays, we all went to our respective parents' rezzes to visit our grandparents and extended families. I absolutely loved getting out of the city to visit everyone. Six Nations is just over an hour from Toronto, and Christian Island is about two and a half. My paternal grandparents in Six Nations lived in a log cabin with no running water and no electricity. We'd use oil lamps when we'd go to bed on the second floor. I told my city friends about using an outhouse, but it was incomprehensible to them. I sometimes added that we had to use newspaper or catalogues as toilet paper … True.

My mom's rez on Christian Island was like paradise for us, especially in the summers, when we'd stay with our maternal grandparents for a few weeks. Those are precious memories of swimming and fishing for perch. Grandma would give us a big jar to fill with blackberries and she'd make us a pie for our dessert after dinner. Those were the days. We were safe and not running on concrete daily.

It was during these trips to the rezzes that I'd hear my dad speak in Cayuga to his parents and my mom speak in Anishinabe to hers. At that time, we had not been taught either language.

Still, I loved watching my parents speak to their parents. My dad became animated and he'd wave his arms, describing what he was talking about. My mom was the same way with her parents. But what I remember best was the laughter. Oh my, could my families ever laugh. No tee-hees here, but laughter that came right from the bottom of your gut. It's been twenty years since my mom passed, but I can still hear her laughter in my mind.

These were the 1960s, a time when Indigenous people were supposed to be 'assimilated' into mainstream Canadian culture. The preservation of our languages was not encouraged. In the last twenty-five or thirty years, however, Indigenous people have been reclaiming these languages, which are now being taught in schools, colleges, and universities across the country. It's cool to reclaim your language, which is what my mom did in 1996.

She applied to – and was accepted into – the Indigenous Language Instructor's program at Lakehead University in Thunder Bay in the summer months for three years.

My mom would say, 'The language may skip a generation, but it will come back to our communities.' She was right, and she would have been proud to see two of her grandsons go to Cayuga immersion school in Six Nations.

It was after her first year at Lakehead that she was diagnosed with breast cancer. She didn't want her instructors or fellow students to know – it wasn't until her third year that she informed them about her illness.

She had a lot of support from our family and friends during her radiation treatments at Princess Margaret Hospital in Toronto. My aunt Debbie was battling colon cancer at the same time, and they would try to schedule their appointments together whenever possible. Because I worked free-lance, I was able to accompany them to most of their treatments.

My mom left quite the life lessons to our family: you're never too old to learn your language, and never too old to go back to school. She graduated from her Anishinabe language program at Lakehead University, but only substitute-taught for one semester before she passed away from breast cancer in 2000, at fifty-nine years of age. My aunt Debbie passed away at fifty.

Today, the Bomberry family has grown; although I never had children, each of my siblings had three. My father, Peter, is happy to have his family all living at home in Six Nations. My brother Mike is father to Michael and Michelle – who has two young sons, Noah and Carter – and Tyler, whose daughter is Zehra. My sister Tracy is mom to three sons – Winter, Jared, and Jayden – and Nancy is mom to Sean. My nieces are Taylor – who just gave birth to a boy, Oaklynd – and Mackenzie, the youngest of the grandchildren.

Most of my extended family live in Six Nations of the Grand River Territory, Ontario, with the exception of my niece Michelle, who lives in Barrie. I am married to Murray Porter, also from Six Nations. We live on the Capilano rez, on unceded Squamish territory in North Vancouver, British Columbia.

DUKE REDBIRD, A MAN OF MANY WORDS

BRIAN WRIGHT-MCLEOD

Many successful journeys have begun in Toronto. The city has served as a launch pad for numerous careers and adventures. Duke Redbird, an Anishnabe born on the Saugeen reserve in 1939, is one of many such stories.

He first came to Hogtown in 1962 to embark on his own intrepid path. Over the years, he established himself as a visual artist, poet, activist, television journalist/host, educator, lecturer, entrepreneur, and innovator who eventually received an honorary degree from the Ontario College of Art & Design in 2013.

It all sounds so simple, but it is the result of a long road.

Duke began sign painting for local businesses while venturing into visual arts as he spent time in the Spadina Avenue area. Most of the shops on the street often had need for show cards and signs.

He needed a studio, and a friend had a trailer full of wood slabs from a sawmill, with the bark still attached. 'I constructed an area in the alley behind the iconic store Honest Ed's,' he recalls. 'People would walk through the alley to the parking lot.'

The store's benevolent owner, Ed Mirvish, gave him use of the area. Duke constructed a makeshift space that looked like a fort. In the summer, he would set up a tipi to attract customers.

'It was known as the Indian Fort where I sold Native crafts and my paintings,' Duke says. 'I stayed there all summer and winter. It attracted people heading to the parking lot or walking through the alley. Ed never charged me anything for the space. That was my first access to Toronto and that's how I made a living at that time.'

Through the Indian Fort, Duke met local Indigenous people, including Wilfred Pelletier from Manitoulin Island, who had been active since the mid-1960s and also wrote *two articles* (Neewin Publishing, 1969) and *for*

every north american indian who begins to disappear, I also begin to disappear
(Neewin Publishing, 1971). Pelletier was involved with the Indian Eskimo
Association that would later be renamed the Native Canadian Centre of
Toronto.

'I was invited to become a member,' Duke says. 'They had meetings,
and I started a local handmade newsletter called the *Thunderbird News*.
And I would distribute it myself and drop copies off at places like the
Silver Dollar. It was more than a bar/hotel, but also a meeting place for
people in the Native community.

'Another popular destination was the Varsity Restaurant, on the
northeast corner of Bloor and Spadina. It kept its 1950s ambience until
it closed in the late 1990s. The original laminated tabletop booths had
coin-operated jukeboxes mounted on the walls. People would go for a
bite of food or a coffee klatch to discuss current events, spiced with
some local gossip.

'The Spadina strip was a very different place before it became predominantly Chinese, which the demographic continues to slowly transform.
Kensington Market was primarily Jewish, with butchers, bakeries, and a
wet market with live animals for sale. It was a lively area.'

The air was thick with the pungent scent of animals, fish, and exotic
spices, he recalls, accented by the cacophony of languages lilting along
to the music of car horns, shouts, and coughing automobiles.

Along Spadina, one could find restaurateurs, shoemakers, tailors,
typesetters, and all manner of entrepreneurs and merchants. But the
nightlife was to be found farther north along Bloor Street and Yonge.

'Yorkville was a popular place,' says Duke. 'I lived on Huron Street.
Joni Mitchell lived across the hall from me and I got to know her. That's
when I started to write poetry. I hung out in the night scene, coffee houses,
and performed recitals at music festivals. I opened the Thunder Bird Club
coffee house, where young people would go after the Silver Dollar closed
at 1:00 a.m. I had thirteen employees at the time.'

The great thing about the Native community was it was just starting
to get respect. The hippie community was embracing Indigenous ideals
and becoming aware of the historical social issues. 'The Ballad of Ira
Hayes' (Peter La Farge) was made popular by Johnny Cash and became
something of an anthem.

Buffy Sainte-Marie and Willie Dunn started to come onto the scene.
Yorkville was the epicentre. A generation of young Native people arrived

and everybody was wearing fringe leather vests. The young middle-class radicals were writing songs and hanging out. The whole scene was anti–Vietnam War. A lot of draft dodgers came in from the U.S. They began to develop businesses. Everything was happening between 1962 and 1968. Expo '67 in Montreal was the place to go that summer. An Indian pavilion was also set up there.

'The police were aggressive, but they didn't shoot you. In the sixties, if you crossed the line, they would beat you up. It's much worse now than it was then.'

Duke went up to Ottawa, where he was invited to join the Company of Young Canadians, established by Bill McWhinney. Through that experience, he met Bill Ayers, co-founder of the U.S.-based far-left extremist organization the Weather Underground in 1969 that launched terrorist attacks on American soil during the 1970s. Other Native members of the organization included Phil Fontaine, former national chief of the Assembly of First Nations from 1997 to 2009.

'We went out to communities in different provinces out west to organize with young people,' Duke recalls.

The message was one of self-determination in order to get out from under the heel of the Department of Indian Affairs and have freedoms like Canadian citizens.

'Residential schools were still operating at that time,' Duke says, 'and many people experienced the brutality of it all. The reality had not been exposed to the public. The government denied what was going on, and denied status to Indigenous women who married out of their communities. We tried to expose the issues and organized politically. I was elected the vice-president for the Indian Youth Council and the Native Council of Canada. We also worked on the enfranchisement issue of losing status. It was a time of heavy political action,' he explains.

Following some successful filmmaking stints with the National Film Board of Canada in the early 1970s, Duke started to put his poetry to music with musicians Willie Dunn, Shingoose, Tom Jackson, and Saskatchewan Cree performer Winston Wuttunee.

'I met Winston in the early seventies,' Duke says. 'He was in the army when I met him when he was on leave. He was in the army band, and when he left the service, he looked me up and we started to create together, doing concerts and recordings. We did folk festivals like Mariposa on the Toronto Islands in the mid-1970s.

'There was a Native stage with performances all day and into the night for two days. The festival organizer, Estelle Klein, decided there should be a showcase for Native music. She invited her friend, filmmaker Alanis Obomsawin, who in turn gathered everyone she knew in the community to take part.'

Featured artists included local Arapaho singer-songwriter Christopher Kearney (founder of Toronto bands Jackson Hawk and China), Willie Dunn, Shingoose, Alanis Obomsawin, Paul Ritchie, traditional Cree performers, and Inuit singers. Sioux folksinger Floyd Westerman and Kiowa/Comanche guitarist Jesse Ed Davis, who accompanied bluesman Taj Mahal, also came up from the US.

(The only connection this writer has made to Jesse Ed Davis appearing at Mariposa came from a conversation with Chris Kearney, who related an anecdote about meeting Jesse at the receiving end of a flying egg-salad sandwich. 'I walk into the performer's tent,' Chris said. 'And wham! I get this egg-salad sandwich launched in my direction and I take one to the chest! Then this Indian guy comes rushing over, saying apologetically, "Sorry, man, I'm real sorry!" He introduced himself as Jesse Ed Davis and explained that the missile was intended for one of the festival organizers he was pissed off at!' A meeting of the minds in a special moment in music history.)

But things worked out for Duke as well.

'Around that time,' he says, 'Shingoose and I got a songwriting contract with country music legend Glen Campbell.' The deal prompted a move south of the border.

After leaving Toronto for the U.S., Duke embarked on another entrepreneurial passion by opening the Harris Club in Lake Tahoe, Nevada. The project would be a useful experience for similar business ventures in Toronto years later.

His book, *We Are the Métis*, was published in 1980 by the Ontario Métis and Non-Status Indian Association. The publication examined self-rule, history, and cultural impacts.

'I met my life partner in the 1980s,' Duke recalls, 'and we moved up to Algonquin Park, where we bought some property and where I created a lot of paintings.'

It was around this time that he ventured back to Toronto, where he discovered the Academy of Spherical Arts in Liberty Village.

'It was a high-end pool hall where all the top players from around the world would come shoot pool or billiards. I'm a decent player and got to meet my future partner, Ron. Together we opened the Coloured Stone on Adelaide Street.'

By the end of the 1980s, alcohol was allowed to be served in establishments where pool was played. Up until then, it was unlawful in Ontario to combine both elements in one place.

'With our combined experience, we ran the venue. It was a nice below-street-level club with an art gallery and restaurant,' he says. 'The ceiling was covered in dried red roses. Native organizations, businesses, and the Indigenous Juno Award nomination celebration rented out the space for events. We had an eight-ball table – it's a smaller table and provided more floor space.'

Duke's experience and determination landed him a fruitful television gig: 'I was a CityTV arts reporter for fifteen years, covering a lot of local Native events.'

He has remained active in the arts. In addition to his earlier recording projects, Duke eventually returned to the studio to create a poetry and music album in 2019 with Toronto's Sultans of String.

Not short on academic exploits, he also received a political science degree, and, in fall 2020, delivered a keynote address at Boston's Massachusetts Institute of Technology, entitled 'Dish with One Spoon.'

For some artist/entrepreneurs, the road seems long and demanding, but Duke's simple philosophy kept his journey blessed and fulfilled, despite the trials along the Red Road of life. It's a journey of inspiration and influence that reached far beyond the Indigenous community and into the hearts of many whom he has influenced with his work.

ROBERT MARKLE: THE POWER OF THE MARK/
AT THE HINGE OF LIGHT AND DARK

BONNIE DEVINE

There was a harsh knot at the core of artist Robert Markle's life. Perhaps he inherited it as an infant, a tight tangled wound in the softness of his newborn heart. Perhaps he nursed and cultivated it for the protection and perverse comfort it offered in the rough, postwar steel town where he grew up. When he arrived in Toronto in 1954, a young man determined to take the Ontario College of Art by storm with his instinctive artistic gift, he had already developed a defiant, confident attitude. He was belligerent and outspoken. He was loud, funny, and charismatic, and stingingly, formidably smart.

> Robert Markle's ancestors were among 20 Mohawk families who settled in the Bay of Quinte, east of Belleville Ontario in 1784. British loyalists, they'd been promised land and a good living in Upper Canada and travelled from New York State to claim it. Their territory was formally recognised in 1793 and named Tyendinaga.[1]

Bruce Maracle, Robert's father, was an iron worker who moved west from Tyendinaga in 1910 to find work in the Hamilton/Niagara Falls rust belt. He married Kathleen Clute, a descendant of the Claus family from Tyendinaga, and they settled in Hamilton, where Markle was born on August 25, 1936. In 1940, to shield her children from the small-town racism they faced at school, Kathleen changed the family name from Maracle to Markle. She chose not to talk to her children about their Mohawk ancestry. Robert grew up aware of, but mostly uninformed about, his Haudenosaunee history and roots.[2]

In 1952, at sixteen, Markle bought himself a vintage Harley motorcycle and drove it on weekends 105 kilometres around the rump of Lake Ontario to take in the jazz scene and night life in Buffalo, New York. John Coltrane, Charlie Parker, and the strippers at the Palace Burlesque were his earliest inspirations.[3] He adopted a beatnik's swagger and an appreciation for the nude female body he saw writhing in the glare of the stage lights.

In 1876, Canada's Parliament voted the Indian Act into law. That same year, the Ontario School of Art (later named OCA, Ontario College of Art) was established in Toronto.

His high school teachers noticed Markle's drawing ability and awarded him a tuition scholarship to art school in 1954. The prize was sponsored by the Hamilton chapter of the Imperial Order Daughters of the Empire – an irony that perhaps he noticed, too. The kindness of the colonizer can be a hard thing to swallow when you're young and strong. Markle was accepted at the Ontario College of Art but didn't last long there; he got kicked out in second year for hurling a bottle of etching acid against the wall in printmaking class.[4]

Maybe he wasn't sorry. OCA was entrenched in a stuffy, parochial aesthetic at the time, dominated by the Group of Seven and traditional landscape painting. Markle was thirsty for speed, freedom, and naked dancing girls.

Paul-Émile Borduas had published 'Le Refus Global' in Montréal in 1948. The manifesto was signed by 16 modernist intellectuals and abstract painters, including Les Automatistes,[5] who collectively rejected Canada's fixed, nation- alistic approach to representational art.

In 1954, Roberts Gallery mounted the first major exhibition of Painters 11,[6] Toronto's first exposure to abstract expressionist art. In 1955, Av Isaacs opened the Greenwich Gallery (later renamed Isaacs Gallery) at 736 Bay Street, near Toronto's Gerrard Street 'Village.' It became a centre of avant garde artistic activity, with regular exhibitions, poetry readings, and discussion nights.[7]

Meanwhile, throughout the 1950s, the Haudenosaunee communities of Kanesatake and Kahnawake resisted the Sulpicians, the British Privy Council, and the Canadian and Quebec governments over the sale of Mohawk territory to construct the St Lawrence Seaway.[8]

Markle's year and a half at OCA was not wasted. He met fellow students Graham Coughtry and Gordon Rayner, who had seen *Painters 11* at Hart House Gallery and were on fire with the group's ideas and gestures. Markle, the jazz lover, understood this kind of fervour. He, too, wanted to make unstructured, complicated marks on paper, play wild unmusical music, and write poems unconstrained by convention or good manners. He had an authentic biker saunter to boot, which somehow suited his skinny five-foot-eight bespectacled frame. And he could draw. He, Coughtry, and Rayner became lifelong friends. He also met Marlene Shuster at OCA, the

Robert Markel teaching at Arts' Sake, an artist run post-secondary art school in Toronto, c. 1980.

beautiful student at whom he had reportedly flung the bottle of etching acid. When he was expelled, Marlene quit school in solidarity. They married in 1958 and remained together for thirty-two years.

In 1958, either Rayner or Dennis Burton (the group's exact origins are uncertain) founded the Artists' Jazz Band, with Rayner on drums, Markle on saxophone and piano, Coughtry on trombone, Rick Gorman on bass, and Nobuo Kubota on saxophone. Harvey Cowan would occasionally join in on electric violin, and Michael Snow (the only trained musician in the company) sometimes played trumpet.[9]

AJB was deeply influenced by Borduas's *Le Refus Global* and Les Automatistes' devotion to 'the liberating necessity of art.' Technical ability or musical training were not required, only a willingness to blast out sounds in total abandon, lurching on the crazed edge of poetic chaos, exploring the potential of complete artistic anarchy. By the 1960s, they had a following at Grossman's Tavern and the Paramount Hotel on Spadina Avenue, where they were favourites with the regulars.

Markle, in particular, fit in among the blue-collar clientele with his easy stream of sarcastic observation, quick-witted banter, and good-natured kibbitzing. The Pilot Tavern, a block from Isaacs's Greenwich Gallery at Yonge and Bloor Streets, was another favourite hangout, where a different crowd tended to congregate, including Michael Sarrazin, an aspiring actor who waited tables at a restaurant across the street, CBC broadcaster Patrick Watson, and other members of Toronto's art scene.

Though Markle drank there with his friends most nights, he had other, darker haunts and deeper personal interests that were neither intellectual nor aesthetic nor abstract. He took to regularly visiting the Victory Burlesque, a strip joint on the corner of Spadina Avenue and Dundas Street, to lubriciously gaze at the dancers in their stiletto heels and G-strings. Their bodies were the subject of his drawings, their sexual contortions the object of his ink and charcoal investigations, their faces smudged out, their cunts splayed spread-eagled across the large black-and-white drawings for which he was beginning to be known. No, Markle was not an abstract artist. His practice was bluntly figurative, his eye steadily trained on the crotches and breasts of

Robert Markle, Denim jacket, c. 1975.
Cotton, embroidery floss, glass beads,
Art Gallery of Ontario.

faceless women. Markle was not interested in – if he was even aware of – the social struggle unfolding in Indigenous communities in Canada.

> *In 1959, Kanesatake and her sister territory Kahnawake challenged the municipality of Oka, Quebec, over the purchase of part of Kanesatake called 'the Commons' where the town planned to build a golf course.*[10]

> *That same year, Long House traditionalists at Six Nations attempted to take control of their territory and declare it a sovereign country. The RCMP was mobilized against them and several leaders and clan mothers were arrested in the council chamber of the hereditary chiefs.*[11]

Markle was interested in solidifying his membership in the group of artists coalescing around the Isaacs Gallery, and in developing a recognizable approach and personal style. His work progressed quickly and became more explicit as he explored – in large drawings, paintings, and lithograph prints – the single female nude or pairs of female figures, dancing, lounging, posing, or making love in bold charcoal and tempera on white paper, their gestures and poses caught in the glaring light and lushly smudged blackness of his quick, confident marks.

In 1965, he exhibited a series of drawings in *Eros '65*, a group show at the Dorothy Cameron Gallery on Yonge Street. The exhibition was raided by the police and several works seized when Cameron refused to remove them from the gallery walls. She was charged and eventually convicted of obscenity and pornography, a decision she appealed unsuccessfully to the Supreme Court of Canada.

Of the seven confiscated drawings, five were by Markle, who became something of a Canadian art celebrity in the wake of the event. Cameron, however, ultimately lost her gallery in the course of the lengthy and costly legal proceedings.[12]

The Toronto avant-garde art scene faded after the Cameron Gallery controversy. Markle, Rayner, and Coughtry accepted teaching jobs at the New School of Art, an alternative art school that suited Markle's irreverent approach to formalism and gave him an opportunity to interact with students and artists. It provided an atmosphere of social and creative licence that often spilled into local pubs after class, where the conversation was frequently laced with bawdy, misogynist insinuations about women and art. Markle was a lusty, witty, bad-boy artist who turned out to be a born teacher.

He taught in two alternative art schools in Toronto between 1966 and 1982, the New School of Art and Art's Sake.[13] Both were built on ideals of creative and intellectual freedom that would offer a less traditional, more unorthodox atmosphere than OCA. Markle's free-form yet skilful approach to drawing translated easily in the classroom. He encouraged camaraderie with all his students, but took liberties with some, indulging in a succession of sexual affairs. Two such relationships lasted several years.

During this period, he found his literary voice – a fluid, unconstructed writing style that was instinctive, incisive, poetic, and direct, like his drawing and his jazz. Words flowed from him in jolts and jabs of gestural depiction, shot through with dark humour, illuminated with bright intelligence. He wrote articles and did interviews for *Showcase Magazine*, *Arts Canada*, *Maclean's*, *Toronto Life*, and other journals, celebrating junk food, music, and motorcycles, with titles like 'The Glory That Is Grease,' 'The Aesthetics of the Drive-in Movie,' 'Chips with Everything,' and an audio guide called 'The Passionate Listener.' In 1974 he appeared on Patrick Watson's television program *Witness to Yesterday*, playing Rembrandt in full costume and wig; he was spellbinding in the role. His posture, the cadence of his voice, and his intuitive grasp of the old master's creative motivation and sensual relationship to light and shadow inspired Watson to christen him 'Robrandt.' In 1976, he impulsively entered a needlework competition at the Art Gallery of Ontario. His closely embroidered figures on a well-worn jean jacket are frankly – and perhaps surprisingly – exquisite.

Markle didn't hide his Mohawk background, but he wasn't interested in exploiting it in his work. His subject was the female body, which he depicted as an exotic sexual instrument – contorted, splayed, examined, and fingered over with the stubby, dripping black shaving brush he liked to tease across the creamy paper. Yet despite his apparent professional indifference, in 1977 he inquired about his Native status at Tyendinaga, the first time he'd addressed his ancestral homeland. He completed the required formalities and was registered within the Indian Act under band number 1358.[14] Markle's June 1980 solo exhibition at Isaacs Gallery was the first time a critic made reference to his Indigenous heritage in a published review.[15] John Bentley Mays, on the other hand, chose to overlook the artist's racial background in his write-up and instead focused on Markle's intimate familiarity with G-stringed female bodies, praising his 'profane, analytic, modern imagination.'[16]

The following decade, though his work remained primarily focused on the female figure in lithograph prints, drawings, and a large-scale commission for the ceiling of a restaurant in downtown Toronto, Markle began to tentatively incorporate Indigenous references in his work. At first, he avoided direct cultural or visual quotations. His initial such gesture in 1980 was a mural commissioned for the Ontario Government Services Building in Hamilton, for which he created an abstract

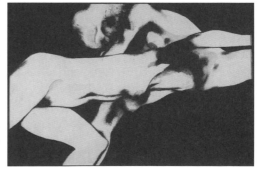

Robert Markle, Lovers II, 1963, tempera on paper,
58.6 × 89.1 cm, Art Gallery of Ontario

structure in steel, neon, and glass. It was entitled *Mohawk* but contained no recognizable Indigenous imagery.

In 1982, the Government of Canada patriated the British North America Act from the authority of the British Parliament and renamed it the 'Constitution Act, 1867.' The new constitution included a Charter of Rights and Freedoms and provisions that recognized Indigenous peoples' and women's rights.

In 1984, 'Norval Morrisseau and the Emergence of the Image Makers,' curated by Tom Hill and Elizabeth McLuhan, opened at the Art Gallery of Ontario.

Tom Hill, director and curator of the Woodland Cultural Centre in Brantford, Ontario, was instrumental in bringing Indigenous art to local and national attention. Located on the site of the Mohawk Institute Residential School on Six Nations territory, the museum and gallery had begun the enormous task of telling the story of the Haudenosaunee people in their own voices and with their own artwork in 1972. By the 1980s, Hill had consolidated the museum's collection of historical artifacts and established an annual exhibition of contemporary Indigenous art. Hill and McLuhan's exhibition, *Norval Morrisseau and the Emergence of the Image Makers*, at the Art Gallery of Ontario, set in motion a reconsideration of Canadian art history that is still underway today. There is little doubt that Robert Markle was aware of the shift in Canadian attitudes and politics.

In 1984, he successfully submitted a proposal for a mural at the Metropolitan Toronto Convention Centre, titled *Mohawk: Meeting Place*, a multipanelled frieze in painted steel and neon. The piece referred to Toronto's two rivers, the Humber and the Don, and contained motifs representing ceremonial figures both human and non-human derived from Haudenosaunee confederacy belts, petroglyph images, and other unmistakable traces of an ancient North American pictorial tradition. He had consulted with Elders from Six Nations and specialists at the Woodland Cultural Centre before designing the piece. In an astounding gesture of self-recognition, he signed the completed installation *Maracle*.[17]

Perhaps the harsh tangle inside him was beginning to unravel, softened by the ardour and labour of cultural leaders like Tom Hill, Norval Morrisseau, and Daphne Odjig. Perhaps it was suddenly less soul-defeating to be a Mohawk in the caustic competitive patriarchal city of Toronto. Or perhaps he'd begun to discern an advantage in his heritage, and the beginning of a diffident pride. Markle's violently sexualized imagery began to transform. Not entirely, as he was still obsessively interested in the female nude. But his drawings began to take her out of the strip club and into a natural setting on the land. In 1985 he travelled to Tyendinaga to receive his official status card and band membership.

In 1990, between June 12 and June 21, Elijah Harper stood in the Manitoba Legislature on eight separate occasions to oppose the Meech Lake Accord.[18] *Harper objected to Meech Lake because it ignored Indigenous peoples' demands that their rights as a founding people be recognized within the constitution of Canada. Because of Harper's efforts, the Accord ultimately failed.*

On the night of Thursday, July 5, 1990, Markle was driving home drunk on a rural road near Mount Forest, Ontario. Reportedly travelling at almost 130 kilometres per hour, his pickup truck smashed into a tractor driven by a local farmer. Markle had been involved in a serious motorcycle accident on the Don Valley Parkway in 1969. In that collision, he had sustained fractures to his arms and hands, and dangerous internal injuries that left him in pain and unable to draw for more than a year. But on this night, he wasn't as lucky. He died at age fifty-three, before the knot within him could be fully activated, radicalized, or bent to the service of his blood and the light in his mind.

Robert Markle, c. 1980.

On July 11, 1990, six days after Markle's death, Haudenosaunee protestors at Kanesatake and Kahnawake made a stand against the town of Oka, Quebec, over the expropriation of the Kanesatake Commons. The town wanted to expand their golf course across a traditional area of the Commons called 'The Pines.' The stand-off lasted 78 days and changed the relationship between the nation of Canada and the Indigenous people of this land forever.

Artists of Indigenous ancestry across the country responded to the events at Oka in 1990 and, two years later, to the five-hundredth anniversary of the Columbus landing, in what became a flowering of political and cultural expression that continues to unfold and expand to this day, heartened and warmed by the joy of unity and the hope for change.

Would Markle's work have flourished and transformed in the surge of this enlightened, infuriated spirit? Sadly, we will never know.

ACKNOWLEDGEMENTS

Thank you to Diane Pugen, who generously shared memories, newspaper clippings, video tapes, and photographs from her personal collection during the preparation of this essay. Thanks also to Sarah Milroy for providing a brief but valuable reflection on the artist and his work. Finally, a sincere thank-you to Marlene Markle, a kind and invaluable source of insight and images. Marlene established a scholarship in Robert Markle's name that was awarded to thirteen Indigenous art students between 1994 and 2008. I was a grateful recipient in 1997.

TOMSON HIGHWAY
AND THE LANGUAGE OF LAUGHTER

DENISE BOLDUC

My first memory of Tomson Highway is of a soft-spoken man with an infectious giggle, wearing a white dress shirt, ripped-up black jeans, and Wellingtons. At the time, he chain-smoked Winston cigarettes (a habit he has ditched for many years now) while working countless hours in the basement back space of the Native Earth office at 37 Spadina Road. I was fascinated by his humour, playfulness, aristocratic charm, and the rhythmic musicality of his words.

It was mere months before that I witnessed for the first time an Indigenous story with Indigenous performers onstage. I had just arrived in Toronto from Northern Ontario and was bouncing around various minor jobs in the arts. I was not aware that Native Earth Performing Arts or Indigenous theatre even existed. The play I saw was *Dry Lips Oughta Move to Kapuskasing*, a co-production between NEPA and Theatre Passe Muraille (1989). Onstage were these incredible and most beautiful Indigenous performers – brown like me, and characters like from back home.

Shortly after I'd seen the play and was volunteering at the Native Centre, the late Pat Turner, then volunteer coordinator, told me about a job posting at Native Earth and suggested I apply. I did and was hired on the spot. My first task was to help the company move from Jarvis Street to the new Spadina office across from the Centre. It was the true beginning of my love affair with Indigenous performing arts.

Tomson is the eleventh of Joe and Pelagie Highway's twelve children. The family lived a semi-nomadic life between traplines and a village called Brochet, located in northwestern Manitoba and bordering Saskatchewan, Nunavut, and the Northwest Territories. He was only thirty-seven when *Dry Lips* was produced. The play won four Dora Awards and was subsequently staged at both Ed Mirvish's Royal Alexandra Theatre and the National Arts Centre in Ottawa (1991). Prior to this success, Tomson had already written and produced six plays, including the highly acclaimed *Rez Sisters*. He was artistic director at Native Earth for six years, from 1986 to 1992, transforming, collaborating, supporting, and nurturing many lives during his six-year tenure. He forever altered perspectives of Indigenous peoples through onstage storytelling. Fortunately, I worked with NEPA during this time, and credit his leadership, as well as that of general manager Teresa Castonguay, with my own development, thereby influencing the work I involve myself with to this day.

So many memories arise as I think back on this time: *Moonlodge*, by the incredibly brilliant Margo Kane, was the first production I worked on. The most memorable was *Son of Ayash*, which was dedicated to the late René Highway (dancer, choreographer), Tomson's brother. Those years were full of laughter, long hours, celebrations, arguments, disappointments, deep loss, more laughter, and great love. There were many parties, fundraisers, and auctions. A who's who of the arts community would dress in their finest and pack the house on opening nights.

Under Tomson's leadership, Weesageechak Begins to Dance, a festival of new works and performance now in its thirty-third year, provided a venue for Indigenous story/play development, with the potential for production in the following season. Weesageechak took place, as did many productions, in the Native Centre, transforming the gymnasium into a theatre.

One year, Ron Cook, who worked days at a hardware store and moonlighted as an actor in the evenings, showed up with the raffle items donated from his day gig. At the end of the evening, winners departed toward the subway carrying their prizes: shovels, rakes, and axes. That was hilarious to see. There were also box socials, where a bidder could win a box dinner with the likes of actors Gary Farmer, Doris Linklater, Billy Merasty, and Graham Greene, and auction parties at the Mirvishes' private halls, with Jack Layton as the auctioneer. As always and through it all, Tomson's playfulness, charm, and wit as the host were as dazzling as I imagined a Trickster to be.

During four decades as a playwright, composer, writer, musician, songwriter, and producer, Tomson has created over one hundred compositions, as well as a highly acclaimed novel, *Kiss of the Fur Queen*, four children's books, and a memoir, A *Tale of Monstrous Extravagance*. He is the author of eighteen plays that have been presented all over the world and translated into at least ten different languages, including Japanese, Tagalog, and Inuktitut. He has received eleven honorary doctorates, countless awards, speaks six languages ('two badly and can fake my way through another seven, including Japanese and Czech'), and has travelled to sixty-two countries. 'I travel so much; I travel for a living,' he says. 'I find it extremely important to speak to people in their own country, their own language, on their land. I believe that and practise this religiously.'

He is a wicked card player, has a memory like an elephant, and is a constant joke teller. A master of exaggerated storytelling, Tomson is a dear friend whom I consider family. I love to listen to him play piano – especially that first composition he plays every morning from the production *The Sage, the Dancer and the Fool* (1989). We definitely do not always agree on things, but we have a silent respect for one another. Although I may roll my eyes hearing a 'story' I have heard a million times, it truly is the greatest privilege to know Tomson.

So I rang him…

Hey, you mentioned the other day you had a funny story you wanted to share about Graham.

Graham Greene is the funniest man alive. He is so funny. His sense of humour is spectacular, honest to god. There are a lot of Native people like that, right. Mind you, there are a lot of white people like that – we know some very funny white people, right? *[laughter]*

Of course!

We also know a lot of funny Black people, too. *[more laughter between us]* Anyway *[more laughter]*, um, well, every time he opens his mouth, Graham Greene, something funny comes out. If he ever loses his career in acting, he could easily, easily become a comedian. A stand-up comedian and a star. He could have his own TV series.

Yeah, he is quite the talented and funny guy.

In *Dry Lips*, he played Pierre St. Pierre. It's a tragicomedy, like all my stuff is. Tragic characters on one side and comic characters on the other side, and in between there are people who are both. Okay. Pierre St. Pierre is a crazy comic fool.

Pierre St. Pierre is the referee of the hockey games on the reserve. So the set designer got this material – Teflon, I think. Anyway, it's an artificial material that functions like ice so you can actually skate on it. He covered the stage at two points in the play – the end of the first act and the end of the second act – as it turns into a hockey rink and Pierre St. Pierre skates. The women are playing hockey, with the commentary being read by Big Joey in Cree. We don't see the woman playing, of course; we just hear Big Joey saying, 'She shoots, she scores, and this and that…blah blah blah.' It's that kind of commentary, but in Cree. At the same time, Pierre St. Pierre has music playing for his skating – it's a clownish-like figure-skating music. *[laughs]*

You just have to see it to see how funny it is. How hysterical it is, and how that performance is the performance of the year – of the decade, in my opinion. Yeah, he won the Dora award for Best Actor of the Year. That is the funniest thing I have ever seen in Toronto in all my life.

Now, I know you brought your mom in from the far north. Was this for the opening of *Dry Lips* at the Royal Alexandra?

No, lots of people get that story mixed up. Brought my mom in twice. First for my brother, when he was dying in bed at the hospital. That was in September of 1990. Then she left and couldn't stay for the entire time. The last period of René's life was six weeks, and then the final visit at the hospital when he started fading away. She couldn't stay for all of that, so she did her best and said goodbye. Then I brought her back in the spring. I had just bought my house in Cabbagetown, my beautiful house, and I wanted her to come and bless it, in a sense. That was in May, Mother's Day in 1991.

At that point, the sky was raining money and I was getting prizes all over the place. I was receiving the Toronto Arts Award. It is a big, big art award, and [included] people like Raymond Moriyama, the architect who designed the Toronto Reference Library and many other incredible buildings all over the world. David Cronenberg was another winner that night, and others. Anyway, there were eight winners in total and the awards ceremony was at one of the theatres on Yonge Street, at the Elgin Theatre, with the after-party at the Carlu.

The organizers loaned each winner a black stretch limo for the evening and we were free to bring friends. The limo would come and pick us up at the house to go to the awards. So my mom, my nephew Billy, and some good friends came to the house and off we went to the Elgin. When we arrived, there were other limos arriving, and a red carpet, lights flashing, television cameras, and everything was there and everybody was there. Yeah.

Mom was pictured like a star, coming out of the black stretch limo arriving into Toronto, and it was just amazing. There was the party afterwards and there were these eight alcoves that were elevated like thrones. They gave each winner one of these alcoves, and I had mine, and my throne so to speak, and my mom was on one side of me.

The most important people in Canada, from what I could tell, were there to come congratulate us winners. So they did this reception line where everyone came to my mother. As her seat was elevated, they came to kiss her hand and congratulate her. There were people like the big bank presidents of Canada and such. I remember Norman Jewison was there, and I remember Mrs. Jewison, the late Mrs. Jewison, saying to my mom, who didn't speak a word of English, 'You have a very talented son.' Yeah. So that was that – the night my mom became a movie star.

Dry Lips *cast, Theatre Passe-Muraille, 1989. (L–R) Ben Cardinal, Errol Kinistino, Billy Merasty, Gary Farmer, Kennetch Charlotte, Ron Cook, Graham Green.*

She never saw the show, she never saw *Dry Lips*. What a lot of people don't know of us northern Indians is that we come from so far north. Did you know that Nunavut is the same distance as Ottawa to Europe?

No, I didn't know that.

Did you know that the distance between the northern Manitoba–Nunavut border, where I come from, to the North Pole is the same distance as from Halifax to Vancouver?

No, wow.

We have those distances to deal with. We are nomadic caribou hunters and all that, and because we were moving around all the time, there was no school to go to. So, in order for us to get an education that my father never had – he had Grade 0, he never went to school and he always regretted that – so he put us on that plane to fly us really far south to go to boarding school. He desperately wanted his children to go to school. People get the impression that authorities came to our house and dragged us out the door to the school, like it was ten blocks down the street. There was no such thing, so we had to leave home to get an education.

We went back and forth as kids. Even when I was a seventeen-year-old, we had to pay $2,000 to get a plane ticket to go back home. That is how much a plane ticket cost back then. I did that all my life. It didn't bother me, and it is just what I had to do, okay? When you live in a local reserve, schools are just ten minutes away and you can walk there. We can't do that.

So my parents never heard me play the piano. My parents have never seen any of my shows. They couldn't speak any English, so they would not have understood.

That is incredibly moving, Tomson. I can't imagine what it must have been like for your mom to come all the way down here and not really know all of your accomplishments that were really from their support, your parents'.

Yes, they were the best parents imaginable. Of course, we went home every summer for two months. The best time of the year in the Manitoba–Nunavut border area in the summertime is exquisite beyond compare … and the land is exquisite beyond compare. I come from paradise. Our summers were so spectacular and so filled with love. My parents had the best life imaginable. I always say my parents had a marriage they could only dream of in Hollywood.

We had two months every year that were so spectacular they would more than adequately replace the ten months of the year when we weren't there with them. For chrissake, in Hollywood, an average kid, by the time they reach ten years old, they have three sets of parents. Can you imagine Father's Day at Elizabeth Taylor's house?

There used to be a joke about that, right: 'What is the definition of confusion?' So-and-so told this, I won't name him. 'The definition of confusion is Father's Day on an Indian reserve.' Now, I don't agree with that at all. I think the definition of confusion is Father's Day in Hollywood.

Good point. Besides the night of the Royal Alex theatre opening of *Dry Lips*, are there any other stories you would like to share?

Well, the publicist for the theatre is a friend of ours who eventually got the job, John Karastamatis – a wonderful and adorable man. But at that time, it was Gino Empry, toward the end of his reign. He led all those venues, including the Imperial Room at the Royal York Hotel. He managed my publicity through that whole period at the Royal Alexandra. Gino is hysterical. OMG, what he was. He has passed away now. I don't know what it was, but he took a shine to me. He used to call me and take me out in his white Cadillac and drag me off to fancy restaurants and we just partied.

I'd love to tell you tamer stories about Gino, but there aren't any. He was wild. I have had a spectacular life – those stories – I have had crazy, crazy times.

Years ago, I remember you saying, 'The Trickster is not well and is passed out under a table at the Silver Dollar, and as artists, it is our responsibility to resuscitate him.' Something like that. Fast-forward to today: where do you think the Trickster is now?

The Trickster is contained. The very centre of the Trickster's existence is in the languages. I speak fluent Cree. I have never lost my

Tomson Highway.

language and am very proud of it. When you start speaking Cree, the second or the first syllable you start to laugh, and you laugh and laugh.

I just have to call up Northern Manitoba and my voice comes on the phone, and they start to laugh as soon as they hear my voice. That is how Cree is. We laugh and we laugh and we laugh. The second we switch to English, we stop laughing. English is not a laughing language. It is a serious language. It is an intellectual language and it's a brilliant one at that, but it doesn't laugh. If English is an intellectual language, French is an emotional language. One comes from the head, and the other comes from the heart and middle part of the body.

So that is the case for those two languages, and guess where the Cree language comes from? From the third part of the body. The part that is most ridiculous-looking. The part that is most pleasurable. The part that scares the living daylights out of the English language. You know, as far as I can tell, this organ doesn't even exist in the English language. It's a shocking idea, a shameful idea, it's the dirtiest idea from that perspective.

From the other perspective it is fun and it's funny.

There is nothing funnier, funnier than a good big fart. It's hysterical. *[laughter]* In English, no you don't do that, as 'fart' is not existence. It's feared and not allowed. So that is where the Trickster exists. In the language, as the languages are still alive – some of them. Trickster is in those that are working that fear, that are keeping them alive, keeping those languages alive.

So as long as the languages are kept alive, so will the Trickster, and that is where he is right now. Sitting up, laughing and laughing his heart out.

Love this. Do you still write in Cree first?

Yep. Well, it depends on what I am writing. Sometimes yes and sometimes no. And now I write in French as well and translate into English.

René, your brother, was also a celebrated dancer, choreographer, and artist. You and René worked on many projects together and he had such an impact on the performing arts, especially in Toronto. Is there anything you would like to share about him or your work together?

The most important thing about him, the most impressive thing about him, was the fact that he was incredibly beautiful. The first thing about him is there was not a single stitch or sign of vanity in his personality. He was humble. He took that humility into his work. He was extremely talented, but humble about his work. He was never arrogant, he was never vain.

He just did it humbly, and did it fiercely. He gave a gift to the world with his short life with such humility. That most impressed me. I like to have that kind of humility. I follow that model to the best of my ability.

There are much more important people out there than I. I am thankful that I got an education. A fabulous one at that. So this is what I chose to talk about. The beautiful things that I have learned. One of the most important things about my residential school experience is that I got to learn a beautiful language, so I can listen respectfully to what you have to say, and I can understand it. That is the approach that he has used. Very humble and quiet, he never flashed it. None of that stuff. That is what most impressed me about him.

Beautiful. Tomson, do you have any other stories or experiences from your years in Toronto that you would like to share?

I think the most important part of that experience is that I got so much love from the community; that includes the non-Native community, too. How much they helped me with my work and with getting it done. How kind they were. That is what I most remember, the amount of kindness I got and the amount of love I got.

That is what I am eternally thankful for. I was just so loved and I still am. That is the gift that life has given me, the love. I am so loved in this country that I escape six months of the year and go live in Europe. I live there for many reasons in the wintertime, and that is one of them. I just can't take it, it's too exciting, it's too much fun. I laugh too much and I drink too much. *[laughter]*

I have to go to a place where I won't do that. I lead a very, very quiet life with my partner of thirty-six years, and just have a wonderful, wonderful life in the arms of love. I am so loved, it's unbelievable. That is what I remember the most from my experiences in Toronto.

It's been four decades since your first play, and there have been numerous productions, compositions, books, tours, travels, etc., etc. As you approach your seventieth milestone birthday, what keeps you inspired and motivated and dreaming for the next few decades?

My aim is always to make people laugh. I think my philosophy is such that my favourite sound in the world is laughter, after the sounds of nature, water and wind. In the human sphere, it's laughter, human laughter. I love that sound so much that I will do anything to get it. Even make a fool of myself in front of two thousand people, which I have done. Get that laugh, get it out, get it out. Get that laughter out and laugh, and laugh and laugh.

One of my philosophies is that if you haven't laughed a hundred times in one day, you haven't lived that life. You haven't lived that day. You and I know people who have never laughed. There are certain people we know in our lives who I have never heard laugh, you know. I find that so sad. I want to make those people laugh. That's what inspires me. Laughter. Human laughter is when the human beings are most beautiful. That is what I want to see. Yes, that is what inspires me.

Our conversation continued, with Tomson telling a knock-knock joke, some funny Cree sayings, and sharing further exaggerated, scandalous stories and laughter. This continued through email exchanges a day or so later.

In closing, I will share a moving excerpt from a short piece Tomson wrote as the address for the Dancers for Life event, in a supplement to *Xtra Magazine* from April 1992.

> … *there is a richness to the very act of living that was not there before; it seems to me that the contributions made to our lives by these departed friends and lovers have left us richer, somehow a more potent magic … magic that was not there before, that we the living have all that much more reason to live the lives of beauty, lives of spiritual and emotional wealth, lives of great vitality and lives of … yes, magic.*
>
> *These are the thoughts and feelings my brother, the dancer René Highway, left with me. That's what he said as he lay on his bed preparing to go away. He said: 'Don't mourn me; be joyful.'*
>
> *Yes! Forgive me for beginning to sound a little like a preacher, but yes, ladies and gentlemen, please, do be joyful! Celebrate life, celebrate your families, your friends and your lovers, celebrate the sunlight, the water, the wind, the laughter of strangers, celebrate the very earth you walk on. Because, indeed, if death is an absolutely heart-breaking, mind-bending, gut-wrenching, earth-shattering miracle, then so is life.*

'I JUST WOKE UP ONE MORNING
AND I WAS A PLAYWRIGHT'

INTERVIEW WITH DREW HAYDEN TAYLOR,
BY JOHN LORINC

Tell me about the moment you decided to come to Toronto and set yourself up as a writer here.

I wanted to be a writer, but unfortunately I didn't know anything about it. I grew up on the reserve during that period when we didn't have internet or that kind of thing. But I was an avid reader. Books took me places I never thought I'd see in life. For a kid, life on the reserve can be very boring, so I decided to ask people about the process of being a writer, to see if it was possible.

The first person I went to was my Grade 11 English teacher. I said to him, 'Sir, is it possible to make a living from creative writing?' And without looking at me he said, 'No, not really.' Then I went to my mother and told her I was interested in being a writer. She looked at me with quite a perplexed look. 'Why do you want to be a writer? It's not going to get you anywhere.' So basically, I was told there's no point being a writer by two very influential people in my life. Therefore, I decided on giving up on the dream of being a writer.

Around this time, I was sixteen or seventeen years old and school was coming to an end. I wanted to leave the reserve and see the world. The best way to do that was to get a post-secondary education, college or university. What should I study? I wanted to be a writer, but obviously there didn't seem to be a point in that.

I went through the course catalogues handed out by all of the universities and colleges. I found one program called Radio and Television. It was at Seneca College, in Toronto, which wasn't too far away. I applied and, surprisingly, I got in. In retrospect, I realize I should have read the fine print – it was actually for radio and television *broadcasting*. Enrolling in that program was one of the worst decisions I could have made. I was inherently shy, and part of the job of being a journalist is basically going up to people you don't know and asking them questions that are frankly none of your business. But I had committed myself, so I moved to Toronto and went to school.

Surprisingly, I did very well. After graduating, I hung around Toronto for a number of years. Even though I couldn't be a writer, I liked the artistic world. I liked artists because the thing about the arts is you basically create, hopefully, great things from just a figment of your imagination. If I couldn't be an artist myself, I wanted to work with artists. I wanted to be a hanger-on, a groupie, a wannabe.

I spent most of my early twenties working for arts organizations in the city. I worked as a trainee producer for CBC Radio and the Canadian Native Arts Foundation, now known as Indspire. I did the location sound on a couple of documentaries being shot across the country. And I ended up working for a film company that was doing a thirteen-part series about Native children in northwestern Ontario, near Lake Nipigon.

It was a children's television series taking place on a fictional reserve. But the thing was, all the writers, the directors, the producers, and a third of the actors were non-Native. I remember just walking up to the door of the production company, knocking, and saying, 'Hi, you're doing a series about Native people, but you don't have any Native people in the cast or crew. I grew up on a reserve and you should hire me.' And they did.

I had no experience in film production per se. So I did most of the lowly jobs – camera assistant, production assistant, casting assistant, etc., etc., etc. But one of the odd responsibilities I had was that I frequently was asked to make sure things were technically accurate from the Aboriginal perspective. They would give me the scripts to read. I was dissecting them, saying to myself, 'Is this accurate? Is that accurate?' But you have to keep in mind that I grew up just north of Peterborough, and this was being shot in northwestern Ontario, way north of Thunder Bay. The difference between Native people in the two places is quite substantial.

Just through osmosis, I learned the structure of a half-hour television show for Canada.

What year is this?

This would have been the mid or late eighties. When the series ended, I found myself unemployed. I had a very hungry landlord who liked to be fed on a regular basis. I was doing only an occasional article for magazines or newspapers, for spare money. One time, I was writing an article on adapting Native stories to a television and film format. I talked with all the story producers I could find at all the TV series being shot here in Canada. I ended up talking with one who suggested I submit some story ideas, just for the heck of it.

I did and, lo and behold, they bought it. I wrote it, they shot it, a season ender for a series called *The Beachcombers*. So I wrote my first television show for one of Canada's most popular television series at the age of twenty-five. Nineteen eighty-seven, I think that's when it aired.

That was when Tomson Highway's *The Rez Sisters* was running. I actually lived three blocks from the theatre – the Native Canadian Centre at Spadina and Bloor. At that time in my life, I couldn't afford theatre tickets. Around this time, Native theatre was getting incredibly popular. And Tomson Highway, the artistic director of Native Earth, had gotten a grant for a playwriting residency program from the Ontario Arts Council. At that point, there were, I think, two working Native playwrights in Ontario: Tomson and Daniel David Moses. I had written for *The Beachcombers* and I was working on *Street Legal*. Tomson asked me if I wanted to be the writer-in-residence.

At that time, I really was not interested in theatre. I thought theatre was pretentious. The number of plays I saw I could count on my fingers. But again, I had that very hungry landlord. So I ended up saying yes. I'm one of those few people you meet who can say they got into theatre for the money.

I became Native Earth's writer-in-residence, even though I didn't know what I was doing. I didn't know how to write for theatre. It was not a good marriage right off the bat, but I did my research. I tried to read as many Native plays as I could. I decided to see as many Native plays as I could. I wanted to understand the structure, the storytelling methods, the genre and why it was suddenly becoming so popular.

I really jumped into the world of theatre and, lo and behold, that was like my third career. I started off with writing articles and essays, I went into television, and now I was writing theatre. And if I'm to believe my press, I was very good at it.

What were you reading when you decided to do that research, besides Tomson? Who was out there?

I read *The Book of Jessica* by Maria Campbell, who wrote it with Linda Griffiths. Of course, I was reading Daniel David Moses, too, and a few others here and there. I was also reading stuff about Native people, but not necessarily by Native people, like *The Ecstasy of Rita Joe* by George Ryga.

Can you talk a little about how you conceived of presenting Indigenous issues and Indigenous lives in this theatrical setting? There wasn't a lot of precedent.

You're making the assumption that it was all a conscious thought. It wasn't. I didn't sit down and say, 'I'm gonna write something that has a political and social take on contemporary Indigenous life.' I'm actually known within the context of Native theatre as one of the more innocuous playwrights, because I've been known for writing comedies. Some of my plays have absolutely no social relevance whatsoever and are celebrations of an Indigenous sense of humour

Even within that context, my work can still attack and ask questions. Issues like father abandonment and other sorts of things are explored with humour. But I found that the vast majority of contemporary Native theatre was highly issue-oriented. In fact, most of the plays for the first twenty years or so of the contemporary Native theatrical renaissance were dark, depressing, bleak, sad, and angry.

To me it seemed there were basically three narratives involved in almost all the plays – they were either historical narratives, victim narratives, or they dealt with some element of what I refer to as post-contact stress disorder. I was doing what I considered glorious celebrations of Indigenous life and Indigenous people through the funny bone. Now, I have been very fortunate to have been to over 140 Native communities across Canada and the United States. Everywhere I've been to, I've been greeted with a laugh, a smile, and a joke, and I wasn't seeing this in a lot of the theatre. A lot of the theatre coming out of our community dealt with dysfunction. It has to be understood that when an oppressed people get their voices back, they're going to write about being oppressed.

That's all understandable, but I would look at my mother, who raised me on the reserve. She was not by any means oppressed, depressed, or suppressed. You saw a vibrant, healthy, strong woman with a good sense of humour. And I wasn't seeing her onstage. So a lot of the work I did celebrated the Indigenous sense of humour. It's my opinion that it's been our humour that's allowed us to survive all those centuries of oppression. But a lot of Indigenous authors and artists think that Native theatre, by definition, should push the envelope, make the audience uncomfortable, ask difficult questions.

What was the response you were getting from other Indigenous theatre people to the work you were doing?

A lot of the actors really liked what I was doing because they got to make people laugh. They got to celebrate life instead of doing sexual abuse or violence or alcoholism. I remember one actor, a few years ago, was doing a role and he said, 'Oh, wow, thirty years later, I'm still playing the drunk Indian.' So the response overall was very, very good. They really liked it, and the audience response is what, I think, made me overcome those sorts of odds, of not being serious. I remember one person from a political organization up in Thunder Bay going up to the artistic director and saying, 'I understand the importance of the other plays, but these ones remind me of my parents and my grandparents, my brothers and sisters, more than the others do.'

My plays are often referred to as 'kitchen-sink drama.' They are more realistic than a lot of the other ones that deal with the negative aspects of the Native community. A lot of my work also does deal with issues. I did a trilogy of plays dealing with the Sixties Scoop, and they have been some of my most successful. *Someday, Only Drunks and Children Tell the Truth*, and *400 Kilometres*.

Then I wrote plays that dealt with Native stereotypes. One of my most recent plays, *Cottagers and Indians*, deals with the disagreement between Native and non-Native people over land and water management. I also wrote a biography of Sir John A. MacDonald. So there is a lot of the exploration of issues in some of my work. But, as I repeatedly say, I like to celebrate the more positive aspects of the Indigenous community.

If you reflect back on the evolution of Indigenous theatre since you began, when it was in its infancy in Canada, where do you see it right now?

Right now, it seems to have plateaued. For the first ten or fifteen years, Native theatre was an exciting new force. I remember an artistic director of a non-Native theatre company saying that was where the really exciting work was coming out, where questions were being asked and spotlights were being held on topics. It was where Canada was getting an opportunity look at itself, both the good and the bad. Lately, there's not been that sort of shakeup within the larger Canadian theatre community that there once was, when Native plays were being produced.

It used to be that the theatre was, in my humble opinion, *the* method of expression within the Native community, because theatre is the next logical progression from oral storytelling. From people like me – I've never been to university. I've never taken a writing course in my life. But I became very good at theatre because I grew up surrounded by oral storytelling. That's what theatre is. You're telling stories through how people talk, how they move, and what they imagine.

I think that's why theatre was so popular. The ways we talk and tell stories are all different and unique. All these generations of people who had gone through colonization, we have something we want to say, and it's not going to be pleasant. But now that the first generation has passed on or moved over or whatever, you've got the generation of writers who've gone through the university system and who are modifying their storytelling techniques as presented to them through post-secondary school education.

I saw *Cottagers and Indians* at Tarragon Theatre. When I looked around the audience, I saw mostly people who are older, white, and able to spend seventy dollars on a theatre ticket. This is the crisis of theatre. Do you think this tradition of storytelling is going to find a new way of getting out into the world that may not involve a stage?

That's a good question. People have been saying that theatre has been dying since they invented movies and television and so on. Theatre's always on the verge of dying.

What's going to happen now? I know the world has been shaken and has had to survive with this COVID-19 thing. One of my plays, the biography of Sir John A., was supposed to be produced by Native Earth last spring; instead, it was recorded online and broadcast by this company that was doing plays that were cancelled. I listened to it and it's like a radio play. But a play is a play is a play. So, will theatre die? I don't know. I doubt it. I think it'll come back. I mean, theatre is so wonderful at interaction, at being there to watch, to see, to get drawn into the story.

Cottagers and Indians **is about a conflict in cottage country over wild rice, but so much more than that. When I saw the play onstage, I enjoyed it because you could see the audience reaction – discomfort. How did the television version come about?**

The video adaptation is not an adaptation of the play itself. It's a documentary about Native and non-Native conflict involving the land and water issues the play was based on. We were using the issues explored in the play as the starting point for the documentary. The wild rice is in Pigeon Lake. We started there with the real people, then went to other areas of the country where people are dealing with different interactions and conflict.

Herbie Barns in the original production of Cottagers and Indians.

How did the play come about?

I grew up in the Kawarthas, where this is all happening. A gentleman was planting all this wild rice, James Whetung. I went to school with his younger siblings, so I've known him all my life. This whole issue has been ongoing for ten or fifteen years. To me, it was old news. It's just a case of not seeing the forest for the trees. A lot of people thought of it as James tilting against his windmill.

But Richard Rose, the artistic director of Tarragon, was sitting at a café in New York City reading some newspaper or magazine. He saw an article on this issue and became intrigued by its dramatic possibility. Then he said, 'Wait a minute, I know somebody from the Kawarthas, from Curve Lake, where this guy's from.' So he emailed me and we chatted for a bit. I said I knew all about this topic, and I even wrote an article on it for NOW *Magazine* a couple years ago. He told me to just sit back and think about it as a playwright, not as a journalist.

He was right. There was a play there, and all the conflict was sitting right in front of me. So I wrote it, and it was actually produced really, really quickly – within a year's time – because there'd been a cancellation in the season. It was a surprising hit and ran for five weeks, sold out four of those five weeks.

Tarragon remounted it the following year, and the play did a small tour of Central Ontario and Eastern Ontario. Then this past year (2020), it was going to be in Thunder Bay, in New Brunswick, and three other theatre companies had picked it up for production, one in Port Perry, one in Kincardine, and one on Manitoulin Island. So it was really, really big and very, very popular.

I've always discovered, as somebody who worked in Native theatre and as a novelist, that 90 per cent of the people who go and see Native plays and buy Native books are non-Native. On any given night, the vast majority – 80 to 90 per cent of the audience – is non-Native.

Some people I had worked with about three to four years ago worked on a documentary exploring the German fascination with North American Aboriginal cultures, called *Searching for Winnetou*, along with the head of CBC's documentary unit, and they came to see the play. They saw the dramatic potential for a documentary. We pitched the idea and they liked it. So we decided to do a documentary using the issue in Pigeon Lake – with James Whetung and the people of Pigeon Lake – as the catalyst for a larger exploration of conflict within Native and non-Native communities, usually through land and water issues.

Have you been pleased with the public response?

Oh, it's been very, very good. Some people agree with James, some people agree with the anti-wild-rice faction. It's set up several interesting discussions.

Is there anything else you want to discuss about your theatre career?

I find it fascinating that somebody who was completely unprepared, untrained, and uninterested suddenly woke up one morning and discovered he was a playwright. Friends of mine who read some of my articles, had seen my *Beachcombers* episodes, and then came to see my very, very first play, *Toronto at Dreamer's Rock*, said, 'Drew, have you finally found your medium?' That's when I had the brutal and uncomfortable realization that I was, my god, a playwright.

When I was working as the playwright-in-residence at Native Earth, part of my responsibility was to write a play. I sat down and wrote this play, having no concept of theatre structure whatsoever. I did what I could, but there's a lot to be said for experience. I wrote this three-act monstrosity that was just all over the place. I didn't know what I was trying to say. I was just doing it to fulfill a contract.

But the funny thing was it got huge laughs. And trust me, I know the difference between laughing at something and laughing with something. I was sitting there in the audience during the workshop of the play, and it was being read. I was so mortified and embarrassed. It was horrible. But the audience was laughing, and a lot of people came up to me who weren't in the theatre community and said I had great potential.

Anyway, I fulfilled my contract and life went on – I was going to write an episode of *North of 60*. While workshopping that play at Native Earth, I met a man named Larry Lewis, who at that time was the artistic director of the Debajehmujig Theatre on Manitoulin Island, the other Native theatre group in the province. He worked on my play during the spring, and he saw potential in it, too. Then somewhere around July he phoned me and said, 'I need you to write a play for me,' and I said, 'No thank you.' I confessed that I wasn't very good at it. And he said, 'I'll pay you in advance,' and I said, 'When do I start?'

I decided to approach this second play differently. I needed to write something I would actually like to go and see. So I wrote a play about two things I'm very fond of. One was science-fiction fantasy. The other one was something of obvious interest to me. It would explore what it meant to be Native, because, if you've never seen me, I've got blue eyes and fair hair. As a result, a lot of my work deals with Indian identity.

So I wrote a play called *Toronto at Dreamer's Rock*, about Rusty, a sixteen-year-old boy who climbs to the top of Dreamer's Rock on Manitoulin Island. And while he's up there, he has this experience where he meets Michael, a Native boy from a hundred years in the future, and Keesic, a Native boy from four hundred years in the past.

Basically, they spend forty-five minutes arguing, fighting, laughing, talking about girls – all these different things. Then, at the end of that forty-five minutes, Rusty, the sixteen-year-old boy from now, comes down. And then all three boys go away with their own definition of what being Native means for them.

There are these three different boys, from different time periods, with different definitions, who meet at the top of Dreamer's Rock and find common ground. As I said, I wrote that because Debajehmujig wanted me to write it and I needed the money. But lo and behold, it was a huge hit. It was remounted about a dozen times in about five years and published. I won a Chalmers Award for it, and that is literally what started off my career.

Like I said, I just woke up one morning and I was a playwright.

DANIEL DAVID MOSES

MNAWAATE GORDON-CORBIERE

Daniel David Moses was born on February 18, 1952, at Six Nations of the Grand River reserve. His father was Delaware, his mom Tuscarora. He was raised Anglican, attending St. Peter's Anglican Church on the reserve. The Moses family were dairy farmers, and growing up on a farm gave Daniel a strong connection to nature. However, he came to appreciate Toronto while working as a page for the Ontario Legislative Assembly when he was in middle school. He would spend his days off at the Royal Ontario Museum and exploring the city.

As a child, Moses loved to read, and in his teens he began to write. He said he knew he was meant to be an artist and chose to become a writer because of his love of words. Moses started off writing short stories and eventually moved on to poetry. After graduating high school, he moved to Toronto to attend York University, where he studied writing and graduated with an Honours BA. He then went on to the University of British Columbia, where he obtained his Master of Fine Arts in creative writing.

After completing his formal education, Moses moved back to Toronto in 1979 to establish himself as a full-time writer. He also wrote poems and, in 1980, published his first poetry collection, *Delicate Bodies*. After this collection came out, he began to learn more about his own style and where he wanted his writing to go. Moses continued working and, in 1982, teamed up with Tomson Highway and Lenore Keeshig-Tobias to form the Committee to Re-Establish the Trickster. The Committee sought to promote Indigenous cultural expression and published a magazine now and then.

The Committee was short-lived, but Daniel took what he learned and incorporated it into his play *Coyote City* (see excerpt, page 141). The play premiered at Native Earth Performing Arts in 1988, contributing to the then-nascent Indigenous theatre scene. *Coyote City* is about a woman and

Daniel David Moses, 2018.

her family going to the city in search of her lover. It explored, among other themes, the urban Indigenous experience. In 1991, *Coyote City* was nominated for the Governor General's Award in Drama. Though it didn't win, it became a fixture in Indigenous literature, and the first in Moses's 'city series' of plays, which included *Big Buck City* (1991), *Kyotopolis* (1993), and *City of Shadows* (1995).

While his plays were garnering attention, Moses continued to write poetry and in 1990 published another collection, entitled *The White Line*. He was becoming a more prominent figure in Indigenous arts, he regularly conducted workshops and attended new performances by aspiring Indigenous artists, wishing to support the next generation.

Over the course of his career, Moses wrote more acclaimed plays, such as *The Almighty Voice and His Wife* (1991), *The Indian Medicine Shows* (1996), and *Brébeuf's Ghost* (2000), as well as two more poetry collections, *Sixteen Jesuses* (2000) and *A Small Essay on the Largeness of Light and Other Poems* (2012). His work often explored themes based on his own experiences, such as gender and sexuality, what it meant to be a two-spirited Indigenous man, and the Indigenous experience in non-Indigenous spaces. Additionally, Moses always made sure history informed his works, no matter what time period they were set in.

Moses was asked to be an artist-, writer-, or playwright-in-residence by various Canadian institutions. In 2003, he was appointed the National Scholar to the Department of Drama at Queen's University. He served on the boards of various Indigenous and literary organizations, including Native Earth Performing Arts, the Association for Native Development in the Performing and Visual Arts, the Playwrights Union of Canada, and the Advisory Board of Oskana Poetry and Poetics. In 2019, Moses was appointed Professor Emeritus at Queen's University. He passed away from cancer on July 13, 2020.

AN EXCERPT FROM *COYOTE CITY*

DANIEL DAVID MOSES

The ghost said to Coyote, 'Here we have conditions different from those you have in the land of the living. When it gets dark here it has dawned in your land and when it dawns for us it is growing dark for you.' (Coyote, and the Shadow People)

To be seen is the ambition of ghosts and to be remembered the ambition of the dead. (Norman O. Brown)

COYOTE CITY was produced at the Native Canadian Centre of Toronto from 17 May to 5 June 1988 by Native Earth Performing Art, Inc. with the following cast:

JOHNNY	Gordon Odjig
LENA	Alanis King
BOO	Tina Louise Bomberry
MARTHA	Margaret Cozry
THOMAS	Ron Cook
CLARISSE	Gloria Eshkibok
Directed by	Anne Anglin

CHARACTERS
JOHNNY, a young Indian man, a ghost
LENA, a young Indian woman
BOO, a young Indian woman, Lena's younger sister
MARTHA, a middle-aged Indian woman, Lena's mother
THOMAS, a middle-aged Indian man, a minister
CLARISSE, an Indian woman, a hooker

The play is set in a darkness complicated only by spot lights and by the shadows of the characters and the few necessary properties. It happens just yesterday on a reserve and then in the city.

Act Two, Scene Four

A spot. BOO *and* MARTHA *wander into it.*

MARTHA: Boo. Boo, I don't like this place. Why are the lights all off?

BOO: It's a bar. It's atmosphere.

MARTHA: It is smokey in here. You think Lena's here someplace?

BOO: That's what she said.

MARTHA: But all they do here is drink.

BOO: I can't see them nowhere. Come on. Here's a seat.

MARTHA: Let's go. We can wait for them outside.

BOO: Ma, you're so tired, you're almost falling down. In here at least we can get off our feet. Come on.

MARTHA: They'll want us to drink.

BOO: What's a couple of draft? I could use one.

MARTHA: We don't have money.

BOO: I've got a few bucks in my pocket. Sit down. Sit down, Ma, please.

MARTHA: Oh all right. But I don't like it, Boo. It's so crowded.

BOO: Ma, there's hardly nobody here yet.

MARTHA: Daughter, tell me the truth. You've been here before?

BOO: Of course I have.

MARTHA: What were you doing here?

BOO: Having some beer. With friends. From school.

MARTHA: But this is an awful place. I didn't bring you up like that. Who are they all?

BOO: They're just people, Ma. Lots of Indians. Look around.

MARTHA: I don't see nobody I know. And it's so dark. Why would anybody in their right mind come here?

BOO: So just where the hell else are they going to go, Ma? They ain't rich.

MARTHA: You watch your tongue, Daughter.

BOO: I'm sorry, Ma. Just relax. I'll go get the draft.

AN EXCERPT FROM *TWO INDIANS*

FALEN JOHNSON

Synopsis: Win lives on the rez and Roe lives in the city. After years apart, the two cousins meet in a Toronto alley to recreate a ceremony from their childhood, but can they remember how? Has the world changed too much? Have *they*? When the words *missing* and *murdered*, and *truth* and *reconciliation*, *occupation* and *resistance* are everywhere, how do two Mohawk women stand their ground?

§   §   §

An alley. Downtown Toronto. Late evening. June.

It's hot. It smells like an alley. We hear music. It begins to fade, replaced by the sound of streetcars, the occasional sound of people having a good time on an early summer evening. Heading to dinner, maybe a show. The street sounds run for the duration of the show, increasing and decreasing in various sections.

The music and sound swell as we see ROE *(Rose) and* WIN *(Winnie) walk into the alley. The alley walls are covered in graffiti and tags. Milk crates sit in a stack nearby. There are mysterious alley puddles and scraps of garbage everywhere.*

We hear voices only; we are not sure if it is WIN *or* ROE *or both or someone else altogether.*

VOICES: Come on, cousin. Little further. You're almost there. It's just down the road.

(The following speech as they enter.)

ROE: I'm trying to convince this guy to buy a pin. On top of all the other shit this guy is buying – leather jackets, sweatshirts, godawful T-shirts – I'm trying to convince him to buy a goddamn pin. It's so effing ugly, too. It's like a, like a pilgrim, like a sexy pilgrim. Her tits are popping out and she's blond, of course, and she's a sexy pilgrim. She's wearing this like sexy pilgrim outfit. Little black shorts, tall high-heel boots, a collar that isn't even connected to a shirt, it's just there to be like sexy. And her hat, her pilgrim hat slightly askew, sexily askew. And she's leaning on this giant guitar. In perfect fuck-me pose.

Then all of a sudden it's like I come back into my body, like I land in my skin and I realize how ludicrous this is. I'm an Indian selling pilgrim pins. Sexy pilgrim pins. Sexy rock 'n' roll–themed Thanksgiving pilgrim pins. I know I shouldn't say it, even before I say it, but I just can't stop myself, it's out of my mouth, I look right into this guy's eyes and I say, 'Dressed like that, no wonder they almost died when they got here.'

The guy just looks at me blank. Totally not getting it. And I start giggling and the guy looks at me like what's-so-fucking-funny? And then I start laughing even harder and then I can't stop. And this guy is confused and then offended and then pissed 'cause I just won't stop. Can't stop. And then my manager walks in. I'm on the ground basically pissing myself, tears streaming down my face and I just laugh harder and harder because what else was there to do? I knew I was screwed. Might as well laugh.

(She laughs; Win joins in.)

WIN: So what happened?

ROE: I got a write-up. My manager said it was not the kind of experience that 'our' patrons are looking for when they visit one of 'our' establishments. Like I'm a stockholder in the company or something. We sell burgers and T-shirts, for chrissake.

I hate my job.

WIN: Yeah, I'd hate your job, too. You work retail in a restaurant. Sounds like a nightmare to me. Why don't you just—

ROE: Why don't I quit?

WIN: Well, yeah.

ROE: Because it pays well, like really, too well. Stupid well for retail. And it is expensive to live here.

WIN: So that is what you moved here for? Retail?

ROE: I moved here for school.

WIN: And now?

ROE: Now I am trying to work in my field.

WIN: Your field?

ROE: Yes.

WIN: You studied art therapy. Seems kinda far away from burger-shop retail. And you didn't even finish.

ROE: I almost did. I'm gonna go back. Next semester.

WIN: Sure, if you can get funding again. The band council doesn't like to fund a dropout cousin.

ROE: Yeah yeah yeah. Jesus. I didn't invite you up here to nag me all weekend. And remind me, where you are working again?

WIN: It's a good job and at least it's tax-free.

ROE: Slinging smokes to the kids.

WIN: Kids even. Mostly old Indian dudes. Too old to quit.

ROE: Well, you better quit or you'll end up all old and leathery like those guys. Smelling like a piece of smoked meat.

WIN: Who's nagging now, hey? And what are we even doing here? I didn't come all the way up to your big glorious city to sit in a dirty stink alley.

ROE: No? What'd you come for then?

WIN: (A few beats.) Well, this I guess.

ROE: Come on. Try and enjoy this. It'll be fun.

(An ambulance drives close by. The siren blares. They pause while they wait for it to pass. Win looks around.)

WIN: This?

ROE: Yeah, dude.

WIN: You wanna tell me why we are here? I see the gross alley. Very impressive. Hooray for pee smell! Can we go now?

ROE: The moon. You will see the moon like never before from right here.

WIN: The moon, cousin?

ROE: Yes, the moon.

WIN: *(Looking around.)* And we gotta do that here? Is this even safe?

ROE: Trust me, they are more afraid of us than we are of them.

WIN: Uh, I don't know about that.

ROE: Just think of them like bears. Make lots of noise and they won't come near you. That's what I do.

WIN: I'm not sure if that's how bears work.

ROE: Come on and rez up.

WIN: What does that even mean?

ROE: You know.

WIN: *(Beat.)* Man, you city Indians.

ROE: What?

WIN: You come up to the city and you act like the moon is this new thing. Like you never seen it before. Like you gotta sit in a dirty alley and see a full moon to feel Indian again. *(Beat.)* You know you can see this kinda thing back home all the time.

(Roe makes a scoffing sound, perhaps a snort.)

WIN: What is that supposed to mean?

ROE: Nothing. This is what it's like here. The sky is small here. You gotta plan how you can see things.

WIN: Mmm hmm.

ROE: Oh Jesus, super Indian over here. So, what at home you, what, pack a bundle and head out on the land and wait for the moon to rise over the trees, then empty your menstrual cup in the snow and howl?

WIN: Eww! What is wrong with you?

ROE: When's the last time you even went outside for anything, let alone to see the stars? And going out for a smoke doesn't count.

WIN: I see them all the time.

ROE: On your way home from the smoke shack?

WIN: What's wrong with that? Seeing the stars on my way home from my job? Is that really the worst thing I could do? Look up as I head home or look up when I go for a smoke?

ROE: No, it's not, but don't treat it like you are somehow better than me or like this means less. I didn't know the moon was reserved for the reserved. (*She grins, waits for a response.*)

WIN: Oh, you are clever. Just hilarious.

ROE: Look. I live here now. Three years now. And yeah, it is different but it's been good for me. It's made me appreciate who I am in a way that home never could. (*She looks up.*) Once you lose the stars, you learn to appreciate them.

WIN: Sure.

ROE: I know it's different, but can you just try to enjoy this?

WIN: It stinks. (*She checks her phone.*)

ROE: It stinks everywhere here. You get used to it.

WIN: I don't think I could ever get used to it.

ROE: Sometimes you have to.

WIN: You have to? (*She looks to Roe. Silence.*) So, how long?

ROE: Not long.

(*Beat.*)

A scene from the production of Two Indians.

WIN: So, we are here to see the moon.

ROE: Not just any moon. A supermoon.

WIN: And what makes it so super?

ROE: It's a really big moon.

WIN: Like a full moon?

ROE: No, it's bigger than that.

WIN: So, the moon is closer to the earth? I don't get it.

ROE: Well shit, I don't know, like the exact science behind it. It's a big moon. It looks big, okay? It's impressive.

WIN: Hold on. (*She pulls out her phone.*)

ROE: Don't do that.

WIN: What? I wanna know. Don't you wanna know what you are out here appreciating?

ROE: No mystery at all.

WIN: *(She googles from her phone.)* Here. *(She reads from her phone.)* 'A super-moon is the coincidence of a full moon or a new moon with the closest approach the Moon makes to the Earth on its elliptical orbit, resulting in the largest apparent size of the lunar disk as seen from Earth. The technical name is the perigee-syzygy of the Earth-Moon-Sun system.'

ROE: Well, that's clinical. Could you maybe read that again, but this time play some flute music underneath? Drums. An eagle cry.

WIN: *(She continues to look at her phone.)* Okay, so … I need a … *(She looks around the ground for something to draw with. She finds an old can of spray paint and goes to a wall.)* So, it –

ROE: Whoa!

WIN: What?

ROE: You trying to get arrested?

WIN: Arrested? For this? Seriously? *(Referring to the graffiti and general disrepair of the alley.)* Look around you.

ROE: I know, I know, but shit, if they see you doing that …

WIN: Come on. Rez up.

ROE: *(Beat.)* Fine. I'll watch.

WIN: *(Referring to her phone occasionally, she begins to draw/paint, as she does the following.)* Okay, the earth is here. And the moon is here. The moons orbit it like this. So, when it's on this side of the earth it is closer and therefore looks larger. There.

ROE: Mystery solved. You really know how to suck the fun out of things, you know that?

WIN: Sorry. *(Beat.)* So, we stand here and wait for the moon to rise. Are we even gonna be able to see it from here?

ROE: Oh yeah.

WIN: You do this a lot? Come here?

ROE: Yep. Just about every month. The winter is the best. Snow makes things quieter. Smells less, too.

WIN: And how'd you find this place?

ROE: This old Indian guy who used to stop in the store. He came in once looking for a gift for his niece and we got to chatting. He's from up north. James Bay area. He would come in and we would talk. He had these really sad eyes. Looked like he had a rough time, like he had been crying for a long time. Years maybe. We'd talk. Sometimes even have lunch on my break. He told me about this spot. Told me where to find it. Said he felt like there was something special here.

WIN: So how come he isn't here?

ROE: I don't know. I haven't seen him in a while … He just stopped coming in.

WIN: Maybe he went home.

(A few beats.)

ROE: Maybe.

§   §   §

Production History: An excerpt from Two Indians *was presented at Wrecking Ball 14 at the Aki Theatre in Toronto.* Two Indians *was then produced by Salt Baby Collective as a part of the 2016 SummerWorks Performance Festival at the Factory Theatre Studio in Toronto, with the following team:*

Rose (Roe): Yolanda Bonnell
Winnie (Win): Darla Contois
Direction: Jessica Carmichael
Scenography Design: Andy Moro
Sound, Design & Original Composition: Patrick Bramm
Stage Management: Brittany Ryan

A second showing of Two Indians took place at the Gathering Place on Six Nations Reserve as a part of the Onkwehón:we (The Original People's) Festival in 2018, with the following team:

Rose (Roe): Samantha Brown
Winnie (Win): Joelle Peters
Direction: Falen Johnson
Scenography Design: Andy Moro
Sound Design & Original Composition: Patrick Bramm
Stage Management: Lindy Kinoshameg

A LIFE IN BUSINESS, CRAFTS,
AND THEATRE

MARGARET COZRY

Our family consisted of twelve children, of which I was the youngest.
We resided on the Ojibway Parry Island reserve, overlooking the
incredible beauty of Georgian Bay, an undeniable paradise where we
swam, skated, fished, and picked berries, apples, gooseberries, and winter-
greens. In the spring, sweet water (maple syrup) nourished our bodies
and spirits. We watched the sunsets and rainbows over the water and
heard the loon calls, the birds chirping, and the fish jumping out of the
water. The boys made tree houses for their own fun and privacy. Two
beaches were close by. We went canoeing and for very long walks to visit
relatives and friends. When the snow blanketed the hills, we sat on cardboard and slid down them really fast, squealing.

My artistic appreciation came from my mother – I watched her and
my two aunts make exquisite birchbark and porcupine quill boxes
trimmed with fragrant sweetgrass. This art predates European contact.
My special aunt Rosie excelled in black ash basketry, as well as making
moccasins and anything her creative hands could pick up, including
making pies. All raw materials were seasonal and all natural, not supplies
you purchased in a store. Not knowing the value of their craft, they sold
their artistry at very low prices, and no one told them otherwise.

In the summers, I worked as a chore girl on an island resort on Georgian Bay called the Yankee Club of Pittsburgh. My mother instilled in me
the importance of work and saving money at a very young age. In 1953,
when I was fourteen, my dad got transferred to Toronto and I was devastated. He worked for the CNR. We were leaving Parry Island to come to a
concrete urban life in Toronto.

We lived in a flat on Baldwin Street on the east side of Spadina and shopped in Kensington Market. My initial observations were of the different types of people, and they weren't very friendly-looking either. When my dad sent me out for a newspaper, I ran all the way to the store and back. Because of the trauma and loneliness, my mother took me home every weekend for a year to visit my relatives and friends and get some clean, fresh air. To this day, I hate the sound of the CNR whistle, as we had to get up after midnight to catch the train.

I found in Toronto that Natives didn't have a community like the European immigrants all had. The Europeans lived together in enclaves and spoke their own languages and never learned who built the foundation of Canada: us.

We didn't know high schools had different subjects. After failing in two different high schools, I chose a secretarial school, Central High School of Commerce. In order to make sure I passed all the subjects, my mother insisted I study after school, from 4:00 to 11:00 p.m. It worked, and I started my career in the business world. One executive I was fortunate to work for was a graduate of Harvard University. He was the vice-president and a chartered accountant. Taking dictation in shorthand helped improve my English vocabulary. He was very patient and considerate, but he told me for the first six months, 'You are the worst secretary I ever had.' I thought for sure I was going to get fired. But later he smiled and said, 'You turned out to be the best secretary I ever had,' and handed me a generous Christmas bonus. I think he recognized my struggle and determination.

Later, another secretarial position required me to organize a stenographic pool for an engineering firm, from 8:00 a.m. to 4:00 p.m. At the same time, I worked for a chartered accountant, typing financial statements in the Manulife building, from 5:00 to 9:00 p.m. Then I went to another floor and typed envelopes from 9:00 to 11:00 p.m. for a personnel placement agency. I made twenty dollars for typing five hundred envelopes, and that made me type faster. I saved this money as I was too busy to spend it.

A staff member was impressed with my ninety-eight-words-a-minute typing speed and sent me to a job interview at Indian Crafts of Ontario, where the executive director was Haida from British Columbia. This wholesale crafts operation was government-funded, but they didn't see it as viable and cancelled the funding. It was another type of experience where I learned to overcome my shyness and how to handle racial discrimination. My boss told me if I had any money saved, I could open a retail store because the government consultants didn't know what they were talking about.

As destiny would have it, I was asked by Ojibway writer and storyteller Basil Johnston to type a draft of his book, *How the Birds Got Their Colours*. This opportunity was at the Royal Ontario Museum, where I met Dr. Ed Rogers, Curator of Ethnology. On my lunch hours, I was able to take in the beauty of the collections. I was disheartened that such amazing hand-made crafts were rarely seen in stores, and the art was being lost. I had already decided my mission would be to open a retail operation where customers could come and purchase authentic original handmade arts and crafts made by true First Nations artists and crafters, as opposed to the Asian imports that are allowed to be copied by machines and sold cheaply to unknowing tourists.

Through Dr. Rogers, I met Robert Liss. He had seven fabric stores. He took me out for lunch and asked me how much money I had for my enterprise and where I wanted my store to be. I said I had $5,000, and I wanted it to be in Yorkville. He said, 'Well, you'd be bankrupt in a month.' He assured me that when you have merchandise no one else has, people will have to come to you no matter where you're located. It's called destination shopping.

Robert suggested I begin with a few years of groundwork, sending hides and beads to fly-in remote communities on the Ontario-Manitoba border, where these supplies are outrageously priced at the Bay stores, which offered little choice. I monitored the designs and quality of the one-of-a-kind items. Every box that arrived contained unique creations never seen down

Tomson Highway and Margaret Cozry.

south. I bought and tested the market. If they didn't sell, I would ask the craftspeople to upgrade their crafts. They were very willing to do that.

These works found a good market, and I was paying more for their crafts, so the artists were very pleased. My stockpiling was done in my apartment. Eventually, I couldn't move. I had too many boxes, so I found a location at 668 Queen West, where I lived and worked. I called it the Algonquians Sweet Grass Gallery – 'gallery' to indicate the merchandise was special.

The landlord was Ukrainian and kind of – what would you say? – suspicious. Being a woman, what was I doing having my own business? He called me 'Mrs.,' as Europeans usually do (assuming you're married). He was also in the textile business. Number 668 was his original store, where he had a large counter where he used to cut the fabric. I said to myself, 'Well, that could be my bed.' I put a futon on it, and that's where I slept. I went to the local community centres and swam at seven o'clock on most mornings. The landlord said I would do well in that block, everyone did, and that he would give me a reasonable rent because tenants stay longer that way.

As a vendor, my first large endeavour was the Canadian National Exhibition, in the Arts, Crafts & Hobbies Pavilion in 1978. I was fortunate because I could get a few extra booths where I got craftspeople to demonstrate porcupine quill work, carvings, and beadwork. I brought in an artist from Thunder Bay, Noel Ducharme. It was a great education process and the best place to test the market. The public became aware of how much time and work went into the making of the crafts and began to appreciate and respect the art. The booths drew a lot of interest, especially with two male Ojibway salesmen with long braids. One was hilarious and he would sell four rings at a time. I could see women nudging each other, and over they came.

I learned how to attract the customers just by observing their interest, and many times I had to change the display to make it work. I also learned that presentation was the most important thing in marketing and that selling is psychological.

I was quite surprised on opening day when some executive directors came by and presented me with an award for the best booth. I was very honoured. I won on many more occasions after that.

Members of the public were very interested in the descriptive signs and write-ups in the booths. Purchases were guaranteed authentic, with an 'Algonquin Product' tag and a biography of the makers of the carvings

Canadian National Exhibition.

and artwork. With soapstone carvings, it didn't occur to the artists to sign their work. So I insisted that everything that came in had to be signed to differentiate them from cheap Asian imports. I even had the artists' pictures taken as more proof, unless they were too shy.

My gallery was not a consignment store. The crafters' handmade merchandise was always COD, as I understood their needs. Other buyers took 30, 60, 90, or 120 days for payment. And in no way was my business government-funded.

I didn't consider the gallery only as a summer tourist business. As with the Hudson Bay, tourists came in the off-season, too. Customers came particularly for Christmas gifts, with November and December bringing the highest volumes. (The Bay also requested I put up a trading post on one of their floors in the summertime. I did that, too, but it took a long time to get paid.)

Because we handed out so many business cards, people were waiting outside to get into 668 Queen on the Tuesday after Labour Day, when the CNE ended. That was awesome. I always identified my proud Native ancestry by wearing the clothing and accessories. A few times, potential customers followed me because they said they knew I would have something really good to see wherever I was headed. My wardrobe also consisted of Native designer clothing that appeared in *Flare*, the fashion magazine.

I began another venue, a wholesale business. I exhibited first in the Toronto Gift Show and later travelled to Edmonton to theirs. The retail-store buyers would come from Canada and the United States, and people were amazed at the volume of authentic merchandise I had, particularly porcupine quill boxes, which they hadn't seen for years.

Retailers were spending anywhere from hundreds to thousands of dollars in my booth. Then there were buyers who reneged because they thought they could get the quill work cheaper from my mother and my two aunts. I said, 'You don't have to buy them, but you won't be getting them from my relatives anymore, because I happen to be Mrs. Cozry's daughter and the niece of my two aunts.' The next year, the buyer put in an order. I always stood my ground. My Chief was happy to collect the quill boxes for me, as it helped the makers year-round.

The prices the makers were getting for quill boxes was doubled, and the stores I sold to were exclusive locations, in high-end, heavy-traffic tourist locations. I didn't sell to stores that sold imported junk and weren't worthy of the quality.

What amazed me particularly was the publicity I received with practically every show I went to. The advertising and promotion came automatically because of my high visibility. I did TV and radio interviews, which were free, as well as newspaper write-ups and free ads in visitors' guides promoting places to visit in Canada. This promotion was also done in Europe and the United States.

Fifteen exhibitors were invited to the largest trade show in Europe. It was in Germany and included a visit to France. Through a German wholesale buyer, I was invited to a German Indian club in Frankfurt, where they made their own Native clothing, dressed up in full regalia, and drummed and danced. They did extensive research and had furnished teepees. There is a German writer by the name of Karl May who had a love of nature and wrote many books on Indians, as we were called back then. Those books were used throughout the school system. If you ever wonder about Germans' appreciation for our people and our crafts, now you know why.

My landlord let me purchase the house my mother and I were renting on Stephen Drive, near the Queensway in Etobicoke. That pleased my mother so much, because she really never expected this. My landlord had a lot of respect for Native people. He told me I was a role model. That year, I did thirty shows, and my accountant told me I had made a profit, which is unusual for the first year. My Native and non-Native clientele wanted my operation to succeed.

The high visibility of my business got the attention of the marketing executive promoting Village by the Grange on McCaul Street, across from the Ontario College of Art. She gave me a store for free. I asked her why. She said, 'Because I see you all over the place, and you'd be a really good drawing card for our location.'

In our culture, we have what we call 'the moccasin telegraph.' It didn't take long for the craftspeople to get word that I was buying. I was getting crafts not only from Algonquin Nations, but also from Six Nations. Sometimes I would go to their reserve to buy pottery, and it was just wonderful. You'd go to one house and they would say, 'You go to that house and that house and that house.' It was like going shopping for all different products. Some were relatives and friends of theirs, and I found they were eager to help, especially when I praised their fine work and didn't beat their prices down.

All the vendors were asked to design and make a Canadian flag for the CNE's hundredth anniversary. I decided I wasn't going to make one because I was too busy preparing for the opening. When I told the coordinator, he said, 'I'm so disappointed that you of all people are not making a banner.' It embarrassed me so much. We had four days to go before opening. I called my crafty girlfriend, who's Ojibway from Thunder Bay, and I said, 'Let's put together a banner.' We put a beaver pelt in the centre of a wooden hoop and made a flag for each side of the banner with owl and wild-turkey feathers. My friend, who is a collector, loaned me an ancient banner stone to put on the bottom of the banner. In the centre, I put an amazing beaded rosette that was about six inches in size.

The next day, dignitaries came to my booth and said I had won the Best Banner award. I was really surprised. Later on, the coordinator said there was a vendor who had worked for six months on a needlepoint banner, but they couldn't let her win, because mine was the most historical banner.

At the Grange store one day, the phone rang and a lady said, 'Are you Margaret?' I said yes, and she said, 'You have a booth at the CNE every year?' I said yes, and she said, 'Well, you remember my aunt? She does the metal booth every year?' She said, 'My husband is a producer and he's written this story on Tom Longboat, the great runner. It's called *Wildfire: The Story of Tom Longboat.*' She said, 'We've been searching the reserves for a Native lady with long black hair to play the part of Tom Longboat's mother. And we haven't been able to find anyone.' I said, 'Well, I'm very busy right now. I can try to find you somebody and I'll call you.' She said, 'No, I don't mean *anybody*. I mean you.' I said, 'What? I don't think so.' I said I had never done that before. She said it was a non-speaking role: 'We'll have you feeding chickens or something.' And I said, 'Oh, you know, I don't think so.' She said, 'Well, how about you come up to our place and meet my husband.'

I thought, maybe I could sell them something for the set. So I filled up my van with arts and crafts and props. Anyway, her husband said, 'Okay, you're perfect for this role. You know, you could make a living at this.' I said, 'Oh, really? I don't think so.' I said I already had a job. *Wildfire* was a very successful film.

Then the next phone call I got was from Denis Lacroix, the actor in *Black Robe*. He said, 'Margaret, TVOntario is looking for someone to play the part of Molly Brant.' I said, 'That's not my career.' Denis said, 'We can't keep having other people playing Native roles. We have to get in there and push ourselves to play Native roles. And it won't take long, you know.' I went to meet Gladys Richards, a producer at TVO, and she hired me after I read a few paragraphs. It was filmed on Centre Island.

The next call I got was from the CBC and director Bruce Pittman. He said, 'We saw you in a film and we would like you to audition.' I said, 'I'm terribly busy right now.' He said, 'Well, could you come down?' So I went down and met him, having no experience whatsoever of how auditions worked. He handed me the script and said, 'Okay, now read.' So I read everyone's part. He said, 'That's fine, now just read the part of Mary, the grandmother.' August Schellenberg's daughter Joanna was cast as my granddaughter. August was a client, and I got a call from him, congratulating me that I was cast for the part.

By this time, I had spoken to the other great actor, Gary Farmer, who had come into the store. He helped me with my actor's resumé and how to how to get principal wages. I thought, 'You know, this isn't too bad.'

One day, a tall, handsome Cree man with flying black hair came rushing into my store, swift as a deer, and came right up to my desk. His name was Tomson Highway. He said, 'Margaret, have you ever done any stage acting?' I said no. He said, 'Well, I wrote this play called *The Rez Sisters*. It's about seven Native women who come to Toronto from Manitoulin Island, to the biggest bingo in the world.' He said, 'Would you like to audition for the part of Veronica St. Pierre, a gossiper?' Shocked, I said, 'I don't know.' I asked Tomson where he got my name, and he said Denis Lacroix. So I phoned Denis up and said, 'Denis, Tomson Highway came into my store. He wants me to do a stage role.' Denis said, 'You have to do it, Margaret. These opportunities only come by once in your life.'

I went and auditioned for director Larry Lewis and Tomson Highway. Larry handed me a monologue said, 'I want you to start reading this together with me, and I want you to read it as fast as you can, and as loud as you can. And I'm reading with you.' I said, 'Okay,' and I did it. We finished right on the same note.

Tomson said, 'We'll let you know in a few weeks.' In a few days, Tomson called and said, 'You're cast as Veronica St. Pierre, but on one condition: you and Gloria Eshkibok will start ahead of time, rehearsing with Larry Lewis for about a month because you don't have the stage experience.' The other actors had over fifteen years of acting experience.

We did that, and then we moved to the Native Canadian Centre to rehearse. It was exhausting, and after one fourteen-hour day, I said to myself, 'I made a mistake.' When the rehearsal was over, I left. The director said, 'Good night, Margaret,' and I didn't answer.

Sensing something was wrong, Larry came running through the lane, and he said, 'You didn't say good night to me. What's wrong?' So I told him. I said, 'I think you made the wrong choice. I don't think I can do this, Larry.' He said, 'You're doing fine!' The next day, Anne Anglin, one of the other actors, told me she thought I was taking it personally that no one liked my nosy gossiper character.

Tomson called me over. He said, 'Margaret, I see something in you that I want to help you develop. How about I come to your store every morning before rehearsal and we'll do your lines?' Well, he and I had so much fun. At least, *he* had a lot of fun, because he knew what he wanted portrayed in these characters. These were actually real-life characters on his reserve.

Opening night came along, and right until I went on the stage, I was practising my lines. Tomson knew you should never let your guard down in learning your lines, even right up until the last minute. According to the director, during one of my first scenes on a veranda onstage, I had my toes wrapped around the leg of the chair I was sitting on because I was so nervous.

I think I was so tired that I couldn't see the success of the play. We had a party afterwards. There was lots of publicity and buzz and eventually sold-out shows. I was especially pleased that, for one evening's performance, a busload of Ojibway came from my home reserve and waited after the show for autographs. It was a joy to see them.

This play, *The Rez Sisters* by Tomson Highway, was the winner of the 1986–87 Dora Mavor Moore Award for Outstanding New Play and was nominated for a Governor General's Award in 1988. It was performed on a cross-Canada tour and represented Canada on the main stage of the Edinburgh International Festival. We were all so very happy.

HOW WE CARRY THIS PLACE

THE ANISHINAABE CITY: OGIMAA MIKANA

HAYDEN KING AND SUSAN BLIGHT

At the height of the Idle No More movement in early 2013, we began thinking about how language revitalization in urban spaces like Toronto was missing from these national conversations we were collectively having about justice for Indigenous communities. And so we decided to intervene, linking our commitment to language revitalization to our refusal to be erased by the city and our thirst for Anishinaabe self-determination, wherever we find ourselves.

The result was the Ogimaa Mikana Project, a campaign to restore Anishinaabemowin place names to the streets, avenues, roads, paths, and trails of the city, transforming a landscape that often obscures or renders invisible the presence of Indigenous peoples.

Ogimaa Mikana consists of a dozen installations in the city itself, and nearly as many in Anishinaabe territory outside Toronto, from Thunder Bay to Ottawa, as well as large-scale murals, banners, countermapping initiatives, or exhibits in gallery spaces. The Project has been prolific, growing to include new members, and has inspired related campaigns across the country. The photos in this series chronicle some of the Ogimaa Mikana Project's early Toronto-specific work.

1. At Queen and McCaul, this was Ogimaa Mikana's first installation. It recognized the leadership of Indigenous women in the Idle No More movement. The Project renamed Queen Street the Leader's Path (or Ogimaa Mikana).

2. There is a cluster of streets, roads, crescents, and groves in the High Park area named after nondescript 'Indians.' Challenging this misnaming, the Project sought to remind the mostly wealthy High Park residents that we are still here, we are not Indians, and this is our land.

3. Ogimaa Mikana works with Elders and Speakers to confirm our translations. In this Queen's Park installation that criticizes the Government of Ontario's lack of engagement on Indigenous issues, we worked with the late Alex McKay, an Anishinaabemowin teacher and a fixture of the Toronto Indigenous community.

4. In 2016, the Project installed a billboard in rapidly changing Parkdale, which was home to a relatively large Indigenous community in the 1970s and 1980s that has since been pushed out due to rising rents and gentrification. We sought to re-articulate old obligations, like sharing, that are captured in Toronto-area treaties such as the Dish with One Spoon.

5. Ogimaa Mikana took over this historic intersection, correcting Spadina (Ishpadinaa) and renaming Davenport (Gete-Onigaming) to reflect their original uses by Anishinaabe as major thoroughfares. The Dupont by the Castle Business Improvement Area later worked to make versions of these signs permanent.

KAPAPAMAHCHAKWEW:
WANDERING SPIRIT SCHOOL AND
THE VISION OF NIMKIIQUAY

KERRY POTTS WITH PAULINE SHIRT
(NIMKIIQUAY)

'We show them spirituality and love and try to teach by example.'[1]
– Elder Vern Harper

'Unless we know the legends and the stories of Creation, unless we know the songs and ceremonies, we don't really know who we are.'[2]
– Elder Jim Dumont (Onaubinisay/Walks above the Ground)

Toronto is defined by its strata of buildings, its paved public spaces, and its hum of human activity. In many ways, this city defines one's connection to the earth. Elder Madeline Skead, from Kenora, Ontario, in awe of the immense and unnatural landscape of the city, once remarked to my father, 'Where can you put down your tobacco here?'

Madeline, who passed away in 2012, was a beloved teacher and rights advocate whose name is celebrated across many parts of Ontario and beyond. She was a mentor and spiritual guide to my own family, and her question has lingered in my mind for the twenty years I've spent living in T'karonto. This city teaches us a way to live in a human-centred environment where the focus is on what humans can build upon and consume, rather than on our responsibilities to the earth. Where can we communicate with what is sacred? Where can we put down our tobacco?

Over the past two decades, Elder Pauline Shirt has been one of my most important teachers, helping me to answer such questions by listening to the Indigenous community, to my own heart, and to the earth. Pauline (Nimkiiquay) is a Plains Cree Elder originally from Saddle Lake, Alberta, Red-Tail Hawk Clan, and member of the Three Fires Society (Midewiwin) and Buffalo Dance Society. Informed by her own Plains Cree culture, Pauline has dedicated her life to providing people with ceremony and guidance, and to cultivating spaces in this city that offer an Indigenous approach to education.

Pauline once offhandedly told me she comes from 'a family of chiefs and go-getters,' but until I sat down with her for this article, I had no sense of the depth of her statement. She is currently the Elder at George Brown College, is on the Elders Council for the Urban Indigenous Education Centre of Excellence, and is endlessly called upon by organizations and community members for her fearless-yet-kind direction and rich cultural knowledge. Pauline's unwavering commitment to education crystalized when she, with support from her late husband Vern Harper, started Wandering Spirit Survival School, a school that would teach children living in Toronto about Indigenous ways of life. It became the first Native-led school founded in Canada.

I wanted to sit with Pauline to understand her vision for the school, and the history that shaped its creation. When we speak, it is in the middle of the pandemic lockdown in May 2020, and she, in her nomadic ways, has moved temporarily to Six Nations. One thing that continuously draws me to Pauline is her buoyant energy, and even my cellphone doesn't stifle the delight she radiates in being able to talk about her 'favourite subject.' Pauline says, almost effervescently, 'The school produced so many successful souls. To this day, there are lots of good stories. So many good things happen that I could just sit here for weeks and tell you all of the beautiful things that happened!'

In my eagerness to direct the interview, I begin to review my list of questions, when she warmly interrupts: 'I will just talk, and the answers will come through in the story.' As I allow Pauline's words to wash over me, it becomes clear that like any river, her story of the school has many tributaries that shape and nourish it. One tributary is her son Clayton, who refused to return to the public school he attended. Protesting against the racist schoolyard bullying and his general disconnection from the curriculum and pedagogy, Clayton's actions, combined with the lack of other culturally safe schools in Toronto and across the country, strengthened Pauline's resolve to start a school where her Indigenous way of life could be taught and celebrated. Though her son's daring protest further stirred her spirit to action, the spirit of the school itself preceded young Clayton by seven generations.

Wandering Spirit (Kapapamahchakwew), a hero of his people, is the school's namesake, and what he represented to Pauline was a spirit she wanted to foster in her children and the larger community. Known as a key player in the Frog Lake Uprising of April 2, 1885, Wandering Spirit was a skilled Cree War Chief whose partner-in-leadership was the famed Cree Peace Chief, Big Bear (Mistahimaskwa), known as the last Cree leader to resist acquiescing to treaty.[3]

The history of the uprising is disputed and most certainly incomplete. In short, dependence on government rations took hold as buffalo became scarce and were killed as a strategy to starve Indigenous bands onto reserves. Coupled with fighting with the neighbouring Blackfoot, Big Bear's band of Plains Cree were relocated by the Canadian government close to Frog Lake, an area twenty-four kilometres long, connected by a creek to the Saskatchewan River. Prior to April 1885, the government had continuously failed to provide promised rations or uphold the agreed-upon rights, leaving the band starving and badly impoverished.

Renowned for his tenacity and strategic intellect, Wandering Spirit joined a group of young braves after they had confronted Thomas Quinn, a reviled Indian agent known to both the RCMP and the Plains Cree band for mistreating Indians and withholding rations. This encounter resulted in Quinn being shot and killed, and in the killing of several other townspeople.

Ten days later, on April 12, Wandering Spirit and two hundred Cree moved on to capture Fort Pitt, which held military supplies and other useful provisions. Sources on this history are again conflicted. Some align Wandering Spirit with Louis Riel and his resistance, while others suggest Wandering Spirit and Big Bear's refusal of Riel's invitations. Following the RCMP's surrender of Fort Pitt, the War Chief and his followers travelled through the woods to avoid imprisonment, but surrendered some months later.[4] Wandering Spirit was hanged at Battleford with others accused of participating in the North-West Resistance (otherwise known as the North-West Rebellion), though none of the accused were provided with translation or legal counsel at their trial. It is said that at his death, while others cried out in defiance, Wandering Spirit sang softly to his wife.[5]

Mainstream schools have taught children that Louis Riel, Big Bear, and Wandering Spirit were traitors, and misunderstandings about the details of these incidents have been retold by community members for decades. Notwithstanding this imperfect historical memory, Wandering Spirit's goal of independence and his fight against starvation were resolute and irrefutably determined his actions. Despite his dedication to his people, Wandering Spirit's name was unspoken on Pauline's reserve for nearly six generations. When she began the school, Pauline was unaware of her close blood ties to him. Her family held their silence for generations as they had been disgraced with the label 'Your Grandfather killed' – a saying that underscored the shunning of Wandering Spirit for being labelled as 'a killer of your own' and the community's cultural prohibition against being the first to raise your weapon.[6] Today, Pauline celebrates his name and the indomitable spirit that sought a better future for his community.

As poet and researcher Sharon Berg writes:

Pauline named her school after him in order to re-establish his name with honour in his own community. In Pauline's understanding, he had shouldered the blame for circumstances that were far beyond his control in 1885. As a warrior, his life was devoted to protecting his nation and Wandering Spirit did his best to protect his band during the events leading up to the Frog Lake uprising and their months-long trek through the forests ... Even with his last breath, Wandering Spirit urged his people to continue practicing their cultural ways in the death song he sang for his wife.

... Pauline heard from people who knew the true story, different than the story recorded for posterity. The shooting of Thomas Quinn was shifted to Wandering Spirit's shoulders to protect a younger brave. That's why his name was unspoken in Pauline's family for almost 100 years. She wanted to correct the wrong done to him, even as she worked to correct the wrongs done to her people.[7]

The story of her grandfather, six generations removed, is certainly a tributary for Pauline's vision. Another is her family in Alberta, and growing up on a farm where she was her father's shadow. She learned 'how to work in a circle, together as a family, to respect and love each other.'

'Being Dad's helper,' Pauline recalls, 'that's how I learned to take care of Mother Earth. Dad was always talking to the spirits, talking to the horses, animals, and plants. He showed me what a relationship to the earth looks like. While he was tilling the fields, he'd talk to the earth. He taught me all the trees, berries, the birthing of animals. As Plains Cree, the horses were such a great part of our livelihood. We have that connection.'

She shares that everyone had a responsibility in the family, and that at lunchtime, everyone would be together. She was also taught that '[e]verything had a spirit – the clouds, air, the wind, water, the wood, the animals. If the spirit is alive, they have their own language, and my father would talk to them in our Cree language, and they understood. I used to love how he would communicate with the horses and run around with them. We would try to imitate him.

'As a little girl, after the rain, I would just run in my bare feet, with my dress flying around, right into the water and meet my father. I will always remember that most beautiful feeling of being connected to water.'

Pauline has always loved learning, and this learning spirit was nourished by her family, by the land, as well as in school. When she was eight, she went to Blue Quills School, a residential school in St. Paul, Alberta, run by the Catholic Church and named after Chief Blue Quill (Sîpihtaka-nep) of Treaty 6 territory. Unlike so many, Pauline's experience of residential school was positive. This was helped by her mother's presence as the school's assistant cook, allowing her a parental connection that most children were denied.

As Pauline recounts: 'They tried to make me a good Catholic girl, but I was traditional and I spoke my language. But I loved to learn. In Grade 11 or 12, I went to school in Edmonton and I just loved it. I continued on to college for business school, and then I came to Toronto in the late 1960s with my three little ones. Going to Toronto was like going to China at that time!'

Compared to rural Alberta, Toronto meant a radical departure from a land-based lifestyle and a separation from a distinctively Indigenous community. Seeking community and family, Pauline became involved with the Native Canadian Centre of Toronto, known still as an important meeting place for the urban Indigenous community. Soon Pauline connected to other Indigenous people, including the respected educators and leaders Jim Dumont, Edna Manitowabi, and Joe Hare. Becoming involved with the burgeoning Indigenous rights movement of the time, they braided politics into their new urban life.

Pauline and Vern became fixtures in activist circles, never shying away from the front lines of the causes they supported. In 1974, along with Louis Cameron (founder of the Ojibway Warrior Society of Kenora), Chief Ken Basil of the Bonaparte First Nations in British Columbia, and others, the two co-founded what would become known as the Native People's Caravan.[8]

'In 1974,' Pauline recalls, 'there was a call-out to organize the Native People's Caravan. Vern and I organized, and we trucked 200 to 250 young people across the country with our Eagle Staff and developed the Native People's Manifesto. Our main purpose was to go on September 30, 1974, to meet the parliamentarians, along with George Manuel and the National Indian Brotherhood [now the Assembly of First Nations].'

The Caravan moved from Vancouver to Ottawa to deliver a manifesto to the federal government about the state of Indigenous lives, including poverty, dishonoured treaties, Métis rights, and other grievances.[9] It became a symbol of Indigenous solidarity and self-determination, and education became a crucial focus, with the demand of 'Indian Control of Indian Education.'

As Pauline recounts: 'We were so young, we said, "Enough is enough, they are not listening to our chiefs, or our people." It was just broken promises, and then [came] the White Paper.[10] In the Caravan, we said we would go for the opening of the parliament and talk to the parliamentarians about our education system, spirituality, and health. It was a very peaceful thing.

'When we got to Ottawa on September 29, we had a peaceful protest, had the drum there, and the women took over. I was the last one to close the doors behind us, make sure nobody had any guns or sticks. We got there around 10:00 a.m. I remember my little boys were playing with their toys, and we made sure that if anything happened, the kids had someone to spirit them away. Then, of course, they sent the riot squad to us. It was really bloody.

'We went back to this abandoned building [on Victoria Island], and called it the Native People's Embassy. We had a big circle, sang songs, gave tobacco, and asked the spirit, "What now, Spirit? They don't want to listen to us, they beat us." So many people were beat up, and Vern was concussed, but we sat in that circle and looked at our manifesto and decided that since the politicians would not listen to us, we would decide what we were going to do for ourselves. I put my hand up and I said, "I am going to put my mark on education. I am going to start my own school in Toronto." That was October 1, 1974.'

Though so many moments in Pauline's life reveal it, perhaps that October day marks the moment when the spirit of her great-grandfather from generations past became manifest. After her son Clayton's refusal to return to school, she eventually established one in her own living room with her children and others, and with supporters who were conscious of what was happening in the education system: nobody was learning anything about Indigenous cultures.

Pauline's school was modelled after the Red School House in St. Paul, Minnesota, part of a project of the American Indian Movement. The founder of that school was her friend and AIM affiliate Eddie Benton-Banai. As Sharon Berg recalls from her time living in the same housing co-op as Pauline in the early 1980s, Eddie had a big sticker across the back of his van that read, 'You are in Indian country.' Sharon writes, 'I couldn't help but think this sticker was notice of Aboriginal resistance to the colonial land grab ... It was also a resistance of the Residential Schools system. That note of resistance was the first seed for the establishment of Pauline's school ... That connection to the AIM Survival Schools is the second seed.'[11]

Self-determination through Native education was a foundational and, at the time, radical idea of the Wandering Spirit Survival School. A 'Native Way Education' for children was at the core of Pauline's vision, grounded in a Four Seasons curriculum,[12] including language, ceremony, community immersion, and love. Obstacles to creating the school were many and included voices from the Indigenous community. At first, Pauline paid for everything from her savings, but soon she found a critical circle of supporters who carried her vision forward.

'The spirit of our ancestors and medicines helped us,' she says. 'I was well guarded. I knew lawyers and knew how I wished the school to be: *To share the spirit of what our ancestors had been, passed on to our future generations.*

'We had people from all the four sacred colours involved. I always had people surrounding me and helping me out, women in particular. Vern helped in the beginning. Lenore Keeshig-Tobias, Keith Lickers, and others helped us to create the curriculum. Everyone listened to my stories and saw how my children were being treated in the mainstream school. There weren't rich Anishinaabe to join us. We were an embarrassment at the time. People were scared of the child welfare system taking their children away if they got involved.

'We called on the parents to be the advisors to us, so we developed a working parents' council, and they were just so lovely. I selected seven people, including Jim Dumont, to be on the council, and we became well-known by the city as politicians. We had meetings at my house at that time with Keith Lickers [an elementary school teacher from Six Nations] and Al Bigwin [an elementary school principal who was First Nations], who both just listened and understood. I then registered with the province,[13] under my name, to continue the school as a private school.

'Roger Obonsawin [executive director] approached me at the Native Canadian Centre, and he said, "The board is offering you a classroom here." We had this big classroom that was spacious and bright. Roger and the Centre helped us with funding and with their luncheon program. So we moved to Spadina and Bloor.'

Pauline believes that people eventually accepted her vision for a legitimate, Native Way school because they were accepting themselves and understanding why they were put on Turtle Island. Due to the success of the model established by Pauline and her large circle of supporters, the Toronto Board of Education in 1977 voted to accept it as an alternative school. She recalls the vote was not an easy win, and it required Pauline to call on her great-grandfather's spirit.

'After a few months at the Native Centre, the Toronto Board approached me to join as an alternative school,' she recounts. 'I remember it was a very emotional day for me. Dale Shuttleworth at the Board of Education stood by me, introduced me to everyone. I'll never forget this one trustee who banged his shoe on the table, just like Khrushchev when he took his shoe off and banged it on the table at the UN. There was a lot of yelling: "Who do these Indians think they are?"

'I had to leave the room when the trustees had to vote. I went out to another building and offered my tobacco, and I spoke to my grandpa: "Grampa, if you allow us to have our school as part of the TBE, we will still maintain our own way. I will not receive a red penny for seven years. Please help us." That was a promise I made to the school. I also remember Irene Atkinson, who was a hell-raiser on the TBE, and a lot of my friends were there, and we won. We named the school Wandering Spirit, and it was the first legitimate Native-controlled school across Canada.'

Pauline Shirt (Nimkiiquay) in front of the Ontario Legistlature.

Eight years after the school was accepted by the board, in 1985, a policy was passed by the TBE entitled 'Wandering Spirit: Self-Determination through Native Education.' This policy aided in the proliferation of a Native Way Education through other public schools, including Eastview Junior Public School, Riverdale Collegiate Institute, the Native Learning Centre, and the Native Learning Centre East.

As Pauline reminds me, near the end of our conversation, 'Things change. Nothing is ever the same.' This isn't a lament, but an acknowledgement of the shifting nature of the school. She eventually had to withdraw from involvement in the school due to illness. In 1989, the name of the school was changed to the more generic First Nations School, and the school grew to be larger in scope, but in some ways it lost its ties to its original spirit. Tanya Senk (Métis/Cree/Salteaux), who is currently the principal, or Kiskitomowin eskwe (Knowledge woman), and the Centrally Assigned Board Lead in Indigenous Education within the Urban Indigenous Education Centre of the TDSB, called to let me know that in February 2019 the school had a reclaiming-of-the-name ceremony. Tanya shared that the renamed Kapapamahchakwew – Wandering Spirit School – has grown from a K-8 to a K-12 school, and is now located at 16 Phin Avenue, in the old Eastern Commerce Collegiate. The academic year 2021–22 marks the first time Grade 12 will be offered.

'Education in this school is about knowing who you are as an Indigenous person, and also thinking about Indigenous futurity, and what it means to be an Indigenous person in the twenty-first century,' says Tanya. She says the aim of education is about 'finding your gifts and then sharing your gifts,' and she centres an approach to teaching developed by Mi'kmaq Elder Albert Marshall called Two-Eyed Seeing.

In essence, this approach is about braiding together the best of Indigenous knowledge with knowledge from other cultures. As Albert Marshall shared in a talk about this concept at Humber College,[14] 'There is no hierarchy of knowledge. We all hold a piece of the puzzle.' As it was always part of Pauline's intention to include the four sacred colours, today's Wandering Spirit School invites learners from any cultural background who seek an Indigenous-focused education.

Pauline's vision circles back to her ancestor Kapapamahchakwew and is carried on through her children, through the people she has taught, and through Wandering Spirit School. Her vision reminds us that, even though this city defines our lives in countless ways, there is still a way of finding the gifts that our ancestors fought for, and an importance in carrying them forward: 'You have to know your creation story. That is where we get our curriculum from, and our songs, and our stories. That's where the spirit comes from. The children who attended never knew their spiritual names or clan systems, and we taught them that. That whole spirituality was embedded in them, and we helped them bring it out. We were just spiritual helpers, and that's all I'll ever be.'

ACKNOWLEDGEMENTS

My endless respect and love go to Pauline and her family, and 'che meegwetch' to Tanya Senk, and author Sharon Berg for their generosity of spirit and careful attention to detail. Sharon Berg's book The Name Unspoken: Wandering Spirit Survival School *(2019) was essential to my research.*

VERNA JOHNSTON, NOKOMIS

MNAWAATE GORDON-CORBIERE

*Some [Elders] were Indigenous leaders; maybe that's what I am. I don't
know what I am. But all my life, all my life from the time I got married I
believed that we had an obligation to our babies, to our children. That that
was our obligation, to teach them something about their heritage.*
— Verna Patronella Johnston,
interviewed by Jocelyn Keeshig (1982)

Verna Patronella Johnston was born on the Neyaashiinigmiing Reserve
along Georgian Bay in 1909 to Charlotte and Peter Naugwen. Her
mother was a white woman and her father an Ojibwe man. They raised
Verna and her fourteen siblings on the reservation. As a child, Verna
spent a lot of time with her paternal Grandmother Jones and Great-
Grandmother Lavallee. From her grandmothers, she inherited a lot of
traditional knowledge that she would carry throughout the years, eventually becoming a grandmother herself.

Growing up, she aspired to become a mother and housewife and, at
sixteen, married Henry Johnston. At the time, there were limited options
for women on the reserve beyond becoming a wife and mother. If women
pursued a career, they would often have to enfranchise, giving up their
Indian status and their homes on the reserve. This is what Verna's sister
Vi did in order to become a teacher off reserve, although she visited
Neyaashiinigmiing when she could. Verna was uncertain about her own
career aspirations aside from being a mother, as Henry was the bread-
winner for the family.

Not long after they had children, Henry moved to Toronto to find
work. Because she missed him, Verna came down to Toronto shortly
after. They soon realized she, too, would need to work so they could
afford living in the city. Verna got a job at a bake shop and was a good

employee. That was one of the first times she felt she truly had agency over her own life and was capable of more than she had realized.

The couple returned to the reserve, and Henry took odd jobs around the province. The two argued often, and Verna wished to stop Henry's drinking. When they were in Niagara Falls for one of Henry's jobs, Verna left him to go work in Toronto. She was scorned by her family for leaving Henry and giving up on her marriage.

Verna worked service and factory jobs, and didn't meet many other Indigenous people. She felt isolated in the city and missed her community on the reserve. When she fell ill in Toronto, her brother Wilmer brought her back to the reserve. But there were few jobs for women there, so Verna decided to make her own job. She became a foster mother, so foster children from Neyaashiinigmiing could stay on the reserve close to their families.

Verna did not return to live in Toronto until 1962, and by that time she was a grandmother. Her granddaughters Lana and Marlene wanted to attend post-secondary school in the city in order to get better jobs. Remembering her past feelings of isolation and disconnection from her community, Verna resolved to go with them to prevent them from experiencing the same thing. The three lived together in a house at Hogarth and Broadview in the east end. Verna cooked and kept their home tidy. Their home was like a sanctuary away from the new and unfamiliar ways of city life.

A cousin of Lana and Marlene's was also living in Toronto and enjoyed the homey atmosphere Verna had created. One weekend, while Verna was away teaching crafts at the Moraviantown Reserve (southwest of London, Ontario), the cousin moved in! It wasn't long until the house became a hangout for Indigenous youth in the city. They felt comfortable around each other, and had a common understanding of what they were all going through. The food, community, and warmth were a welcome escape for new-to-the-city 'Urban Indians.'

Verna began taking in more boarders who were unhappy in their other rented digs, were just visiting the city, or simply needed a place to stay. She headed the only Indigenous-run boarding house at the time.

Word spread of the important work Verna was doing. North Toronto resident Roy Ramsey learned of her boarding house and arranged for Verna to use his house on Blythwood Road, which was currently empty. It was much larger than the house on Hogarth Avenue, allowing Verna to take in more people. Indian Affairs learned of what she was doing and began referring people to her boarding house. They never provided compensation, though. When federal officials did offer to take over the house and pay Verna to run it, she refused, wary of the regulations she would have to obey.

To create a home for her boarders, Verna cooked reservation favourites like corn soup, bison burgers, and bannock. Aside from a few house-keeping rules, her most important rule was no alcohol in the house. Verna would talk with her boarders, counsel them, and connect them to services if needed. Many affectionately called her Grandma – or Nokomis in Anishinaabemowin – because she treated them like her own grand-children and was their connection to an Elder while in the city. Though some of her boarders made mistakes, she was able to understand why they were struggling and she could be empathetic.

Verna put these skills to use in many Indigenous organizations across the city. While running the boarding house, she managed to find time to work or volunteer in the Indigenous community. She continued offering crafting classes that would allow women to make their own income and gave talks around the province on Ojibwe history and culture. She volunteered at Wigwamen Housing, Anduhyaun Women's Shelter, the YWCA, and the Royal Ontario Museum. Later, she worked at Anduhyaun Inc. If this wasn't enough, it was also during this time that Verna began raising her great-granddaughter Randa, fortunately receiving help with this from her boarders.

When Mr. Ramsey died, Verna had to give up the Blythwood home. But she continued to run her boarding house, moving to McGill Street, at the site of an old Ryerson Polytechnic residence. It was closer to more of Toronto's campuses and could take in many people. Verna had room for up to ten boarders at a time, charging them twenty dollars a week, and was willing to forgive late payments. She made extra money teaching crafts and giving talks, and used some of her savings for her boarders' birthdays, giving them a nice dinner and a small gift. Though not all were her grandchildren, she treated them all as if they were.

As she became a Nokomis and grew more into her Elder role, Verna decided she would like to write a book containing all the stories her own grandmother had shared with her. She had many fond memories of her Grandma Jones telling her and her siblings Ojibwe stories. Each story had a moral to it, and Verna felt they ought to be recorded and shared.

She believed it was important that Indigenous people know their own culture and that non-Indigenous people learn about Indigenous culture, too. The book, *Tales of Nokomis*, was published in 1970. Verna hoped Indigenous children would have a higher self-worth after learning their own traditions and culture.

In 1973, she became sick and her boarding house had to close down. When Verna recovered, she decided to retire and return to Neyaashiinigmiing. There, when she was in better health, she started a new foster home. But, due to an unfortunate accident, the house burned down and Verna was unable to run her foster home. She took it easy in Neyaashiinigmiing for a while, but eventually returned to the city. Always wanting to do something to help her community, Verna took a job at the Anduhyaun shelter for Indigenous women. As she was so skilled at caring for and helping others, it was a perfect fit.

Verna Johnston passed away in 1996. Through her lifetime, she had helped many Indigenous youth live safely in the city and complete their post-secondary educations and/or find jobs. She helped to create the Indigenous community that we know today in Toronto. Verna made a difference with her volunteer work, doing her part to preserve Ojibwe culture. She was the only Indigenous woman to run a boarding house for Indigenous youth in Toronto and was certainly deserving of the name Nokomis.

MILLIE REDMOND: THE FLAME

MILES MORRISSEAU

The young man could not believe his eyes. It was Grandma Millie in ill-fitting second-hand clothes, sitting on a piece of cardboard and begging for change on the streets of Winnipeg, Manitoba. How did this happen and, more importantly, how was she going to make it? Winnipeg's Main Street is a tough place for the homeless, especially when you are new in town and don't know who's who, what's what, and where to go. She looked like a flightless little brown bird, holding up her cup to the wage slaves scurrying about on their noontime feeding breaks. How could she have fallen so far? It was only a few months ago that she had been serving soup to him and dozens of other homeless Indigenous peoples back east. She had offered warm and hearty respite from the streets of Toronto during the bitter cold winter. Now she had hit the skids of Winnipeg. What went wrong?

Millie Redmond was born on October 12, 1917, on the Walpole Island First Nation. The island is located at the top of Lake St. Clair, on the southern tip of Canada, where the St. Clair River carries water from Lake Huron to Lake Erie. It is this unceded territory that members of the ancient Three Fires Confederacy – Ojibwe, Potawatomi, and Odawa – call home. In the Anishinaabe language, they call their land Bkejwanong, meaning 'where the waters divide.' Millie's family was Potawatomi and traced the family lineage back to Ohio and the Potawatomi Trail of Tears.

Although she was taken away from home at a very young age, Millie held idyllic memories of life in the community. 'One of my earliest recollections was maple sugar time, when we would go and collect the sap from the pails. I can still smell the aroma of the burning logs boiling the large black kettles of maple syrup,' she said in an interview.

Millie vividly recalled her grandmother as a powerful person. 'It was our grandmother who always seemed to dominate the scene. A bag of Indian medicine hung near the doorway ready to be picked up at a moment's notice and I can still see her going down the road with her long cotton skirt.'

Unlike their peers, Millie and her six siblings did not go to an Indian residential school. After her parents died, she and her siblings were sent away to an orphanage run by the Independent Order of Foresters in Toronto. She was four years old. Her grandmother insisted that the children not go to residential school. 'She had to send her, one or two of her children, to a school in Muncey, and the youngest daughter died and she was never informed of that, until after the funeral,' Millie recounted.

Millie grew up in the orphanage and as a young woman began clerical work in its administration. Soon she was on her own and performing similar administrative duties at the Peek Freans cookie factory. She enjoyed her work, and it would not be long before she would have a family of her own. Yet she wanted something more: she wanted to build community. Millie would use her clerical skills and community service ethic learned in the Order to create the community she had lost.

Like her grandmother had done so many years ago, Millie filled her medicine bag with all the good things she had collected and went out to help her people. She recalls the early potlucks she hosted that formed the North American Indian Club of Toronto. 'Native people getting together to have a good time, to do social work with each other, to know each other,' she said. 'And I wanted to know more Native people. It's a sense of belonging.'

The first potluck was held on her birthday, October 12, 1957. During these early gatherings fires were lit that still burn across Indigenous Toronto today. For some of the city's most important organizations, it was Mildred 'Millie' Redmond who carried and cared for that flame. For those who found themselves on the lowest rung of Canadian society, she was the Council Fire.

In 1962, five years after the Indian Club of Toronto was formed, the Indian (Native) Canadian Centre of Toronto was founded, and Millie served on its board of directors. As a volunteer, she organized the Ladies Auxiliary. One of the first programs at the Centre funded an Indigenous court worker. For the next eight years, Millie worked with Indigenous men and women who found themselves alone and entangled in a justice system created to incarcerate them.

She worked mostly with young women and was shocked and soon disheartened by how many young Indigenous women she saw over and over again. But encouraging words from a co-worker kept her going. 'Today may be the day they change,' she said. 'One word from you just may cause them to change. You know, from their way of life. And not long after, about a year, I hardly saw any of those women there.'

For nearly a decade, she worked in the courts and continued to volunteer and support the growing Indigenous community, with the Ladies Auxiliary hosting events like Christmas feasts and Halloween parties. Not having a home must have had a significant impact on how Millie prioritized the work she would do. In 1972, she helped form Wigawamen, a co-op housing service for Indigenous peoples. It remains the largest and longest-established urban Indigenous housing co-op in Canada.

Millie wanted to do something to support young Indigenous women before they ended up in the system, on the streets, in jail, or missing and murdered. In 1973, Millie, along with three other Indigenous women who became known as 'the Original Grandmothers,' formed Anduhyaun, a safe place for Indigenous women in crisis. It is Canada's oldest emergency shelter for Indigenous women. In the decades before the crisis of Missing and Murdered Indigenous Women and Girls was acknowledged, Millie was on the front line. There is little doubt that the safe place the Grandmothers created saved lives.

In 1976, she started Council Fire to give support to the most disadvantaged in society, and though no one was turned away because of race or gender, the majority were Indigenous men. Over decades of service, she became auntie, mother, and grandmother to thousands with nowhere to go. It was her great passion.

She didn't just support the homeless. Actor/producer/musician Gary Farmer recalls the warm welcome he received from Grandma Millie as a young man in the city – 'Mother Teresa to Toronto's Native community in the 1970s,' he calls her. Gary drove a cab while taking night school at Ryerson Polytechnic for film and photography. 'I'd always be rushing around downtown during the week and would spot Millie and pick her up and get her where she needed to be. Toronto was such a smaller town back then.'

In 1981, she was chosen as a Woman of Distinction by the YMCA of Toronto for Community and Public Service. 'Council Fire offers Native people in Toronto a haven and more,' the YMCA stated. 'For a young man from the reserve, it can be transit fare he needs to find work. For a woman in hospital, it's a visit arranged from a friend. It's food, bedding, help to find a room. It can be part of an ongoing series of lectures on nutrition or Native crafts. Most importantly, Council Fire is kinship.'

Two years later, she received the Order of Canada for Public Service. 'Millie Redmond began working nearly thirty years ago with the organized Indian movement in Toronto, helping found and serving in the Indian, now the Native Canadian, Centre,' the award noted. 'She has since founded a housing corporation for Native people, a residence for girls and an ecumenical Christian welfare service which is in the front line of the fight against alcoholism and destitution.'

I moved to Toronto in 1989 to begin working in radio at CBC's national documentary program, *Sunday Morning*. It was a crucible. A recent shift in power brought me into a newsroom that was seething with bruised egos and back-stabbing venom. I had been called in by James Cullingham, whose recent appointment as executive producer had not won the hearts and minds of the assembled.

I was not his first choice. He had called my partner, Shelly Bressette, who was laying the groundwork for *Nativebeat* newspaper. She passed but told James I had worked at CBC Winnipeg and soon the offer was mine. Could I be in Toronto in two weeks?

It was a huge opportunity, but the job may as well have been on the moon. We had no money. There was no way I could travel to the city, find a place to live, and pay first and last months' rent. I didn't know anybody and had only been to Toronto a few times in my life, mostly as a stopover between Greyhound buses. This position would not happen unless I could find someone who would let a strange Indigenous man stay in their home for free.

It turned out that Shelly's sister-in-law, Carol Peters, had an aunt in the city who might be able to help out; she would not be put out that I wouldn't be able to pay her until I got paid. That's how I came to live with Millie Redmond.

Millie's house was in a perpetual mess, with full garbage and grocery bags taking up every available space, including the living room furniture. The bags were stuffed with donations of clothes and other soft household items like towels and bedding. It was a kind of hoarding, but she wasn't holding on to anything; it all kept moving from her tiny hands into more vulnerable ones.

My time at the CBC was challenging in the regular ways that working at the national network can be. But it was also challenging in ways specific to being an Indigenous journalist working at the CBC. First was the attitude or opinion that I didn't deserve to be there, and that I was merely a token. This attitude was most acutely felt during my time at *Sunday Morning*, thrust into a poisonous atmosphere where there was a new poison to share.

The other burden was the belief that Indigenous journalists could not be trusted to cover Indigenous stories, an outlook I felt most bitterly during the time of the Oka crisis, when I would not be allowed to cover the story for almost two weeks. My job at the time was National Native Affairs Broadcaster.

There were many nights when Millie would be in her home with a cup of tea and an offer to cook me food, no matter how late in the evening. She had that warmth that let you talk to her about anything. I would talk to her about my problems at work and she would listen, and she would encourage.

When my wife became pregnant with our sixth child, the burden of maintaining our home and the newly launched newspaper had become too much. I gave my notice at the corporation. I had covered history for the CBC and now it was time to tell it from our perspective.

When I had my office going-away party, I received a twenty-pound frozen turkey as a present. I am not sure why. I had made a joke about missing the office Christmas party, but I think the gift had more to do with the fact that I was moving back to the reserve and my wife was expecting our sixth child. I didn't know what to do with the bird. I was travelling on the Greyhound, and I was not going to lug a twenty-pound frozen turkey onto the bus.

How else could it turn out?

Millie was happy to receive the turkey, and there were some folks in need who got an early Christmas dinner that year.

How did Millie end up on the skids of Winnipeg?

It was a story she loved to tell, the story of when she joined a group of professionals and academics representing various ecumenical groups in the Christian Urban Training Course in Winnipeg and had a chance to learn what it was really like to live on the streets.

Millie found a spot on Main Street, put up a little sign asking for money, and held up a plastic cup. She had spent two nights on the streets of Winnipeg when 'one of my skids found me.' Millie would chuckle when she described how concerned the young man was for her situation. He could not believe that this woman, who helped so many street people in Toronto, had now fallen on such hard times. She would whisper conspiratorially when she explained that she was undercover, and chuckled warmly when relating that, at first, the young man did not believe a word she said.

Millie shared this story when receiving the YMCA's order of distinction. 'Part of our training,' she recalled, 'was to experience what it would be like to be in a city with no money. I decided this was a chance to experience what many Native women and girls face on the streets. Since I was in Winnipeg and not in Toronto, I did not expect to be recognized. I slept on the street in an alleyway for two nights. One night after dark, four young Indians went by. One stopped, hesitated, and then said: "Mrs. Redmond, what are you doing here?"'

It is easy to acknowledge the young man's perspective. Millie Redmond could surprise, even astonish.

One day, while still in Toronto, I returned from work and there was a dishevelled white boy sitting at the kitchen table. He was in his early twenties, with the dirty blond, badly cut hair and grungy look popular in those days.

I was never surprised to find anyone at Millie's house at any time. If someone needed help, Millie would open her heart and her home. What was surprising was how consistently she would maintain that level of care. This particular instance was one where I would be stunned by how deeply she not only cared, but trusted in the basic goodness of people.

She introduced the young man and went into some details about his court case. While she offered soup to us both, she casually dropped a bomb. He needed someone to bail him out and act as surety. When no one would do it, she signed him out and put the house up as collateral. The Kurt Cobain wannabe did not lift up his head from the soup. He just kept on eating like this kind of thing happened to him all the time. I could not believe what I heard. I am sure I asked her to explain the word *surety*. It all meant what it meant. She had signed him out of jail and put her house up as bail. If he didn't show up for court, she could lose her home.

This young man needed help, and no one was going to help. No one but Millie.

Millie completed her circle, returning home to Walpole Island First Nation, where she would build a home along the St. Clair River. She lived there for nearly ten years, until her death.

Niece Carol Peters recalls her auntie, then into retirement, continuing street-level action: 'She had a friend who donated some land in the city and Auntie would gather people off the street and take them to work in a garden.'

It was a small expression of her one unattained goal. Mille had learned through her work in the jails and her work on the streets that there was something that could not be achieved in the city. Indigenous peoples needed to connect to the earth. They needed to get back into the bush. They needed to get down on their hands and knees and dig in the dirt and plant seeds, pull weeds, collect medicine, and smell the sweet aroma of maple syrup in the air.

'What I have in my mind is that farm,' she once said. 'There is a need for Native people to leave here and go into the wide-open spaces and see nature at its best. And that's my ambition, anyway.'

DR. JANET SMYLIE AND
'OUR HEALTH COUNTS TORONTO'

ERICA COMMANDA

When approaching solutions to Indigenous health, Dr. Janet Smylie, a Métis physician and research scientist, draws on a key concept: *Nothing about us, without us.* Smylie's mother was one of Canada's very few Indigenous nurses and her father was a scientist. Both parents inspired her to pursue a career in health research.

In her early years as a family physician, Dr. Smylie witnessed conspicuous inequities in health services and outcomes for Indigenous people. She became determined to help close this gap and founded the Well Living House, an Indigenous action research centre at St. Michael's Hospital that is co-governed by a board of Indigenous grandparents.

Through Well Living House research projects, Dr. Smylie was able to assist with the development of the Toronto Birth Centre, a non-profit agency that uses traditional Indigenous knowledge to create culturally safe birthing spaces for families of all nations, advance Indigenous midwifery as a best practice in addressing Indigenous/non-Indigenous birth outcome disparities, and support community-based gathering and application of traditional parenting and birthing knowledge.

Starting in 2008, the Well Living House team began to partner with urban Indigenous health service providers to gather, analyze, and apply population-based health determinants, status, and service use information for First Nations, Inuit, and Métis people living in cities. From 2014 to 2018, Dr. Smylie led the 'Our Health Counts Toronto' (OHCT) survey, the largest urban Indigenous population study ever conducted by Indigenous people for Indigenous people. The study was a collaboration with the Well Living House and Seventh Generation Midwives Toronto. By taking an inclusive, community-driven approach, the research painted a more reflective picture of the urban Indigenous population in Toronto than recorded by Statistics Canada.

According to OHCT, between 34,000 and 69,000 Indigenous people live in Toronto today. These population statistics conflict with Statistics Canada's 2011 National Household Survey, which grossly underestimated Toronto's Indigenous population at 15,650. The discrepancy reflected the disparity between the socio-economically privileged minority sub-population of the total Indigenous community and Indigenous people not accounted for in the NHS.

The OHCT points out that funding allocated on the basis of these early Statistics Canada numbers has been far from adequate to address the health needs of Toronto's Indigenous residents, many of whom were not counted because they move frequently or are homeless.[1]

Statistics Canada's data has also significantly understated the prevalence of poverty among urban Indigenous populations in Ontario, according to OHCT. This gross underestimation represents a gap in the knowledge and understanding of the history of Indigenous communities and their health needs in Toronto.

Among the OHCT's findings:

- Only 14 per cent of Indigenous adults in Toronto completed the 2011 Canadian Census. A representative sample would have required that 70 per cent of households complete the census.

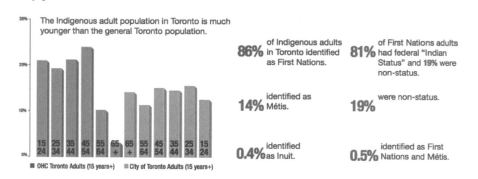

Identity Age

The Indigenous adult population in Toronto is much younger than the general Toronto population.

■ OHC Toronto Adults (15 years+) ▒ City of Toronto Adults (15 years+)

86% of Indigenous adults in Toronto identified as First Nations.

14% identified as Métis.

0.4% identified as Inuit.

81% of First Nations adults had federal "Indian Status" and **19%** were non-status.

19% were non-status.

0.5% identified as First Nations and Métis.

As the report points out, 'the impacts of colonization and colonial policies, such as the Indian Act, residential schools, the Sixties Scoop, and continued exclusion of Indigenous people from the Canadian economy, are reflected in the higher rates of unemployment and lower socio-economic status.'

Our Health Counts Toronto included the following population findings. (The full report can be found at welllivinghouse.com.)

- Indigenous households had elevated rates of extended families living together that included grandparents, aunts, uncles, and cousins.
- Eighty-seven per cent of Indigenous Torontonians live at or below the before-tax low-income cut-off level.
- Over half of the Indigenous population in Toronto believed that financial hardship affected their health and well-being by limiting their ability to partake in preventative health measures.
- Experiences of discrimination by health care professionals were reported by 28 per cent of Indigenous adults, and 71 per cent of these adults did not want to return or continue health services after their experience.

Education

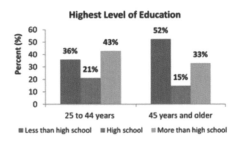

OHC Toronto found that the education levels were increased among the younger (25-44 years) generation compared to the older generation (45 years +).

Indigenous adults aged 25-64 years in Toronto had a lower rate of high school completion (57%) compared to the general Ontario population (90%).5

Among Indigenous adults who did complete high school there was a high rate of completion of at least some college or university (65%).

The study made several important recommendations to address barriers in accessing health services for Indigenous people. One was a call to implement Truth and Reconciliation Calls to Action:

- #7: The federal government must prepare and publish annual reports comparing educational and income attainments of

Indigenous people to non-Indigenous people, as well as comparing funding for the education of Indigenous children off and on the reserve.

- #23: The federal government must provide cultural safety training for all health care professionals.

Our Health Counts Toronto also recommended that all three levels of governments must partner with urban Indigenous organizations to develop and fund sustainable income support and specific Indigenous education programming for Indigenous parents, families, and communities.

JOE HESTER:
ANISHNAWBE HEALTH TORONTO

BRIAN WRIGHT-MCLEOD

Toronto is Canada's largest and most diverse city, with 34,000 to 69,000 Indigenous residents, comprising one third of Ontario's total Indigenous population. This community is alive with cultural, educational, business, and other capacities, yet the health sector is not as vibrant.

Studies conducted by Anishnawbe Health Toronto found that almost 90 per cent of the city's Indigenous residents live near or below the poverty level. Since 1987, AHT has been the sole provider of Western medical and traditional health services to an ever-increasing Indigenous population. Nearly thirty thousand client visits were recorded in 2018–19. About a fifth of all visits are clients under the age of twenty-one.

Three of AHT's health units operate out of different locations providing a variety of services: 225 Queen Street East, 179 Gerrard Street East with sweat lodge ceremonial grounds, and 4 Charles Street East. Waash-Keshuu-Yaan Unit delivers primary care, education, and management; Babishkan Unit oversees mental health, addiction, and homelessness. The Training Unit operates in partnership with Miziwe Biik Aboriginal Employment & Training and George Brown College.

AHT provides sixty programs and services, from prenatal to palliative care, with three full-time traditional healers on staff and one part-time healer along with Western health nurse practitioners and doctors.

Born and raised in the Cree community of Waskaganish on the southeast shore of James Bay in northern Quebec, Joe Hester first moved to Toronto in 1967. Ten years later he began working at Anishnawbe Health, where he is the current Executive Director.

'After attending university, I was asked to do policy work for Anishnawbe Health that led to a full-time position as Director of Programs and Services,' he explains.

During his tenure, Joe has seen crucial changes in health services. 'There were no services delivered by the community,' he says. 'The diabetes study showed community leaders on reserves that community-based health centres were a priority. Providing primary health care with nurses and doctors was an initial step. Gradually, other issues such as homelessness were addressed.'

Additional services, most notably health care from a traditional approach, include the use of traditional healers. AHT has also established partnerships with colleges for chiropractic and naturopathic practitioners, mental health, addiction, dental care, transgender and LGBTQ2 programs, child care, and palliative care.

'With a growing population,' Joes tells me, 'there are demands for more community needs, like long-term-care facilities and end-of-life care that embraces both Western and traditional Indigenous ways. We have to look at resource allocations and better planning of service delivery.'

AHT offers workshops in financial literacy and smart food purchasing as part of an educational effort to further assist its clientele. 'Our clients in the diabetes program, or people with special training (physicians, nursing, tradition healers, and nutritionists), manage a healthier lifestyle in terms of food sources and costs,' Joe explains. 'Many people in our community take advantage of that. And working toward education and employment to create a good home and family is important.

'There's always disparity,' he adds, 'but we try to make sure the programs are there and services can be accessed.'

Racism within the medical community toward Indigenous people has been an ongoing problem, and AHT strives to address the issue. 'It's important for our people to know they can go to a place where they see themselves reflected in that environment, which helps them be confident in accessing health care,' Joe says.

People who come to Toronto from First Nations across the country represent a changing population with diverse needs and traditions. Economics also has a large influence on low-income families and individuals, who end up in poor areas of the city.

The diversity of nations and their traditional approaches to health and healing can be facilitated in practical ways. 'Our traditional healers administer to anyone, regardless of First Nation affiliation,' Joe says. 'We don't advocate anything but offer introductions to those ways.'

Meanwhile, AHT is planning to implement a college curriculum focusing on traditional healing, and encourages students to enter into a relationship with a traditional healer.

What is a traditional healer?

'We don't have all the answers,' Joe says. 'Some people carry gifts that mark them as traditional healers and others can develop those talents. The cultural approaches to traditional healing are different in each community. It's important to preserve traditional knowledge – it must be concrete like an educational program. It's past the time to take on that work to ensure that those resources will always be there.'

By 2018, AHT realized it had reached a critical milestone in meeting the health care and spiritual needs of Toronto's urban Indigenous community. Combined with the historical traumas visited upon Indigenous people, their health needs are unique. In response, AHT launched a bold initiative to address those concerns.

'All of this leads to the establishment of the new health centre,' Joe explains. 'We looked at three different locations because we had to find facilities that can handle the growth of the health centre with integrated health services of both Western and traditional models. Also, the community members who have to access more than one service at different locations become an economic burden in terms of transit cost, child care, or what have you.'

The Anishnawbe Health Foundation initiated a $10 million fundraising campaign to build a central health centre for AHT and purchased a one-hectare parcel of land from the Province of Ontario, located in the West Don Lands, adjacent to the Distillery District. While a central site is integral to AHT's efforts, satellite outlets will continue to operate in various locations across the Greater Toronto Area.

'All services, from primary to long-term, and comprehensive programs will be located in one facility instead of clinics spread across the GTA,' Joe says.

The groundbreaking for the central health centre was planned for the summer of 2020, and the new facility was expected to have been completed by 2022. But the COVID-19 lockdown halted construction.

Regardless of the momentum, changes will arrive.

RENEGADE RADIO: A VOICE OF DISSENT IN A WORLD OF COMPROMISE

BRIAN WRIGHT-MCLEOD

In the 1970s and 1980s, the Toronto airwaves had a sparse Indigenous presence predominantly on CBC Radio, with hosts Ivy Chasky and Bernelda Wheeler. As meagre as the choices were for Indigenous programming on the radio dial, there was an obvious gap that needed to be filled.

I entered Ryerson University's campus/community radio station CKLN 88.1 FM in 1983. Beginning with a bi-weekly, fifteen-minute Saturday-morning bulletin, my on-air presence morphed into various shows, from a one-hour weekly program to a monster two-hour broadcast that became *Renegade Radio*.

My first foray into the basement studios at 380 Victoria Street, on the north edge of Ryerson's campus, was an immersion into a journey through many cultures and experiences. The entrance to the downstairs area was blocked off by a black metal cage that was locked for exclusive host access. Everything was painted black, with metal filing cabinets covered in band stickers and other promo. The on-air and production studios were outfitted with dated equipment donated by CBC Radio and other stations. The analog equipment proved effective for eclectic, innovative, and groundbreaking broadcasts that were live 24/7.

I stumbled my way through the learning process, but managed to hang in and create a more established profile. At first, my delivery was a bit dry and somewhat inhibited. But that would all gradually change as a chain of public events dragged me from self-imposed obscurity into a blinding light of notoriety.

Part of the public dissemination of activist information, alongside the radio gig, involved my profile as a visual artist and poet. I had been invited to several events around the city for about five years at this point. In 1991, the initial First Night Toronto celebrated the incoming new year with a variety of street events. In promoting my spot among two hundred other artists, the *Toronto Star* interviewed me about one of the most memorable new years I had experienced. I related the tale of a hiking trip through Nevada's Death Valley and spending the night of December 31 under the cold stars, listening to the music of distant coyotes. '[T]he artist, broadcaster and poet … [will] be far from the desert, because on Tuesday night at 8 p.m., Wright-McLeod will read his poetry at the Metropolitan United Church, Queen and Bond Streets, in "First Night Toronto,"' Doris Giller wrote in the *Toronto Star* on December 28, 1991.

Other events included an evening in solidarity with Oka that featured the Raging Grannies, the Royal Canadian Air Farce's Luba Goy and Don Harron (as Charlie Farquharson), who emceed the night at the Euclid Theatre. After finishing my poems, I left the stage to thunderous applause. In the wings, Luba grabbed my arm and exclaimed: 'Do you hear that? Do you hear that?' Her expression changed and she asked soberly, 'But why so stiff? Where's all the jokes, man?' That did it for me. Humour. Yes, it's the best medicine. Her remarks became an inspiration for deeper creative development of what would become *Renegade Radio*.

There is a tale among the Huichol of Mexico, the peyote eaters. Apparently, they host a communal event where they share stories of sexual encounters and exploits, no matter how embarrassing. Utilizing this practice as a catalyst for changing the dynamics of *Renegade Radio*, I began to explore.

That experimentation resulted in outrageous exploits and bits, including an in-studio interview with none other than Dominatrix Phoenix. She was instructed to make baloney sandwiches with mustard on white bread.

'This is not the strangest request I've ever had,' she admitted, 'but it's certainly an interesting situation. And why am I doing this?'

'Well,' I began, 'it's symbolic of the history of Indigenous people who have been dominated, squished between white bread, and fed baloney for far too long,' I replied. The mustard was for flavour.

'Oh, I get it,' she chuckled. After slicing and stacking bread and baloney smeared with the yellow condiment, she queried with a devilish tone: 'What do you want me to do with them? Shall I step on them … or what?'

'After the show, we'll gather them up and deliver them to the homeless,' I said.

'Cool!' she replied.

There we were, a leggy blonde and a Renegade Indian, walking along Yonge Street, handing out baloney sandwiches to the less fortunate.

The breathtaking yet apparent symbolism of the interview with Phoenix had to be explained, as Peter Goddard pointed out in his review of *Renegade Radio*: '[B]right with ideas and feisty opinions and rarely heard Indian music; what it isn't about is compromise ... and [Brian] has some wicked ways of getting his point across,' he wrote in the *Toronto Star* on July 3, 1999.

The dominatrix bit was a seminal moment. It dragged me out of the world of the introverted, stolid amateur and thrust me into a vast unknown. The Rubicon had been crossed.

I decided to be direct but not overbearing while providing as much pertinent informa-

Brian Wright-McLeod doing live broadcasts on *Renegade Radio*, CKLN-FM.

tion as possible on issues such as nuclear weapons testing on U.S. reservations, sterilization of Indigenous women, prison and justice, myths, prophecies, and music industry gossip. Broadcaster/journalist Errol Nazareth was writing for the *Toronto Sun* and often plugged the show in his entertainment column.

Meanwhile, the University of Toronto's CIUT had an Indigenous show that aired from 6:00 to 8:00 p.m., preceding *Renegade Radio*, which aired from 8:00 to 10:00 p.m. every Monday night. The four hours represented the only Native radio on the local dial.

By this time, Gary Farmer, who hosted *Moccasin Telegraph* on CIUT, had departed after landing his breakout role in the film *Pow Wow Highway*. He went on to create his first magazine, *The Runner*, which became *Aboriginal Voices* and then led to the creation of the Aboriginal Voices Radio project.

Indigenous programming at CKLN continued to grow. Along with Doreen Silversmith from Six Nations, we created a half-hour Sunday-night news program, *Gah-townya Ongwe Hongwe* (All Native People Talking Together) that aired at 6:00 p.m. We alternated hosting duties each week until Doreen left the station a couple years later. I eventually transformed

Ad, *Renegade Radio,* CKLN-FM.

the time slot into an on-air training ground for aspiring radio journalists from the grassroots Indigenous community.

At CKLN, we had free rein over programming, approach, and direction. *Renegade Radio* experienced few complaints and enjoyed lots of love. Of course, there were equal bits of hate, but they were from those who never mattered.

Live listener call-ins developed a community in its own right. One night, a disgruntled male caller identifying himself as Avatar issued an on-air grievance regarding the content. After he hung up, a flurry of female listeners barraged the airwaves in support: 'You can tell Abattoir to fuck off!' The women came up with their own pet names for the caller.

The lad was a hit. His malfeasance became weekly fodder for satirical bits, wherein he was characterized as sitting in a dank, dimly lit basement dissecting the show with sneering delight. He became known as Ass Guitar. It was a lethal mix of Hunter S. Thompson meets Howard Stern meets Crazy Horse.

One sunny summer Queen Street West kind of day, Denise Donlon popped out of the MuchMusic studios. Identifying me from across the way, she shouted with a wave: 'Brian! Your ratings are up!'

After acknowledging her with a grand hello, I quickly eye-scanned my body for anything unusual, then asked myself: Ratings? What's that? Am I being spied on again?

There was an intentional yet sublime point to everything presented on the show. It was designed to reveal the absurdities of the controlling powers through editorials, rants, satire, sound effects, relevant music, and listener call-in comments. Live on-air music mixes of powwow and techno with sound effects, as well as other tantalizing clips comprised an experimental segment that wove in and out.

Program IDs also became an anticipated highlight. Mostly well-known musicians, actors, writers, and other celebrities were given a well-crafted script that would promote them promoting the show. The fifteen- to thirty-second clips were played as the host introduction or prior to a music set, an ad, or station break.

One example included a female vocal trio from Australia, the Stiff Gins: 'We're the Stiff Gins from Down Under. And now a man who's always stiff down under, Mr. Brian Wright-McLeod.' They added a growl: 'Rowwrrr.' However, their manager was not amused and summarily scolded the Gins for doing the bit. Their handler sounded like someone more suited to being a reform-school matron than a serious person working in the entertainment industry. It takes all kinds.

Renegade Radio continued to grow. Rarely traversed musical paths for Indigenous radio programming featured the stylings of Kay Starr, Jesse Ed Davis, Jim Pepper, and a raft of icons. On-air mixes of rock, techno, powwow, and sound effects brought the culture to life. Various musical guests flew in from Los Angeles, New Zealand, Australia, and Peru for interviews and live in-studio performances. A short list includes Buffy Sainte-Marie, Blue Rodeo, Bruce Cockburn, Robbie Robertson, Willie Dunn, Billy Ray Cyrus, the Last Poets, Rita Coolidge, and Chuck D, as well as activists John Trudell, Leonard Peltier, Angela Davis, and multitudes of others, especially local talent.

Toronto activist and ceremonial leader Jimmy Dick, with his drum group Eagleheart, came in a couple times to sing on-air. Jimmy provided a background to the songs and how they fit into the modern world. There were many local performers, both amateur and professional, representing all genres of music, sharing their licks with the listening audience. Just like the good old days of radio – only *Renegade*-style.

Live phone interviews with grassroots activists and artists from across North America added a special spice to the mix, especially when they were under fire on the front lines.

Combining biting satire with relevant hard core, politically driven music painted a solid picture of resistance. It affected the *Renegade Radio* crew to the point of excitement. A co-host trainee who employed the nom de guerre MC Kaddafi provided insight from his activist experiences. Another of my streetwise trainees, who preferred the moniker K-9, left the building with me following one of the more intense broadcasts. Once we emerged outside, he heaved, 'After that show, I thought the cops would be waiting for us.'

There was no questioning *Renegade Radio*'s motto: 'A Voice of Dissent in a World of Compromise.'

Call-in segments were sometimes explosive, unexpected, and organic. What else could they be? It was unfiltered and uncensored. And the odd television crew would burst into the studio to record a segment.

Duke Redbird was working as an arts reporter for CITY-TV and wanted to do another interview with me, this time at the CKLN studios. That night, I had a guest from northern California scheduled for a phone-in. It was my dear compatriot Agnes Patak, who hosted her own program, *Heart of the Earth* on KMUD, 'the Voice of the Redwoods.' She was always good for environmental updates. But on this occasion, I made the mistake of telling her about the TV crew that was in-studio to do a profile on the show.

To understand Agnes is to understand the power of a hurricane that smiles gently through a haze of the most excellent northern Cali home-grown, but with an energy unmatched by any natural force of this world.

Once the interview began, she quickly flew into high gear. Instantly, Agnes burst forth like a long-restrained volcano that suddenly found unbridled freedom. She flipped her 'on' switch to become a non-stop chatterbox. Without pause, Agnes careened with the speed of a Formula One race car for many minutes on end without pause. Any attempts to interject with a question became instant roadkill. I had lost control of the interview.

Agnes continued seamlessly with near-panicked delivery. All of my interruptions and yelling her name into the phone went unheard. In a futile effort to grab her attention, I swung into action and began issuing sound effects of gunshots, sirens, screams, and explosions. She never heard a thing. Uncontrollably, she continued at a frantic pace.

Fifteen breathless minutes later, Agnes finally stopped to catch a second wind. Immediately, I grabbed the reins and pulled it all together to finally bring the segment to a long-awaited closure. During the music break, the well-entertained camera crew wrapped up their gear and prepared to leave, when Duke commented, 'That was great!'

Renegade Radio wasn't confined to the studios. Through various organizations, I attended out-of-country excursions. CKLN sent me to an annual gathering of the World Association of Community Radio Broadcasters.

The umbrella organization represented community radio stations world-wide and had organized a 1992 Columbus quincentenary meeting in Oaxtepec, Mexico. Indigenous programmers from Australia, South America, and the United States attended. Oddly enough, I was the only Indigenous representative from Canada.

Perhaps the most death-defying adventure occurred in the Mexican province of Chiapas following the Zapatista rebellion that began on January 1, 1994. A few years later, the Native American Journalists Association, Servicio Internacional para la Paz/International Service for Peace (SIPAZ), and U.S.-based humanitarian agencies sponsored a group of Indigenous and non-Indigenous journalists and activists to a fact-finding mission to the province.

These meetings with the people were a surreal Magnificent Seven moment. We danced to their music, ate their food, and were accorded a grand tour of their villages, led by the children, who proudly showed off their new friends. We also encountered terrified people fleeing for their lives, desperately asking us for a way out.

We were twice held at gunpoint by the Mexican army brandishing fully loaded .50 calibre machine guns mounted on armoured personnel carriers, aimed at the people. Officers and their armed troops pushed their way into the anxious crowd and began checking everyone for ID. Brushing me aside, they searched my fellow visitors for passports, made a list, checked it twice, and left.

They returned the following day to repeat the same exercise. One of the young boys who had attached himself to us stood beside me. I moved in front of him to block any possible gunfire, if such an incident occurred. Knowing full well that the ordnance would easily rip through me, I figured it might give the kid at least a chance of survival. It seemed that the officials had one less in their official head count. Realizing who they were looking for, I stepped forward and presented my credentials. They had found the missing foreigner. Check and depart. Sigh of relief.

The third and final occasion of intensity transpired on our day of departure, June 27, 1998. Again, army vehicles approached and strategically blocked any exit. Our group of journalists, fact-finders, and humanitarian aid workers were herded into what looked like a garage. I was thinking, St. Valentine's Day Massacre. Inside the building, these people were rude and dangerous. We were invited to seat ourselves in chairs arranged in a wide circle. The pro-government locals, military personnel dressed in civvies, and our crew sat and tried to engage in some sort of communication. A tall, gangly, middle-aged American humanitarian aid worker tried his best to make things worse with terrible apologies and excuses.

I sat thinking of the possible days ahead, when I would be sun dancing in the scorching deserts of Big Mountain, Arizona. Heaven compared to this. Everyone was parched and perturbed. I had a full two-litre bottle of water. After taking a drink, I noticed a nasty local who by now was melting into humility by the oppressive heat. I thought of our ceremonies and offered a drink. He looked surprised but thirsty. After a quick swig, he attempted to hand it back. I motioned him to pass the bottle on to his fellow villager seated next to him. The humility of the moment prompted that individual to hand it back. Again, I motioned them to continue with the process around the entire circle. The container completed its journey and returned empty. Tensions and confusion had vanished along with the bottle's contents.

In the end, things were finally sorted out. It all ended like Joseph Heller's *Catch-22*: 'All we want you to do is like us. Go back home and write nice things about us.' Consider it done.

Did I get any prime recordings during the show's run? You bet I did.

Sometimes we broadcast ambient recordings collected from the streets of Toronto or Rome or Sturgis, South Dakota, during the massive motorcycle rally. They were all played for the sake of sharing an audio experience. A summer storm in Chiapas, where accordion music haunted the background as mothers called out to their children who splashed and laughed amid tremendous thunderclaps, immense waterfalls of rain, and sharp cracks of lightning. This, too, was *Renegade Radio*. 'We take you there.'

But ballsy hosting skills and taking risks comprised the compass for the journey. It was a ride for its time, and one that could never be repeated. The show was much-loved, sometimes reviled, innovative, and adventurous. A mythology almost evolved around it.

In addition to programming at Rye High, I eventually landed a spot on the newly established SIRIUS Iceberg 95 from 2003 to 2006, along with freelance stints for CBC Radio and BBC Radio in London, England.

Many of the interviews would be spun into articles for various Indigenous publications in Canada and the U.S. to help promote an expanding music scene. The collected material became the fertilizer and seeds for a much larger initiative.

I was no stranger to music writing. Fresh out of the journalism program at Canadore College in North Bay, I wrote several pieces for the *North Bay Nugget* from 1979 to 1981, including concert reviews and interviews with subjects like Trooper, singer Lisa Dal Bello, guitarist Domenic Troiano (the Guess Who, the James Gang), members of the Stampeders, Lighthouse, and small touring bands and local musicians. It was where I learned my chops.

In 1998, I was recruited to serve on the Aboriginal Music category jury for the Juno Awards, and later assisted producer Tom Bee in creating a Native American category for the Grammys (2000–10). Bee had founded the 1970s all-Indigenous group XIT and also wrote '(We've Got) Blue Skies' for the Jackson 5.

Over those years, I accumulated the largest private collection of recorded Indigenous music to be found anywhere. It included vinyl LPS, 45 RPMS, 78 RPM recordings, cassettes, reels, and associated paraphernalia representing traditional, mainstream, and small independent studios from reserves and reservations across North America. The library was not only a source of in-depth radio programming, but also the foundational source for the research for *The Encyclopedia of Native Music* (University of Arizona Press, 2005) and the seventy-track, three-CD companion set *The Soundtrack of a People* (EMI Music Canada, 2005).

The Soundtrack of a People featured original recordings from 1905 to 2005, profiling music of the Arctic Circumpolar Region to the U.S. southwest, in all genres, including traditional, archival, flute, folk roots, powwow, and numerous forms of contemporary, featuring icons like Mildred Bailey, Jesse Ed Davis, Willie Dunn, Buffy Sainte-Marie, and Link Wray. The double-barrelled project went on to become a pillar for the Smithsonian's National Museum of the America Indian exhibit *Up Where We Belong: Native Musicians in Popular Culture* (2010–15), which begat the feature documentary RUMBLE: *The Indians Who Rocked the World* (Rezolution Pictures, 2017). The film won several awards, including three 2018 Canadian Screen Awards, and garnered a 2020 Emmy nomination.

Renegade Radio was also a training ground for the Aboriginal Voices Radio project that recruited some young aspiring talent. But AVR was a playground for failure. The licence was scooped up in 2017 by the Aboriginal Peoples Television Network, which launched ELMNT FM 106.5 in October 2018. Designed to compete within the largest commercial radio market in Canada, it provided a whopping 20 per cent Indigenous music content. Not bad for an 'all-Native' radio station.

On April 15, 2011, CKLN closed its doors and *Renegade Radio* passed into legacy. For years after, dedicated listeners would stop me on the street and recall their favourite *Renegade* moment, as if they had just finished listening to the show. In a chance meeting with someone who was purchasing my artwork at an event, he made the connection to who I was in radio and exclaimed: 'You're the guy that hosted that show! Man, I was driving my car and listening to the program one night and almost drove off the road I was laughing so hard. That was a great show!' Some memories are made to last.

In 2021, *Renegade Radio* became the focus of a collaborative documentary project with the experimental ethnomusicology media lab at the University of Berkeley, California.

Currently, the path of Indigenous radio in Toronto has changed with markets and technology. CIUT maintains a one-hour show. CBC Radio's Indigenous content has expanded with a variety of programs and hosts, including Rosanna Deerchild, Falen Johnson, and Jarrett Martineau, with content recycled on SiriusXM.

Wherever this medium is heading, one thing remains clear: Indigenous people can access or create whatever programming they want on a multitude of platforms. There's a never-ending journey ahead in a changing world. So, what the hell, eh? Hoka Hey!

SERENDIPITY VOICES

ANDRE MORRISEAU

I'm short, gay, balding, French, Scottish, and Ojibway: I am Canadian. I was born a member of the Fort William First Nation (FWFN) in Port Arthur, Ontario (Thunder Bay). I was raised in Kenora, where my father was one of the first Indigenous conservation officers on Lake of the Woods. He was the great outdoors. I was the great indoors. More likely drawing or reading than hunting or ice fishing.

I left home in 1976 to move to Winnipeg, where I finished high school. My adventures took me to Vancouver, and I lived seven of the best years of my life there. I worked at the Hotel Georgia for Eleni Skalbania. Later, I became part of the opening team for her new boutique hotel, the Wedgewood. I was the only male waiter in a sea of beautiful women in the Bacchus Bistro. Those were different times.

I got into acting and stand-up comedy with the Jim Scotland Film Artists Workshop. In the spring of 1985, I moved to Toronto to summer with my best friend, Dudley, and his new partner. I never regretted my decision to move to downtown Toronto. It's home and I love it.

In 1993, I went from high-end restaurants to the CN Tower's 360, where I was the world's shortest manager, managing the world's tallest restaurant.

In 1997, I noticed a TV show called *Aboriginal Voices* on Sunday mornings before my 360 brunch shift. The show opened my eyes to the disconnect I had to my culture, my First Nation, and Toronto's Indigenous community.

My family had moved back to FWFN from Kenora in 1978, while I continued my journey in mainstream society. My search for Indigenous connection began when I quit my job at the CN Tower at the height of my game. *Aboriginal Voices* had awakened a yearning and need for me to find the Indigenous community in Toronto. The question was, did this community exist and how would I find it? Where were the Indians?

My love for acting led me to the Centre for Indigenous Theatre's (CIT) summer acting program. My starry eyes and overblown ego saw this as a fast track to more than one love – for *myself* and for Indigenous thespians.

I threw myself into getting eight-by-tens done, preparing for my big audition with CIT. The theatre's staff became my new best friends. Kind and understanding, they launched me into Toronto's Indigenous arts community. Like most Indigenous organizations, they worked in a constant battle zone of funding shortfalls that fuelled common bonds and mutual foes.

I waited days to hear if I had been accepted into the program. The call, from a phone connected to a wall, changed my life forever. I had been accepted. Overjoyed, I could see a new life emerging. I was a waiter doing double shifts. I could see my Indigenous culture and personal world coming together on my way to perceived stardom.

The life we have is not always the life we planned. The next day, I received a call from Brian Wright-McLeod of *Aboriginal Voices Magazine*. He asked if I would like to be part of the Aboriginal Voices Radio (AVR) project. I knew nothing about radio. I had never done anything with a radio other than turn one on. He said, 'Don't worry. It's a training program. You'll learn.' He asked if I could come down to the office the next day for an interview. I thought, Why not? What do I have to lose? I was on EI at the time and registered with Miziwe Biik Aboriginal Employment and Training, which, as it turned out, was funding the AVR program.

As the theatre program didn't start until July 1 and it was only March, I wondered what I was going to do in between. Out of curiosity, I decided to just go to the interview and see what it was all about. The next day, I scaled the well-worn marble stairs in a red-brick-and-beam building on Spadina Avenue. The *Aboriginal Voices Magazine* office, on the second floor, turned out to be a world of people, paper, phones ringing, and flourishing activity.

Andre Morriseau, 1979.

I was taken into a large warehouse room filled with furniture and desks surrounded by a graveyard of electronic equipment piled on tables. It looked like a repair shop. A young man with striking long black hair and reading a paper was leaning back in an old office chair, his cowboy boots propped up on a table in front of him. He looked at me through eyes that asked, Who is this shaganosh (Ojibway for white man)? I looked at him through the eyes of someone who had spent five years in a corporate environment filled with do's and don'ts. This was my first meeting with Chris Spence. He gave me the once-over and grunted a few words. In my colonized mind, I thought, What the hell is this all about?

He explained the radio program. It was the dream of Gary Farmer, who developed a national radio network that gave voice to Indigenous peoples across Canada. Our job would be to take all the donated radio equipment, refurbish it, and produce radio programming. A lofty idea. Chris swung his boots off the table, and we chatted. I asked questions, eyeing all the comings and goings. My curiosity grew. Literally the ground floor of an exciting project, albeit on the second floor, with a neon Aboriginal Voices sign facing Spadina Avenue's bustle. I left feeling a little bewildered, wondering what was I doing there.

The next day I received a call from Wright-McLeod, who, as it turned out, was one of the most acclaimed Indigenous radio journalists in the country. He became my teacher and mentor for the project. He informed me that if I wanted to be a part of the radio project, I would have to start in the next few days. Should I wait for July and the CIT summer theatre program or would I take this step into a complete unknown and join the AVR radio project? I decided to accept the offer – it was a path that would change my life forever.

My learning curve was swift and intense. It was 1998. The digital revolution hadn't really arrived yet. The donated equipment allowed us to produce rudimentary audio. It was a world of splicing and taping together our interviews. I remember the first telephone interview I did with Ila Bussidor, an Indigenous woman who wrote a book about a house fire that took her family. My eyes teared as I asked my questions and listened to her story. In my heart, I felt radio connected me to another human being in a way that had eluded me in life. This became the passion behind my work for years to come.

A few months into the job, Chris and I went to the Native American Journalists Association convention and special radio project at Tempe University in New Mexico. At the Walter Cronkite School of Journalism we were introduced to a new magic, Pro Tools. Back in Toronto, Spence ordered the demo CD. Within days, we went from tape to digital. I took money out of my RRSP and bought a small digital recorder, stereo mic, and an Apple computer. I had what I needed to start years of interviews all over Turtle Island, and especially Toronto, allowing me each day to share the lives of Indigenous people through their music, art, politics, successes, and challenges.

This was a time when I found a new family to embrace. Spence and I became fast friends, shooting pool, drinking beer, and exploring radio. His genius with computers and electronics inspired and guided the project all the way to the realization of the AVR network.

I met talented people like journalist Minnie Two Shoes, of the American Indian Movement; Toronto writer and photographer Millie Knapp; Indigenous-music trailblazer Elaine Bomberry; Aboriginal AIDS activist Tony Nobis; and others. They shared their stories while I embarked on my education about who I was in my own culture. I learned new words, like miigwetch (thank you), and directives, like always capitalizing Aboriginal.

A few months after I'd started at the radio project, everyone was out front of the office having a cigarette when this large man lumbered down the stairs. He stopped. Someone introduced me to the legend himself, *Aboriginal Voices Magazine* founder and visionary of the radio network Gary Farmer, actor, musician, and activist. He looked at me and said, 'Oh, you're the guy who wrote the beautiful letter.' The letter I had written months before, which failed to make the connection to Aboriginal Voices television show, by serendipity had landed on *Aboriginal Voices Magazine*'s desk. I had made a left turn just when I thought I was going to make a right.

Looking back to 1999, I fondly remember the first Aboriginal Voices Festival at Harbourfront Centre. We had a one-week radio broadcast licence, so we set up a mobile station in the front window on York Quay. I jogged down at 6:00 a.m. every morning of the five-day festival to start the broadcasting day. We featured singers, actors, politicians, and characters who came by our booth to be interviewed. It was a marathon learning moment.

One memory resonates across the years. I was asked to interview a young man whose auto-documentary *Deep Inside Clint Star* had just wowed audiences at the Sundance Film Festival. He landed with a thud in the chair in front of me after having had something more than orange juice at breakfast. The first thing he said was, 'Are you gay?' I responded, 'Are you interested?' So ensued the most intense interview I ever did. Live radio was all so new to me. Right before me was a chance to express my new voice. This was *all* so new to me. Clint provided me the opportunity to respond in real time, checking my timidity while embracing my new voice. I'd never been asked if I was gay in such a public way.

Those early AVR years, and the cast of characters who nudged me along my quest to learn about my culture and ultimately about myself, are golden. I hear the sound of a 49er in Hayward, Wisconsin, when a fortunate few attended Honor the Earth Pow Wow. Drumming floated through warm moonlit air. Serendipity had touched my life, giving me opportunities to build an unexpected future. I say chi miigwech to the Creator who gifted me Toronto, which is not only my home, but a place that brought me home to an Indigenous world.

HONOUR THE EARTH:
ACTIVISM IN THE EIGHTIES

BRIAN WRIGHT-MCLEOD

The only way to tell this thing is from personal experience. So sit tight and follow along as best you can.

It was 1982 when I moved to the Big Smoke at the encouragement of Indigenous gallery owners in Yorkville who were buying my paintings before pigment was slapped to canvas. No, I don't really paint on canvas; it's just a good turn of a phrase. Actually, it was 100 per cent rag paper with watercolour and guache, just so you know.

Since I had already been writing entertainment pieces for the *North Bay Nugget*, combining my visual art with publishing was an easy fit. But it was through the visual arts that I landed a gig producing illustrations for a Native magazine called *Sweet Grass*, the reincarnation of the defunct *Ontario Indian*.

The women who managed the publication were determined and focused. Rounding out the team was editor Juanita Renee, along with poet/writers Lenore Keeshig-Tobias, Nancy Paul-Woods, and Verna Friday. In addition to freelance contributors, additional staff included local American Indian Movement activist Jay Mason and designer David Beyer, who eventually went on to oversee *Aboriginal Voices Magazine* and *Smithsonian Magazine*.

Published by the Union of Ontario Indians, the magazine Ontario Indian *was relaunched as* Sweet Grass Magazine *in 1984.*

I soon found myself immersed in the Toronto AIM community, utilizing my training as an illustrator and journalist. The connections led me to a popular Native coffee house, the

Trojan Horse on the Danforth. The venue accorded anyone an opportunity to jump up onstage and try out a new song, read poetry, or deliver stand-up comedy.

Around that time, I was introduced to Tomson Highway through his cousin, actor Billy Merasty. Billy brought me to a three-storey Victorian brownstone on Church Street. The third floor was being used by Tomson as a studio, where the polished wooden floors were washed to a high gleam by the fresh afternoon sunlight filtering through abundantly large windows. René Highway, Tomson's brother, was twirling and gliding with delicate precision, wending his way through a dance rehearsal as Tomson played a baby grand.

Tomson invited me to a writers' workshop he organized at the Native Canadian Centre of Toronto (NCCT). There was me, Jay Mason, Daniel David Moses, Drew Hayden Taylor, and other aspiring talent. Tomson also organized a special Native poetry edition of the magazine *Poetry Toronto* to highlight his gaggle of budding writers.

The special edition of Poetry Toronto, No. 135, March 1987, *edited by Tomson Highway, featured local Indigenous poets.*

The NCCT was a bustling community hub where people enjoyed social and cultural activities or connected with out-of-town visitors and guests. Weekly community feasts opened with the big drum; Christmas concerts included Buffy Sainte-Marie or Winnipeg's C-Weed Band. It was a vibrant location where the office of the Canadian Association in Support of Native Peoples was located, in order for the organization to operate locally with a global scope.

CASNP was co-founded by Dr. Ed Newberry, Ojibway Elder Art Solomon, Native activist Wilfred Pelletier, and others in the 1960s. The objectives were to build awareness about the pressing environmental and political issues facing Indigenous peoples and taking direction from those affected communities.

Led by Jay Mason and the indefatigable Kay Murphy, a change of name – to the Canadian Alliance in Solidarity with Native People – was a formative shift to more grassroots initiatives. The organization was buoyed by a small core of paid staff, a national network of volunteers, and an active board of directors.

The Alliance produced a series of bulletins, newsletters, press releases, petitions, workshops, press conferences, and rallies to assist communities in struggle. The Friends (Quakers) had a long association since the beginning and maintained an important role in various capacities of financial, legal, and political support.

Yet there was no shortage of character assassinations originating with the mainstream media in the 1980s. In particular, Doug Fisher and Barbara Amiel barraged the public with denigrating and scathing anti-Indigenous editorials in the *Toronto Sun* and *Maclean's* magazine. They had crossed the line one too many times. Writer Lenore Keeshig-Tobias, Jay, and others organized a string of protests outside the publications' offices to demand retractions, apologies, or some sort of an accounting. It was a grassroots call to expose racism in mainstream media.

In a culturally autonomous expansion, Jay and visual artist Mike Cywink created the Native Education Society of Toronto (NEST). Direction came from Elders Max Ireland (Oneida), Vern Harper (Cree), Eddie Benton-Banai (Anishnabe), Philip Deer (Muscogee), Leonard Crow Dog (Sioux), Nellie Red Owl (Sioux), and Kahn-Tineta Horn (Mohawk).

The NEST settled in at 18 MacDonnell Street, near Lansdowne and Queen Street West, a former Katimavik house. The four-storey pad was originally used as a transit residence for the kids involved in Prime Minister Pierre Trudeau's outward-bound initiative for Canadian youth in the 1970s. The house was equipped with an ample kitchen and other facilities outfitted accordingly.

One additional comfort was knowing that, whatever happened, there was a cadre, a backup system to assist in times of need. In terms of street smarts, the NEST consisted of a loose network of activists, working stiffs, artists, musicians, and veterans who comprised an Indigenous family connected by culture, societal conditions, and a common direction. The lifestyle was basic, the possessions few, but morale, stamina, and awareness were high, and combined with a strong cultural and spiritual direction from deep within the AIM leadership.

Through NEST, we organized a weekly fifteen-minute radio segment on the fledgling campus/community radio station CKLN 88.1 FM. Initially, the effort was designed to issue news items and updates on the land struggle. It would transform into other programs over the years, establishing a solid presence on the airwaves. CKLN was an incubator during the embryonic stages of hip hop in Toronto, and a staunch advocate of all things odd. For us, it was a perfect fit.

Another small coup was achieved when Toronto City Council recognized October 12, 1985, as International Day of Solidarity with Indigenous Peoples. Meanwhile, the local anarchist community created inroads to work with Indigenous grassroots activists. The ACT Fallout Shelter, what I referred to as the Circle-A Ranch, was located above the El Mocambo on Spadina Avenue. It had been turned into a little hot spot for political activities, with films, workshops, and guest speakers. The open-stage nights featured local artists and international activists such as Floyd Westerman and comedian Charlie Hill.

Summers were hot and bright. Kensington Market was alive with everything that could move in an international marketplace cadenced by languages and products from near and far. Punks, anarchists, Rastas, rockers, skinheads, bikers, artists, musicians, wannabe cowboys, trippy-hippy-dippies, and off-the-grid entrepreneurs had established digs of one kind or another in the Market.

Haunts like the Lisbon Plate or the Tropical Paradise could provide anything anyone wanted, if one knew the right patterns. To add to the circus of this reality, Bunchofuckingoofs were ever apparent. The resident punk band and their retinue always dressed in the persona of *Mad Max: Road Warrior.* Mohawk haircuts, black leather pants and vests, knuckle gloves, kicker boots, metal studs, shoulder and shin pads cannibalized from sports equipment, wrenches and other tools hanging from custom-made utility belts, eyeshadow, and real jail-time attitude, which added a tinge of apocalyptic immortality. It reflected their lifestyle. But they were pussycats compared to the real bulldogs. And better yet, they were all on our side – all of them.

CASNP's newsletter The Phoenix *represented grassroots Indigenous issues and current events.*

The Leonard Peltier Defense Committee of Canada was headed up by Frank and Anne Dreaver, an undertaking deserving of a book all its own. Their events and campaigns were intense, vibrant, educational, and transformative. Yet, in the end, they produced little achievement in their sole purpose: to free Leonard Peltier. He remains in Leavenworth Penitentiary serving two consecutive life terms as a result of the shooting of two FBI agents in 1976 in South Dakota, amid questionable trials and evidence.

Art Solomon led ongoing prison support work with Indian brotherhoods in the institutions at Guelph and Kingston, including the latter's notorious Prison for Women. His philosophies were written down in two books of poems and essays: *Songs for the People: Teachings on the Natural Way* (N.C. Press, 1990) and *Eating Bitterness: A Vision Beyond the Prison Walls* (N.C. Press, 1994). Art also headed up the Burwash Native People's Project, a cultural program for former inmates re-entering society.

The combined efforts of CASNP and NEST included school visits with lectures and cultural workshops, street demonstrations, and the humble beginnings of a street patrol. Fundraisers, concerts, and showcases were organized at various clubs, including the Cameron House, and venues such as the Euclid Theatre, to raise further awareness of the struggle.

Ad: Honour Mother Earth Day, Algonquin Island, May, 1987.

Every Mother's Day in May, from 1985 to 1988, CASNP hosted Honour Mother Earth Day on Algonquin Island. We wrangled harbour ferries and water taxis to ship the sound equipment and other gear, as well as food donated from various businesses and home-kitchen cooks, volunteers, and artists. A daylong roster of local musicians and poets from Indigenous, Black, and white communities performed on a hand-constructed plywood stage. We organized our own on-site security, designed and distributed flyers, and got the word out in every which way we could through event listings and interviews in print, radio, and television. Some notable guests included poet Clifton Joseph, singer Faith Nolan, the powwow group Eagleheart, and painter Norval Morrisseau, with his protege Brian Marion.

Awareness campaigns around NATO overflights in Goose Bay, Labrador, and the land issue with the Lubicon in Alberta, as well as the uranium mine protests in Wollaston Lake, Saskatchewan, were ongoing. But perhaps the largest international campaign drew around the Relocation Act, Public Law 93-531, in Arizona. The 1974 legislation sought to remove (by force if necessary) ten thousand traditional Navajo from their ancestral lands and a self-subsistent life, and into government track housing in surrounding towns. The area known as Big Mountain was destined to be sacrificed for the sake of mineral extraction by international companies such as Kerr-McGee and Bechtel. In an effort to expedite the process, the U.S. government framed the situation as a bloody range war between the Hopi and the Navajo.

International support efforts increased as tensions grew around the July 1986 relocation deadline. In addition to people travelling to the area, CASNP hosted a special Toronto screening of the Academy Award–winning film *Broken Rainbow*, with a Saturday matinee showing at the Bloor Cinema. Nobody complained about the summer heat. During the following weekend, a peaceful border action at Niagara Falls was wildly popular and effective, as tourists from both sides of the 'medicine line' were informed of the situation in Arizona. The journey to Niagara Falls was made a bit easier with the loan of Bruce Cockburn's tour bus, the Silver Eagle.

The petitions, flyers, and cards attached to balloons were graciously received by the long-weekend tourists. Many were very receptive, due in part to the inviting festive nature of the action. Equally, most were shocked at the information about what was transpiring at Big Mountain. The entire affair generated an outpouring of sympathy and support.

There was always a lot going on, including a determined focus on environmental issues such as plutonium overflights across Arctic Canada, with information derived from the First Global Radiation Victims Conference held in New York City in 1987.

Attendees included Saami representatives, whose reindeer herds were decimated by radiation fallout from the Chernobyl nuclear reactor meltdown, survivors of the Hiroshima nuclear

CASNP's newsletter featured the writings and artwork of Indigenous people incarcerated in prisons within Canada and the United States.

bomb attack in 1945 Japan, and Indigenous peoples from across North America who had survived the devastation of uranium mining, nuclear testing, and nuclear waste.

An international contingent of women activists from Greenham Common in England detailed their experiences of being 'zapped' by electromagnetic pulse waves from experimental riot control technologies.

By this time, NEST had faded. Some people moved out of province or elsewhere, while others, like me, had career paths to pursue and families to raise. Despite personal requirements or decisions, nobody abandoned the direction or spirit of the movement.

Things were not always peaceful. One night, I found myself alone with a group of non-Natives. After a series of seemingly innocent verbal exchanges, I was summarily beaten – kicked, punched, and pummelled into a blackout. I was left for dead before an ogling audience. I don't recall how I made it back home, but I arrived. It took me a few weeks to recover.

During a fundraising event for Big Mountain not long afterwards, I was onstage and recognized the soundman. He was one of the assailants. After informing the AIM organizer, the brother said, 'We've got this.'

I never saw the soundman again. But on another occasion, while seated at a restaurant west of Spadina and gazing out the big bay window that provided a south-facing vista of Bloor Street, I saw one of the other thugs. He was running for his life, shirt half torn away and with a look of absolute fear in his eyes. Following close behind were three Native brothers who seemed determined to nab their prey. That, too, was the last time I saw that individual.

I guess the lesson is that one should be very careful whom one decides to assault. Such cadres of solidarity hardly exist anymore. Our isolation is perhaps a greater threat than anything else in the Indigenous community. It exists in part due to the deliberate societal and political divisions introduced through scientific social engineering that have divided us all. In reality, it was child's play compared to what was to transpire later in life.

When 1990 rolled around, it marked the South Dakota ride for the hundred-year anniversary of the Wounded Knee massacre of Chief Big Foot and his people. Soon after, we became immersed in sun dance and peyote ceremonies from the Dakotas to the U.S. Southwest. And two years later, the 1992 the Columbus Quincentenary – marking the date when Indigenous peoples discovered Europeans – drew protests and awareness campaigns that created a deeper look into transformative historic events.

Into the 1990s, some of the local activists began confronting self-proclaimed white supremacists headed up by Wolfgang Droege and his meagre gang of sandbox Nazis. Activist Rodney Bobiwash took it upon himself to address the issue in a drawn-out back-and-forth telephone war between the hate group and himself. We went to one of the public meetings in the east end that was organized by the neo-hate group. One of their members was sitting by himself outside, where I spoke with him briefly.

He said, shaking his head, 'I can't understand why people hate us. They think we're scum.'

Yes, I laughed, too.

The December 'grand entry' into the Revenue Canada building that was occupied by Indigenous demonstrators for several weeks in 1994.

Prior to the opening pitch at an Atlanta Braves exhibition game against the Toronto Blue Jays in 1993, the special event was met with protests organized by Minneapolis AIM director Vern Belcourt, actor Eric Schweig, and other supporters. The issue of the Braves' mascot was finally raised to public attention. Other actions and campaigns included Revenue Rez, the 1994 occupation of an uninhabited floor and courtyard of the downtown Revenue Canada building in protest of tax legislation aimed at diminishing Indigenous rights.

Individual actions never went unnoticed. The Buffalo Jump project created by visual artist and long-time AIM brother Simon Paul (Dene) utilized satirical imagery to draw attention to legislation that sought to nullify Indigenous rights. The effort grew into an artistic movement in its own right.

AIM activist/poet John Trudell appeared with Australian aborigine music sensation Yothu Yindi and headliners Midnight Oil at Maple Leaf Gardens. A quick hello with John on the tour bus was cut short by the group's departure back to the U.S. Trudell was legally and officially banned from Canada, with the exception of an authorized twenty-four-hour stay-over, all stemming from a political decision based on his effective and tragic high-profile relationship with AIM in the 1970s.

At various points, everyone and everything intersected time and again. Trudell returned to Toronto during an Aboriginal Voices Radio event at the Harbourfront Centre, where I interviewed the brother for the fifteenth time. The encounter underlined the vast history of activism in North America and showed why 'the meeting place' has been the site of many encounters over generations for that purpose.

By 2000, CASNP had been dissolved as an organization. It had been a crucial rallying point that brought hope, activity, and awareness to an uninformed public and a broader profile to Indigenous issues that, otherwise, would have been completely ignored.

Much of the inspiration for my graphic novel *Red Power* (Fitzhenry & Whiteside) was derived from these experiences and dedicated to those people. Some of my original art from *Red Power* was included in an exhibition, *Direct Action Comics: Politically Engaged Comics and Graphic Novels*,

at the University of Massachusetts, Amherst. The show also included original works by Joe Shuster (*Superman*) and Art Spiegelman (*Maus*) – a very humbling experience. I credit the spirit of the activists who illuminated a path for their stories to be told.

Mexico Native Rights/Free Trade demonstration on the Danforth, February 12, 1994. Fernando Hernandez (centre left) Vern Harper (centre right).

The events described here represent an iceberg tip of the numerous activities that abounded during this time. Many of those people have since gone on into the spirit world. Their teachings, their words, and their actions are not forgotten; although not often apparent, they continue to resonate. As my time nears, I remember a traditional Lakota song: 'Only the Earth Endures.'

TRANSFORMING THE CITY

CONCRETE INDIANS

NADYA KWANDIBENS

Concrete Indians is an open-call portraiture series started in 2008 that focuses on reflections of contemporary Indigenous identity and decolonization. Many portraits are of people in traditional regalia at major recognizable intersections and neighbourhoods in cities throughout Canada. Several portraits convey unity and solidarity amongst our own people, while others are personal reflections and expressions of decoloniality; all are assertions of the strength of Indigenous culture and identity through resurgent acts of resistance and of reclamation of Indigenous space(s).

When I initially started editing this series, I wanted the portraits to stand out from the vibrancy of my other work, to use black/white in a way that challenges historical uses of the aesthetic format – mainly the black-and-white portraits of American photographer Edward S. Curtis that deemed Indigenous Peoples 'the vanishing race' – and to disrupt the simplicity and one-dimensionality of the medium itself by presencing and juxtaposing Indigenous people within contemporary urban spaces to state: *We are still here.*

This series aligns itself with the works I created over the past fourteen years via Red Works Photography. Red Works seeks to implicitly point out the dark history of colonialism and explicitly call out the historic and current stereotypical depictions, which are based on the Eurocentric approach of appropriating our culture and telling our stories for us. Red Works aims to eradicate those negative stereotypes by highlighting the complexities of Indigenous Peoples, of Indigenous realities, and our resistance to ongoing colonialism.

Nadya Kwandibens.

Series: Concrete Indians
Tee Lyn Duke
Toronto, ON
March 2010

Series: Concrete Indians
Rosary Spence
Toronto, ON
May 2010

Series: Concrete Indians
Lisa Charleyboy
Toronto, ON
November 2008

THE GREAT INDIAN BUS TOUR OF TORONTO

REBEKA TABOBONDUNG
INTERVIEWS BY ERICA COMMANDA

The most subversive act for Indigenous people is to just be who we are – speaking our language, maintaining our ties to the land, eating our traditional food ... Wealth should not be measured by GDP, but rather by the wealth of our culture and languages.

– Rodney Bobiwash

In 1999, at age twenty, I came to Toronto from Vancouver. After I'd moved around Alberta and the West Coast, Toronto was calling me to become closer to my Anishinaabe roots, as my family were a few hours north, in Wasauksing First Nation on Georgian Bay.

I transferred my university credits from the self-certified Institute of Indigenous Government in Vancouver's Gastown to the Aboriginal Studies Program at the University of Toronto. I immediately felt at home at the Aboriginal Students Services Centre, known as First Nations House, on Spadina Circle. One of the first of many welcoming people I met was Anishinaabe scholar, visionary, and activist Rodney Bobiwash, who headed the Toronto office of the Centre for Global Indigenous Studies.

What ensued was a mentorship and friendship that introduced me to the vast richness of Toronto's powerful, inclusive, and diverse Indigenous community. Bobiwash, a member of the Mississauga First Nation on the north shore of Lake Huron, was a special person. Highly intuitive, funny, and intelligent, he could connect the many dots about the impacts of colonization, all the while wearing a 'Token Indian' pin. His vision included coalitions between Indigenous and non-Indigenous activist communities.

I am so grateful to have been able to walk in his world, albeit for too short a time, and contribute to one of his many legacies, the Toronto

Native Community History Project (now called First Story Toronto), and his genius approach to popular education, the Great Indian Bus Tour of Toronto. Sadly, Rodney passed away in 2002, at the age of forty-two, from complications due to diabetes. In his honour, a sacred fire burned at the Native Canadian Centre for four days, and over seven hundred people attended the service. Rodney's work continues to reverberate across the city and globally to this day.

When I was invited to co-edit this book, many stories of historical places and community knowledge sprang to mind, much of it learned through my involvement with Rodney and the History Project. For this essay, I decided to interview Rodney's partner and Indigenous studies scholar, anthropologist, co-founder of the Toronto Native Community History Project, and activist in her own right, Heather Howard-Bobiwash; long-time volunteer, researcher, scholar, and First Story bus tour operator Jon Johnson; and a next-generation tour guide, Kory Snache. Erica Commanda helped lead the interviews. What follows is the story of how the Toronto Native History project came to be, and how it has fanned the sparks of Eighth Fire.

§   §   §

In 1995, Heather Howard co-founded the Toronto Native Community History Project with Rodney Bobiwash while she was pursuing her PhD in anthropology at the University of Toronto. Currently, she is an Assistant Professor of Anthropology at Michigan State University and focuses her research on Indigenous women's activism in urban community organizing, and community-based health and social service programs. She has also been an affiliated faculty member at the University of Toronto with the Centre for Indigenous Studies since 2009 and was a visiting scholar at the University of Oxford in the Institute for Social and Cultural Anthropology in 2016 and 2017.

Heather Howard-Bobiwash: Back in 1995, I had just come to Toronto. Rodney and I had decided to get married, and he had taken up the job of directing First Nations House at the University of Toronto. I decided to pursue my PhD at the U of T. We had initially met through our anti-racism work prior to that. We were both involved in a lot of work around the country organizing anti-racism activities, through an organization called the Canadian Centre on Racism and Prejudice. Rodney came to be a speaker at a public event we had organized in Montreal, where I lived.

As the years unfolded, I decided to move to Toronto [from Montreal]. When I got to Toronto, I was surprised to find that the U of T did not have [funding] to support my work, so I needed to find a job. Rodney said, 'Well, why don't you go see Gayle Mason?' At that time, Gayle was the director of the Native Canadian Centre. So that's what I did. Gayle hired me to work a couple of months on sustaining the Native Canadian Centre's publication, which at the time was called the *Native Canadian Magazine*.

I put together a plan and revamped the publication. It was really important to the Centre to continue to have that communication with its members and the public. When I was doing that work, a maintenance guy named Gerald Williams came into my office and said, 'You have a whole bunch of boxes in the basement.' I thought, what the heck is he talking about? I'm working on the newsletter. I didn't know what boxes he could be talking about, so I went to see. It turned out there were about a hundred or so bankers boxes full of the Native Canadian Centre's records, and work related to the Centre's publication.

The Centre had continuously had a publication since even before it was founded. Prior to the Native Canadian Centre, there was a club that ran out of the YMCA. Before that, there was kind of a club organized by families in their homes. And that was all interconnected. They had formed a typed-up newsletter that they circulated. It was called *Beavertails* back in the 1960s, then the *Toronto Native Times*, which was appropriately called TNT during the explosive 1970s and Red Power movement. The magazine was briefly called *Boozhoo Magazine*, and then *Native Canadian Magazine* in the 1980s. Getting into the 1990s, it was really facing difficulty.

That's what all those boxes contained: all that history.

The Native Canadian Centre as an organization has changed dramatically over the last thirty years or so. In those days, there was a sense of connection to the previous generation, who had done so much to make these organizations and that kind of capital available in the community, coming out of the Red Power movement and empowering the community with services provided for Indigenous people by Indigenous people.

There was the occasional non-Indigenous person like me working there. But really, the Centre was an Indigenous-led organization. It had a completely Indigenous board, a very active Indigenous Elders Council that invested a lot into really making sure that Elder knowledge was available and then using it in daily practice in the way we carried out our work, and in the way we carried out our responsibilities to people in the community.

In the meantime, I was advocating to save the boxes and do something with them. We managed to secure space in the Centre to bring those boxes up out of the basement to start to figure out what was in them. There were videotapes and audio tapes as well. We recognized the historical relationship the Centre had had with the Toronto Public Library's Spadina Branch next door through a series of oral histories conducted in the 1980s.

Rodney was teaching in addition to directing First Nations House at U of T. He was trained as a historian and he thought, 'I'll run a community popular education history class.' We actually had a lot of people sign up! I think it was maybe forty or forty-five people. It was pretty much half-and-half, Native and non-Native, and people paid forty dollars or something like that to take this eight- or ten-week course. Included in that course, Rodney designed the Great Indian Bus Tour of Toronto. So that's how that started, as part of the class.

One of the things that first class did together was really establish the vision and the mission of the Toronto Native Community History Project. We started to apply for small grants from the city to hire youth. It was important there should always be this engagement with youth – inter-generational engagement, and ways in which they would be meaningfully incorporated into having a say about how the history of Indigenous people was represented, and also having a role in creating that. They had jobs they had to do: coming up with oral history projects and carrying those out; learning how to organize archival materials and how to use those records and articles.

I think our office in the Native Canadian Centre was the first in that building that had an internet connection. So the youth at the time really liked coming in there because they could use the internet to chat with their friends. The office was always busy with youth who were in using the computer. But while they were waiting their turn to get on, they'd be looking through all this stuff that was sitting there and saying, 'Oh, hey, that's my grandfather, that's my uncle.' They felt this material, and that was a way of getting them interested in what it was about.

That was really how things began. It had this two-pronged piece, where we had the archive and the collections that became increasingly important in recognizing the role that the Native Canadian Centre had in stewarding the history of the Toronto community. A lot of the records there have to do with programs that eventually became other organizations that really formed the network or the backbone of the community.

The Great Indian Bus Tour of Toronto postcard design. Artist: Sue Todd.

Erica Commanda: What did you find were the most significant stops or sites along the tour?

HHB: The University of Toronto has an underground river that runs through the middle of the campus. There are places where very important council meetings happened, talking about the Mississaugas' displacement from Toronto. One of my favourite spots was an arrangement with the Royal Ontario Museum. There used to be displays; they were part of the archaeological gallery in the basement of the museum. We didn't have the galleries that are now there. Back then it was down in the basement, with old-fashioned archaeological dioramas, like a guy in buckskins.[1] You'd see a square dug in the display, where the archaeologists would have, quote unquote, dug up this information, and the archaeologist's tools, like a trowel and a camera and stuff like that.

This display was to demonstrate and try to convey to the viewer the work of the archaeologist. It probably had mixed reviews. For some, it might have been clear that the purpose was to engage the 'presence' of the archaeologist, while for others they probably just wondered why there were 'modern' items in with the 'primitive' display.

On top of all that, the gallery was called the Beringia gallery, referring to the Bering Strait. It was really racist and problematic on every level – even the fact that it was in the basement, out of the way, where nobody learned about Indigenous people. Rodney liked to go there [with the tour] and one of the things he'd love to say was, 'Here you have it, folks, absolute proof that we're from Asia.' And he pointed to the Nikon camera that was on display.

I think another important dimension about what he did was his sense of humour. You know, that really got the word around, about how much fun it was to go on tour, even though he spent a lot of time calling people out on their racism and getting people to try to see the world with a different set of eyeballs. We worked with ROM staffer Trudy Nicks, and the ROM gave us free passes for the people who participated in the bus tour. And they did that, so every time we had passes, we could give them out to everybody and they could go back to the museum later.

In a way, Rodney really straddled appealing to the non-Indigenous people to take up their responsibility while also advocating and elevating Indigenous voices. Some people have criticized it in retrospect for relying too much on going to archaeological sites or going to look at the colonial history ... bringing in that non-Indigenous framing. The initial stops on the tour did tend to go to some of these places where particular colonial events occurred, or where archaeologists had dug something up.

But I think it was important to also remember that at the time, this was a five-hour tour and there was a lot of getting on and off the bus. Rodney spent a lot of time also sharing traditional Anishinaabe teachings and understandings about engagement with places like Baby Point. When Rodney started this, all Baby Point was known for was its archaeological significance, rather than for being a site of Indigenous heritage. He would go to the Wendat burial site in Scarborough and get people to take tobacco and understand that this is a burial ground and what that meant, rather than it just being an archaeological site. He went to these places that could serve as a hook for the participants, drawing them into the archaeological mystery, and then take them on a different journey so they could see it through a different set of eyeballs.

§   §   §

Jon Johnson is the lead organizer for First Story Toronto. He has been teaching at Woodsworth College since 2018 and focuses his research on urban land-based Indigenous knowledge in Toronto and its representation through oral and digital forms of storytelling.

Jon Johnson: I've been with First Story Toronto even before it was called First Story Toronto, since about 2003, when it was situated at the Native Canadian Centre, and have taken on increasing amounts of roles and responsibilities in that project as people came and left. I kind of just stuck around the longest. I ended up doing tours and a lot of historical research, and a lot of archival and oral research with the project and learning from other guides who had come before me, and eventually came to steward the tours.

In the time I've been working with First Story Toronto, I've managed to learn a lot from a lot of different people about the histories of Toronto, and that's the work I essentially do – trying to find ways to introduce people to those stories, to those knowledges, to those histories and presences, and ways that hopefully will transform how we think about the city.

Rodney passed away in 2002 unfortunately, and while he couldn't continue the tours, other people continued the tours in his stead. Alanis King started after him because she had been on tours with him, and I learned the tours from her. The project was stewarded for a time by Monica Bodirsky. She was the coordinator as well for the project.

I came to Toronto in 2000 to pursue a PhD and I was working in the area of Indigenous storytelling, trying to think about land-based knowledge in the city. I ended up volunteering at the Native Canadian Centre as a way to form a relationship with the community because I hadn't been there before. I started volunteering with the project through Monica and of course I learned about Heather as well.

Around 2008, Monica ended up leaving her position to pursue her own career in art. There was no one really left because the Native Canadian Centre didn't hire a new coordinator. Monica, and Heather as well, in their own ways, asked me to steward the project in the short term. I did the best I could to continue on with caring for the archive and the stories on the tours.

The majority of my focus has been definitely on the tours, to try to ensure that those kept going in any way possible. My involvement since 2003 has been to learn from people like Alanis and other tour guides I've since become involved with, like Phil Cote, Jill Carter, John Crouch, and Amber Sandy. There's a whole bunch of people I could list, like [public historian] Victoria Freeman, who I've been lucky enough to work with. Over time, in addition to the bus tours, we started doing a lot more walking tours.

Because of all the work we were collectively doing, there was more and more knowledge of how expansive the Indigenous geography was. We were able to be in places where there were particularly rich narratives and a high density of stories and past presences. We were able to spend more time in one place and really walk around.

The first walking tour I ever did was in the area of Deer Park, in the Yonge and St. Clair area. There's the INAC [Indigenous and Northern Affairs Canada] picnic every year [at Wells Hill Park]. They've asked for several years in a row for a walking tour of the valley because that whole area has a really strong Indigenous history.

We talk about Indigenous history generally and look at plants and medicines. We were all working together on tours and knowledges and projects, and people were asking us to do collaborations. It was a really exciting time and there was a lot of fluorescence around the project. Even when Rodney created the Great Indian Bus Tour, he didn't just come up with it on his own. He was drawing from community histories, oral knowledges, as well as his own archival and historical research that he was able to give.

That has always been a community history. It expanded to the point where we're able to do a walking tour pretty much anywhere in the city now. There's a lot more awareness that the city has a very, very rich and long history – that the city's narrative doesn't start just with colonialism. You know, people now are at least aware that there is Indigenous history and that it's expansive, even if they don't know what it is exactly.

Eventually, we changed the name to First Story Tours and rebranded because there were people at the Native Canadian Centre who felt that the Great Indian Bus Tour was no longer an appropriate name. It was always a tongue-in-cheek sort of name, but we understood, so we changed. We had always been based out of the Native Canadian Centre and maintained a loose partnership, like they were our institutional partner.

The Native Canadian Centre is a great place, and I have nothing bad to say about it. We just weren't able to go further. So more recently, because a lot of us are at University of Toronto and we have an institutional affiliation there, we've established a partnership with U of T, and they have become our main institutional partner.

It's been hard for us to continue to meet the demand for tours. We were able to get a grant to train twenty new guides, all Indigenous youth from the community, as well as from U of T. We're also doing virtual tours, because of COVID-19, so we've had to retool that grant a little bit to make space for virtual storytelling.

EC: As a guide with the tour, what do you consider a few of the significant stops?

JJ: I always liked starting at the Native Canadian Centre because that's a really important centre of community activation for the contemporary community here. I like the Davenport Road and Spadina intersection, where you see those two signs are now in Anishinaabemowin. Spadina is also labelled as 'Ishpadinaa' and Davenport is labelled 'Gete-Onigaming.' It's a really cool intersection because those two signs tell the story of the original landscape of Toronto, its trails, and how cosmopolitan and happening Toronto was before Europeans got here.

It was a place of movement and action. Spadina/Ishpadinaa means 'going up the hill' and refers to that bluff that Casa Loma sits on. Then you have that other sign, which is a renaming of Davenport Road, which runs along that bluff. Gete-Onigaming means 'old, old road' and refers to the fact that there was this really amazing path on Davenport Road that connected across the whole of Lake Ontario and intersected so many other paths. It went all the way from Lake Ontario to Lake Simcoe and then into Northern Ontario.

That was a huge series of trade routes that facilitated massive amounts of Indigenous movements for probably millennia before Europeans ever got here. It made Toronto a strategic place for Europeans to settle for trade and military and economic purposes. Even the name Toronto itself comes from those roots and where they lead. So to me, that's a really cool story and place, because it goes back 13,000 years to when that bluff was a lakeshore. It's a really long presence of Indigenous peoples there that you can really feel.

EC: **What is your understanding of the Indigenous meaning of the word *Toronto*?**

JJ: *Toronto* is a really big word because that word encompasses so many different interpretations and different stories and ideas of what it means. I think we can enter a space of understanding that there's not just one right interpretation and get away from arguing over which one is the right one but understanding how they can all be, in their own way, right and interrelated understandings.

Probably one of the most common or widely accepted interpretations of what *Toronto* means is that it refers to trees standing in the water. There are variations on that, like some Haudenosaunee people talk about a log that means log or a fallen tree – possibly in the water, possibly not. In the Haudenosaunee interpretation I've heard, the log wouldn't have just been some random log. It would probably be a very prominent marker of a tree that had fallen, possibly a bridge over a river. Or maybe it would be in the water in part, but it would be a meeting place within Indigenous geographies that would be of importance as a gathering spot.

Another interpretation is of trees standing in the water, which refers to that fishing weir at the north end of Lake Simcoe. The French, when they first recorded the name of that lake, called it Lac Toronto. A fishing weir is a construction of stakes or poles you place across the water for fishing. On that same map, they noted these stakes in the water on the lake. It's almost definitely an Iroquoian word, but no one can say for certain whether it's Mohawk or Seneca or Wendat, because these words get filtered through English and French speakers who don't render the pronunciation properly or the spellings, and so it becomes kind of hard to trace exactly because they become Europeanized in some ways.

EC: **I've never heard of those specific fishing weirs …**

JJ: It's one of the oldest existing wooden structures in the world – a completely underacknowledged world heritage site. There are still wooden stakes that exist in the narrows below the water. They dated them using radiocarbon dating to five thousand years ago. The fishing weir was being used up until the 1800s, but the wood was five thousand years old. So that place was being continuously used as a fishing weir and a meeting place for five thousand years.

It's right between the north end of where Lake Simcoe meets Lake Couchiching. There's a place called the Narrows where those two lakes meet. That's where the fishing weir was, and it was a really, really big construction situated right along all of these north-south routes that go through what is now Toronto, following the river basins of the Humber, the Don, and the Rouge from Lake Ontario, all the way up to Lake Simcoe. The fishing weir is located along those really well-travelled routes.

Those routes were the fastest way to get from Northern Ontario into the northern United States, so that's where a lot of the movement was going. That fishing weir was a place for seasonal fishing by Wendat, and certainly also by Mississaugas/Anishinaabe and probably also Haudeno-saunee people, during the time that they understood that this was their territory, in the 1600s.

It was always also a meeting place. You could be there for a season or for at least a few weeks predictably around a seasonal excursion, so people would know they could meet people at that time during those seasonal periods. They would gather there for trade, and they would probably also gather for treaty and council, all kinds of important discussions.

I think *Toronto* also means 'fishing weir where the trees gather in the water.' That's why there are different ideas of what *Toronto* means, but they all relate to the same story of Toronto being this place of meeting, a place of plenty, a place of gathering, not only of minds, bodies, and spirits, but also fish and the abundance of the place. All of those different words are bound up in that word *Toronto*. Toronto is a really cool name because it's definitely an Indigenous word that is very much reflective of Indigenous understandings of what this place is all about.

EC: **In what ways do you witness passengers benefiting from taking the tour?**

JJ: That depends on who the passenger is. For non-Indigenous folks, most of them are in a good place, I think, when they take the tour. A lot of folks who end up taking the tour are already on a path of understanding that there's this thing called colonialism and are working to figure out what that is, their relationship to it, or their complicity, and hopefully trying to dismantle it.

They really appreciate learning about the histories of place and the stories of Indigenous presence in Toronto, and how the whole history of colonialism across North America is manifested here. A lot of people are not really aware of the expanse of that history and they're blown away by it. They ask, 'How do we not know this? Why aren't we talking about this in school? Why has this history been erased?' They come away with a new understanding that is reparative and generative, helping them to think about their positionality with Indigenous peoples, Indigenous communities, and maybe toward something we might call reconciliation.

Sometimes we do tours with young kids. They're not doing it because they necessarily know anything about Indigenous peoples, but because their teacher thought it was a good idea. That starts them on that journey as well, thinking about social justice issues. It's really nice to see that kind of transformation. Sometimes we have to do work with people who had really, really negative perceptions that come from colonial misrepresentations of Indigenous people. So we do the work of trying to unfold or disentangle those things and re-educate people about different ways of thinking about and undoing that misrepresentation.

Then, for Indigenous folks, I think a lot of Indigenous peoples in the city are also in a space where they might be new to the city. They want to get a sense of what this place is, from an Indigenous perspective: What are the spots? Who are the peoples? What is their relationship to the traditional territories they are within? It really helps a lot of people who feel like maybe they come from small communities, like reserve communities.

They're in the city and they're feeling out of place. To feel grounded in places in the city, to understand that there are land-based relationships in the city that are operative here, too.

It helps to bring them in a good relationship to this place. When people discover that one of the interpretations for *Toronto* is that it means 'meeting place,' that's really profound for a lot of people, because they're like, 'That's what I'm here for. I'm here to take advantage and learn from this diversity here in Toronto, and to meet with diverse Indigenous and non-Indigenous peoples and do good work.'

That's where a lot of activism comes from – those meetings, those connections with different Indigenous folks from across the territory. That's where a lot of the most amazing activism has happened, from those really good meetings, different peoples and different perspectives and sharing, right? Which colonialism undermined, quite frankly, by forcing people to be isolated on reserves.

I think there's a space in the storytelling for sharing knowledges, engaging with community, engaging with stories of mutual interest, helping to support ongoing identity work, and language work that a lot of Indigenous folks are engaging with from their own backgrounds. It's a great educational enterprise for non-Indigenous folks who need to know this stuff so that they don't reproduce colonialism.

EC: Your PhD thesis included the Seventh and Eighth Fire Prophecy teachings. Why was it important for you to connect with these teachings?

JJ: Those prophecies are about the future and they are about the present moment. I felt like there are so many layers of depth to those prophecies. When I read them, and as I started to learn more about urban Indigenous knowledge and storytelling, I connected it in different ways. I was talking before about ongoing resilience, ongoing action and activism: that's what those prophecies are about. They talk about the whole history of colonialism and then a sort of moment where Indigenous peoples begin to pick up what was left by the trail and reconstitute community, culture, language, knowledge.

At the same time Indigenous peoples would be picking up that knowledge and reconstituting those knowledges in relationship to their communities, that knowledge would not only be important for Indigenous peoples, but also for non-Indigenous peoples. Not in an extractive way, not in an appropriative away, but in a way of informing a genuinely different anti-colonial, anti-extractive, anti-destructive way of relating to land and the world we live in.

I think that's one of the biggest strengths that Indigenous peoples and Indigenous philosophies teach us. There are many different possible ways of relating to land and engaging land that are not extractive and destructive of those land-based relationships. That's something that Westerners really need to understand because we're all heading toward some really negative consequences from the expansion of that really destructive way of thinking in the Western world.

For me, that prophecy connects to what is going on in North America today in relation to Indigenous peoples and urbanization. I was working on Indigenous urban knowledge and urban Indigenous storytelling, and it didn't seem too coincidental to me. A lot of people have different ideas of when the Seventh generation starts, but a lot of people trace it back to the 1950s and authorities in the 1950s. In the 1960s and the 1970s, people really started to do that active work of reconstituting culture and community. That's the same time that Indigenous peoples were urbanizing. There were a lot of people coming back to the cities after being incarcerated, in some cases on reserve territories. Not that they're bad places necessarily, but they were used as holding places for Indigenous peoples.

Coming back to the city, there was all of this knowledge sharing and sharing of different perspectives from people all across Canada. I think those good conversations really highlighted for people not only the shared experience of colonialism, but the need to band together against it in strategic and thoughtful ways. To me, that Seventh Fire was lit in large part by the work of people, Indigenous peoples, who ended up in the cities who were having these amazing conversations and knowledge sharing, which is what Indigenous peoples have always done before colonialism.

To me, urban Indigenous knowledge, and the ways that urban Indigenous peoples create community and share knowledge, is really important for creating the spaces necessary to do the work of bringing the Eighth Fire to fruition. How else are Indigenous peoples and non-Indigenous peoples going to have conversations? Where else are they going to have those conversations that need to fulfill that prophecy?

§   §   §

Kory Snache worked for First Story Toronto as a bus tour guide when he lived in Toronto. He is Anishinaabe from Rama First Nation. Growing up, he learned traditional hunting and gathering skills and gained experience as an outdoor adventure guide and survival instructor. He completed the Aboriginal Teacher Education Program offered through Queen's University and currently works with Indigenous youth as an outdoor education teacher at Rosseau Lake College in Parry Sound, just north of Toronto.

Kory Snache: The name of my being is Ginew, which means Golden Eagle. My family comes from the Sturgeon Clan of the Ojibwe people. And my family comes from Mnjikaning, place of the fish weirs at Rama First Nation. I moved down to Toronto back in 2010. I was a student at the time at York University and I was majoring in history. I've always been a big history buff, especially around Indigenous history, and especially Anishinaabe history, learning about anything and everything I can. So I heard about First Story just by meeting people in the Indigenous community around Toronto, and it sparked my interest. I've always wanted to give, and I've been leading tours as an outdoor adventure guide, so I already had some of the skill sets to be guide.

EC: What is the biggest misconception about Indigenous people in Toronto?

KS: The biggest misconception is that there are no Indigenous people around Toronto anymore, like they're all gone. That's a large one. Another one is the only Indigenous people in the city are homeless. That's another one I encounter. And another one is, 'How can we claim ownership of the land when we're not visibly around there anymore, or we gave it up in a treaty?' That just goes to the lack of knowledge and understanding of what a treaty is in that relationship. I'd say those three go hand in hand.

EC: What is a significant stop of the tour that you find most interesting or that stood out with people?

KS: The tour stop I liked was St. Lawrence Market, because of the prominent Toronto history there. It started as a trade market originally and was the site of Toronto's first [recorded] murder – the murder of Chief Wabakinine, one of our prominent leaders, which almost led to a war.

For people on the tour, when they learn about Toronto's first murder, it's usually a big realization of how close history is, like right at the doorstep. Right underneath their feet, really. That's typically a big, big discovery for the participants on tours, for sure.

EC: **Last question. How would you like to see the tour evolve?**

KS: I would love to see it more advertised and have more public offerings and have public schools to high schools access the tours. I think starting younger could be even better – looking at ways we could adapt it into curriculum, and have a curriculum package be based on this tour. We can facilitate biking tours as well as walking.

§ § §

I remember Rodney Bobiwash often referenced Ogitchida, an Ojibwe warrior. *Ogitchida* means big-hearted, and its members are those who are brave enough to fight for their people until death or victory. Rodney wasn't afraid of standing up for the right thing, which includes asserting Indigenous rights and presence in the City of Toronto and across Turtle Island.

While few people may have the courage to be trailblazers, Rodney's work with the Toronto Native Community History Project certainly sparked a fire within the hearts and minds of many individuals seeking to learn and share a history silenced by colonization. Hopefully, the fire grows stronger each day. What appears idealistic and altruistic, a lost cause to most, was totally logical to Rodney. 'There is either justice or there isn't,' he said. 'We fight for our survival or we don't survive. We are the canary in the mine. Once Indigenous peoples are gone, the planet is gone.'

MARJORIE BEAUCAGE, THE RUNNER

JASON RYLE, WITH EXCERPTS FROM MARJORIE BEAUCAGE'S MEMOIR

OPENING SCENE

It's summer 2017 in Wanuskewin, and the June breeze gently lifts the aroma of sweetgrass into the air. Marjorie Beaucage stands, speaks, and is heard, as a cinema screen rises on the Saskatchewan prairie. The Runner, as Marjorie came to be known, shares her stories of a journey still in motion, and recalls her years in the big city by the water, far away from home.

THEN: *NEW LOVE: CINEMA*

> *Autumn Equinox: Here I am in Toronto lighting fire, sweetgrass, offering tobacco and blessing four sacred blue corn seeds from New Mexico – to be placed in desert sand and earth. I ask Corn Woman to guide me and fill my dreams and thoughts with creation. I want to make images that embody Light and Vision. I ask these humble little seeds to release their energy so I can learn from them. They are not in their 'natural environment,' far from their homeland. I ask them to guide me and help me grow.*

Tkaronto/Tsi'tkalù:to/Toronto in the late 1980s was decidedly smaller, perhaps more intimate, and not yet celebrated for the cultural diversity it wears broadly in the 2020s. Like today, however, it was Indigenous land and was always home to those from many nations.

Marjorie Beaucage came to call the city home in the autumn of 1987. 'I am at my best when I do not know,' she says. 'When I was younger, I felt I knew everything but that didn't really help me. But if I don't know and have a question, then I go deeper and go into unknown places and find different truths. It feels better to be at not knowing, where you can let the story or moment drive you.'

One of these moments led her to pivot her life to film. In Winnipeg, Marjorie was needing to recharge her batteries after a career working tirelessly and passionately as an adult educator. Burnout loomed as a call to a new kind of activism beckoned. Encouraged by a co-worker to pursue a film degree, she enrolled in Ryerson Polytechnic's film program. 'I was a techno-peasant,' she recalls. 'I knew nothing about film and so didn't think I could. Turned out to be the best thing I did for myself.'

> *Dream: My feet turned upside down – like in the womb – swimming in new waters of life. Get earthbound feet later … Yellow credits and titles rolling up at my waking: Happy New Year.*

> *Ryerson Film School. Industry-oriented. Challenges to my inner strength and vulnerability of spirit at same time … alienation and anger at teachers' threats and warnings. Watching films with world views that are not mine … discovering the wonder of cinema and dancing with Light. Will my technical skills match my 'big ideas'? The camera feels like a foreign object in my hands. A horrible sensation. I am learning.*

Confronting a foreign structure and an industry in opposition to her Métis and Two-Spirit world views taught Marjorie how to fight and, through her struggles, how to feed her soul in the edit suite. Her 'first-born' was *Bingo* (1991), a short social justice documentary – as much her creative milieu as her conviction – that explored the victim mind and the culture of poverty. It screened to great acclaim and represented a shift in how Marjorie felt she was perceived. 'I had a product and I was a filmmaker,' she says. 'I was still me and didn't feel any different, but other people saw me differently.' They saw in her a glimpse of a changing landscape. They saw a glimmer of a different world, where Indigenous voices rise in a chorus of beautiful revolution.

With *Bingo* complete and work on new films underway, Marjorie found a way to express her creativity and activism, and along the way to fill a gaping void in Toronto's media arts community, which was still almost exclusively white. The conversation about ethnicity and diversity was only starting to emerge, and Marjorie was a force who rallied for equitable access to production. Irrevocably at odds with Ryerson's structure,

Marjorie left film school after two years to turn her attention full-time to working within the Indigenous media arts community. Mentoring others was a deliberate and intrinsic part of her practice and mission.

New Moon. Plants sprouted. New growth. Two leaves each. I love the drops of water delicately balanced on translucent new greenery. I feel joy.

INT. NATIVE CANADIAN CENTRE OF TORONTO – DAY

It's now October 2018, and Marjorie Beaucage is honoured with a blanketing at the imagineNATIVE Film + Media Arts Festival, an organization and event that came to life through the seeds she sowed. Over a generation after she left film school to pursue a path in service to her community, her acknowledgement and retrospective at imagineNATIVE was a long-overdue recognition and celebration of her contributions to the Indigenous media arts sector in Toronto and beyond.

'When I look at my work today, I see that it's still relevant and that the issues are still the same,' Marjorie says. 'Land and our struggles have still not been resolved. But now people are more willing to engage with our stories than before. They want to learn more and understand more, which is a good thing.'

At the start of a new decade, despite global challenges, Indigenous screen storytelling remains strong and continues to gain momentum. This reality would not have been possible without those who cleared the path in the decades before the twenty-first century. Marjorie Beaucage, Cat Cayuga, Willie Dunn, Maria Campbell, Gil Cardinal, Loretta Todd, and Alanis Obomsawin are some of the first screen warriors, fighting to regain a space of our own to build a fire, share food, and experience the power of our stories.

THEN: THE ART-IVIST EMERGES

'In the last few years, there has been a movement toward screening our own works and developing our own networks,' Marjorie says. But this reality was not the case in the early 1990s. In addition to the lack of production resources available, she and others working within an Indigenous community-based way found themselves at odds with artist-run centres that did not consider their work to be 'professional' and whose rules alienated Indigenous filmmakers. This scenario was replicated across the country.

In response, Indigenous artists gathered in Edmonton in April 1990 at the National Alliance of Aboriginal Filmmakers Symposium, the first event of its kind that coalesced the growing conviction of what was referred to as 'self-government in art,' or what today we refer to as 'narrative sovereignty.' From this event, the Aboriginal Film and Video Art Alliance was born, a transformative moment in collective Indigenous screen culture, and Marjorie was part of its beating heart.

AFVAA– *Aboriginal Film and Video Art Alliance*

We fought
We screamed
We cried
We prayed
We gathered
We created together
Where are our stories
Our ways
Our faces
Say their names
Those who went before
Those who betrayed our trust
Those who sold out
Those who persevered
Those who sought
Those who continue

'As artists, it is our responsibility to put forward our visions for others to see,' Marjorie says. 'That is the stuff that movements are made of. Self-government in art … to tell our stories our way. By, for, and about us. To rediscover our own structures and paradigms from oral traditions. And develop our own independent resources so we develop on our terms. That was why the Alliance was formed: to remember this energy of creation and restore the place of artists. To create a gathering place, a homeland, where we can remember ourselves.'

The Alliance was truly a revolution in our communities, coming at a time – post the Oka uprising – when Indigenous activism was gaining greater momentum. It acted with immediate intent to impact generations.

It also called for the formation of a Native Film Development Fund, a funding body controlled by Indigenous people to support films made by Indigenous people, and to create film festivals and distribution partnerships to support our films. Thirty years later, the Indigenous Screen Office has become a vital institution that holds the promise to fulfill these long-held goals.

INTERVIEWER: What do you remember most about your time in Toronto back then?

MARJORIE BEAUCAGE: The first few years, I was immersed in the filmmaking process. Then I started to connect more with artists and other Indigenous people, including the youth. We always included youth, like Darlene Naponse and Bear Witness. There weren't many opportunities, so I always mentored somebody, from the time I left film school, so there were more people doing stuff. It was very intentional. It was part of my practice.

INTERVIEWER: It was such a different landscape then. There were so few opportunities to share our stories …

MARJORIE BEAUCAGE: The only Indigenous art form that was really thriving was theatre. There were the artist-run centres for film, but the structures didn't work for us and so we started organizing. We knew we needed to create our own spaces. I love film. I love the whole medium and sharing of life in that way. And I love doing this in a cinema with other people and feeling that energy.

It was 1992, and the world was celebrating the five-hundredth anniversary of the most famous false discovery in settler history. Toronto, too, was getting in on the game. Public funds were offered to commemorate Christopher Columbus, and the Harbourfront Centre provided the opportunity for a truly exceptional event. Marjorie and her contemporaries – through their art and activism – were holding ad hoc screenings of Indigenous films throughout the city and surrounding regions during this time. Marjorie was invited to a meeting at Harbourfront, where the idea of a film festival was discussed. She was on board.

'We didn't really have our own curators and critics at the time and we had to do things by the skin of our teeth,' she says. 'Fortunately, I could put things together. I just wanted people to know what we had and how different and important our work was.'

What emerged in the summer of 1992 was Reel Aboriginal, Toronto's first film festival showcasing Indigenous-made screen stories. It was the ancestor of imagineNATIVE and the starting point of the city's contemporary relationship with Indigenous film and filmmakers. Reel Aboriginal was held over two weekends, with a focus on North America one week and on South America on the second. 'It was amazing,' Marjorie recalls. 'We screened films no one had heard of. It was a gathering, and people sat around and talked about the stories. We had food, and it was a community kind of feeling. It was awesome.'

Shortly after the festival, Marjorie left Toronto.

… what I know about filmmaking

The first mystery is Light …
the visible coming into being
light in time and space
the power of authentication
not re-presentation
with edges to look inside
to look beyond the frame
provoking the fusion of questioning
constructing meaning
to look
to re-discover
to salvage the essence of everything
that overflows the outline
of reality as an imaginative construction
of what remains within
after the film is over …

What is real?
Is it this or that?

LOCATION: SASKATCHEWAN

That summer, Marjorie was called to northern Saskatchewan, to the blockade at Meadow Lake, at the request of the Elders and her long-time friend and collaborator Maria Campbell. With a borrowed camera, she came to document and witness the Protectors of Mother Earth camp's defiance against colonial aggression and abuse. 'There was a feeling of homecoming – tall pines, white birch, gentle moss, soft sand,' Marjorie recalls, but also something else. 'Clear-cut. Mother Earth massacred, ripped open, and spilled out.'

This was the same time Rebecca Belmore was travelling across Canada with her iconic work *Ayum-ee-aawach Oomama-mowan: Speaking to Their Mother*, a giant wooden megaphone created in response to the Mohawk uprising in Oka and in support of the nation's warriors. Marjorie invited Rebecca up to Meadow Lake, and for three days the work overlooked the clear-cut forest. The event is told in Marjorie's 1992 work *Speaking to Their Mother*. 'A lot of her work wasn't documented at the time and I just wanted to give her something,' Marjorie says. 'I pretty much try to be in the moment all the time. The biggest lesson of all is to be present in the moment and not change anything else.

When you see something, you respond and it leads you to where to go. I trust those moments.'

I have been led to the right paths, friends, meaningful work. I have been blessed many times when I trust this flow, depend on the Universe to take care of me. This flow of Grace moving me moving me to the right livelihood, companions, destiny.

Marjorie grew up in Vassar, Manitoba, a Métis village near Buffalo Point – 'the bush was my foundation,' she says – and she now calls Duck Lake, Saskatchewan, home. She remains as active and vital today as during her days in Toronto. 'I'm the Grandmother for the Two-Spirit community in the region,' she says. 'As a Two-Spirit person, it's a gift to stand in the middle – to stand in between – balancing the circle and those energies and making that medicine that the people need. That's what we as Two-Spirit people were supposed to do. I've come to understand that over time.'

Marjorie was chosen by the community of filmmakers centred on the Aboriginal Film and Video Alliance to be a Runner, a cultural ambassador between arts institutions and our communities of artists. For Two-Spirit ambassadors, serving as Runners for important gatherings and negotiations, their gift of diplomacy was a key. 'As tradition has it, the Runners were the ones who went ahead to prepare the place and the people for what was to come,' she says. 'As a Runner, I was always negotiating, making room, or protecting our space so we could create together. My biggest gift is the ability to question, and I question everything. With questioning, I can create spaces for people to raise their own questions and to search for themselves and their answers. I think stories are at the heart of who we are, and they heal us as we share them and open up to each other. They are very powerful.'

NOT THE FINAL ACT

We return to the plains of Wanuskewin, and those gathered to hear Marjorie speak in the summer of 2017. For some, this is the first time they have heard the Runner's journey, a story of resilience, artistry, and commitment to survival. It is now late 2020, and Marjorie's legacy continues to unfold as she takes new steps into a future she helped create.

To Marjorie:
Thank you. For everything that you have done, and all that you will do. Your gifts are cherished. Your stories are medicine.

This work contains excerpts from Marjorie Beaucage's unpublished memoir of her life.

NOW THAT WE KNOW

LILA PINE

When I first accepted a faculty position at the downtown Tkaronto university where I now work, I was unaware of the legacy of the man whose name the institution bears. I didn't know the significance of the statue I pass dozens of times each day. I didn't know that this man, who as Chief Superintendent of Schools for what was then called Upper Canada, advocated free compulsory public day schools for white children only. I didn't know he had a different vision for Indigenous children – a vision that would pave the way for the Indian residential school system.[1] I didn't know he wrote a piece of legislation[2] that resulted in the 'legal' exclusion of Black children from public schools in Ontario and forcing them to attend segregated schools in communities across the province. I didn't know he opposed education for girls beyond the elementary level,[3] his opposition grounded in the belief that a woman's place is in the home. I didn't know he found 'hermaphrodite spawn'[4] a fitting insult to hurl at his enemies, an insult that amplifies the transphobia that settlers brought to the Americas.

In 1847, this man penned a letter that would seal the fate of thousands upon thousands of Indigenous children and their descendants – if they were fortunate enough to survive long enough to have descendants – for years to come. He proposed a method of establishing and conducting industrial schools for the 'benefit of Indian children' that were reminiscent of British workhouses. These schools would not 'contemplate anything more in respect to intellectual training than to give them a plain English education adapted to the working farmer or mechanic.'

They would, he continued, provide training in 'agriculture, kitchen-gardening and mechanics so far as mechanics is connected with making and repairing the most useful agricultural implements.'

To attain this objective, he argued, it would be necessary for the students to live away from their families, with provision being made for their domestic and religious education. As a devout Christian minister of the Methodist Episcopal Church, he was particularly concerned with religious indoctrination for Indigenous children. He insisted the only way to 'civilize' Indigenous children would be to remove them from the influence of their families. In other words, remove them from the influence of their languages, spirituality, ceremonies, culture, and all their relations. He wrote: 'With him nothing can be done to improve and elevate his character and condition without the aid of religious feeling.' He stated as fact that the 'North American Indian cannot be civilized or preserved in a state of civilization except in connection with, if not by the influence of, not only religious instruction and sentiment but of religious feelings.'

Therefore, he reasoned, the running of the schools 'should be a joint effort of the Government and of the Church.' Ultimately, the goal was to use education, particularly religious education, to assimilate Indigenous peoples in order to produce industrious farmers. Instruction would be provided only insofar as it contributed to the making of farmers, and nothing more. No time or money would be spent on any other area – only agriculture. He noted that children should be put to work from eight to twelve hours a day during the summer; only two to four of those hours would be for instruction. In the planting and harvesting periods, instruction should be removed altogether. He was detailed in his recommendations, down to prescribing the daily schedule. He would have the children wake up at 5:00 a.m., work all day, and go to bed after prayers at 8:00 or 9:00 p.m.[5]

This letter of 1847 set the stage for the forced removal of Indigenous children from their 'uncivilized' homes. It set the stage for the horror of residential schools.

You might argue that this man did not intend for any children to be sexually abused by their teachers. You might argue that he did not intend for children to be starved, that he did not intend for them to be used in experiments. You might argue that he did not intend for them to be ripped from their mothers' arms. And you would, no doubt, be right.

You might argue that his intentions were good.

I would argue back to you that his 'good intentions' paved a road directly to a living hell on Earth from which Indigenous people all across Canada have not yet recovered.

You might argue he was a man of his time and that you cannot judge the past by the standards of the present. My argument back to you is that the only way to judge the past is by the present. My argument back to you is to let history be the judge. In my culture, we are taught that our actions must be guided by the impact they will have for the next seven generations. This man's actions do not stand the test of time.

So you might excuse me if I cringe as I walk by his statue. Now that I know.

Colleagues tell me that this man was a friend to Indigenous peoples. His best friend, they say, was Peter Jones (Kahkewaquonaby). He even invited Peter into his home to convalesce. Proof, they say, that he was not a racist.

Let's look a little more closely at this claim. As a child, Peter Jones was raised by his Anishinaabekwe mother in the traditional culture and spiritual beliefs of his people. But when he was fourteen years old, he went to live with his United Empire Loyalist father, from whom he learned the ways and language of the white Christian settlers of Upper Canada. Peter converted to Methodism as a young man and became a preacher, giving the Methodists an inroad into both the Mississaugas of the Credit and the nearby Six Nations of the Grand River communities. He, along with his best friend, was instrumental in leading the conversion of the Mississaugas of the Credit to a European lifestyle of agriculture and Christianity.

It is disingenuous to claim that our institution's namesake was a friend to all Indigenous people based on his friendship with one Indigenous man who converted to Christianity and essentially became white. That he lived among the Mississaugas of the Credit for a number of years, teaching them how to farm, is also held up as proof of his friendship to Indigenous people. His belief that Indigenous people should adopt the 'civilized' values of hard work, as opposed to what he must have considered the 'uncivilized' work of hunting and fishing, is further proof, in their minds, that he was a friend. Everything he did for Indigenous people, they say, was for their own good. He wanted them to survive in a rapidly changing industrial society. His heart, they say, was in the right place.

I am left wondering what kind of friend sees no value in his friends. What kind of friend would force his own religion, education, and language on his friends? This man was no friend to Indigenous people – he couldn't see them. He couldn't see their generosity and lack of greed. He couldn't see their sophisticated governance structures. He learned their language but couldn't hear its beauty, nor understand its knowledge. This man was no friend to Indigenous people because he didn't love them enough to understand them. Like his god, he only wanted to make them over in his own likeness.

So you might excuse me if I choke on his name each time it passes my lips. Now that I know.

He was a friend of Sir John A. Macdonald, a man who openly held Indigenous people in contempt, calling for their starvation and confinement. This friendship calls into question the good intentions we attribute to our namesake.

My colleagues have yet to come up with a justification for his position on segregated schools for Black children. His own justification resulted in institutionalized racism. He claimed that segregated schools were necessary in some jurisdictions because 'the prejudices and feelings of the people are stronger than law.' In the jurisdictions that had segregated schools, Black kids were not allowed to attend white schools. In jurisdictions that had no segregated schools, Black kids had to sit on separate benches. He urged Black taxpayers to sue for the right to attend segregated schools 'for their own good.'[6] It is worth noting that the 1850 Common Schools Act would remain on the books for over one hundred years. In post-Confederation Canada, only Ontario and Nova Scotia had legislated school segregation.

Let's turn for a moment to his position on educating young women. The only thing he had to say about that topic was, don't do it. They belong in the home. Not only did he oppose the education of women beyond the elementary level, he opposed the participation of girls at grammar schools. He ended co-education at the Upper Canada Academy and insisted on the separation of girls and boys in common schools.[7]

You might excuse me if I come to the conclusion that this man, for whom the university in downtown Tkaronto where I work is named, laid the groundwork for anti-Indigenous and anti-Black systemic racism. You might excuse me if I ponder the origin of the intersectional pay inequities that still exist to this day at this institution named after a man who was openly racist, sexist, and transphobic. Now that I know.

The thing about knowing is that once you know, you cannot unknow. And so, you might excuse me for questioning the president of the university (as of 2020) for claiming that equity is in our DNA, while at the same time upholding its name. Now that he knows.

In 2017 my dean asked me, as Director of Saagajiwe, to do something to commemorate Canada 150. Saagajiwe is the Indigenous Research Creation Centre within the Faculty of Communication and Design of the university where I work in downtown Tkaronto.

At first, I was stumped. How *does* one observe 150 years of genocide? I called my friend, and then-Saagajiwe artist-in-residence Billy Merasty. We agreed to meet at Glad Day Bookshop on Church Street in Tkaronto to toss around ideas. There, in the backroom with the pink walls, we discussed what we could do to both respect our dean's request and be true to who we are as Indigenous people. We talked about what Canada means to us. Billy said the only safe place for Indigenous people in Canada is home in community. We thought about what could symbolize home and decided to set up a tipi on campus, but we could not ignore the connection of the university through its name to residential schools.

We decided to bring the children, who died in captivity, home. I spent the next couple of weeks combing through residential school records and archives. Of the more than four thousand names I found, I laser-printed 150 of them (one for each year of confederation) onto cedar planks and hung them inside the tipi. We burned a sacred fire for four days and four nights to honour the children. Each day, twice a day, Billy told stories

Statue dripping in red paint. Image by Lila Pine and Laura Heidenheim.

inside the tipi and NishDish brought soup and bannock for the people who gathered there. On the fourth day, we spoke each name aloud and put it on the fire. NishDish prepared a feast. The ashes were carried to Lake Ontario. We named our installation *Survival through Sovereignty*. Its next phase will be a wall made from the four-thousand-plus names built around the statue. To honour each of the children in turn, we will light an eternal flame and put one name up every four days. The wall, which will take four years or so to build, will, once complete, hide the statue.

Perhaps you will accuse me of cancel culture, of wanting to airbrush this man from history, of falling victim to a trend. Rather than erase him, I would like to see him take his rightful place in history. I want to acknowledge the impact his actions had on the children of future generations. I want to tell you how it makes me *feel* in my mind, spirit, and body to walk through the halls of a place that bears his name and to pass by the statue that bears his likeness.

I am not the only one. Many of my Indigenous and Black colleagues will tell you the same. Black and Indigenous students are already telling you how they feel as they rise up and throw red paint on the statue – paint that, to them, symbolizes the blood of the children who went to residential schools. The statue that, to them, symbolizes violence on *their* bodies. I know of one Annishnaabeg student in the School of Journalism who left the university simply because he could no longer bear to walk by that statue. Once he knew.

Now that we know, I want us to choose a different name for this university in downtown Tkaronto. I want us to choose a name that celebrates Indigenous and Black cultures. I want us to choose a name that honours women and trans folk. A name that speaks to diversity and inclusion in all its complexity. A name that reflects the values of the Indigenous peoples of this land before settlers arrived – values that were woke before woke was a thing. I want us to choose a name that will stand the test of time. A name that has the courage to let history be its judge.

Postscript: In the wake of revelations about unmarked graves of Indigenous children who died in residential schools, the statue of the man for whom the downtown Tkaronto university is named was brought down. Calls to rename the institution, initiated by Indigenous faculty and others, have intensified and gained widespread support. The administration announced the statue would not be replaced but remains, as of July 2021, noncommittal about the name.

NO THRILLS AND BOUGIE BANNOCK

SARENA JOHNSON

Toronto has an invisible east-west barrier at Yonge Street. Downtown people might be immune to this, but east enders become immobilized at the suggestion of crossing it while west enders laugh at the thought of going east for pretty much anything. It doesn't get much more east ender than being born at the Toronto East General Hospital and growing up in Scarborough, so I'm an east ender. In particular, I lived around Kennedy and Eglinton until I moved out to attend college.

My default grocery store throughout that time was the No Frills at Kennedy and Eglinton, also known as Rob's No Frills. When I was little, I called it 'No Thrills.' But that yellow-and-black sign comprised what I knew of groceries and where food came from. Occasionally, I'd be taken to different grocery stores and notice how clean and fancy they seemed. No grimy yellow turnstiles upon entering. No mountain of used boxes by the door. You didn't have to scrounge for a quarter to get a cart; they just let you take a cart if you wanted one. What freedom. Their produce sections gleamed with robust, exotic offerings. Some of them even gave out free snacks.

Not to complain. I'm fortunate to have had all those trips to the grocery store – unlike so many children, especially Indigenous and other marginalized kids who experience food insecurity as a result of systemic inequities. Despite being one of three daughters of a single mother, I've always had access to food. At our place, and also at my grandma's – the command centre of the family – a short Grandpa taxi away at Warden and Eglinton. There were always kids there, family coming and going. Christmases and other holidays were jam-packed with laughter, aunts, uncles, parents, often a dog or two, cousins running around screaming, playing in the field out back. And always tons of food.

I don't remember the first time I ate bannock but I remember it being around whenever I went to visit either grandmother. The Plains Cree Métis one, who was never far away, or the Lenni Lenape and Caldwell First Nations one whom we had to take long rides on the 401 to visit. Those trips were always such a cause for celebration. Indian tacos, fry bread with corn soup or stew, having a piece of baked bannock with 'butter' before everyone woke up and real breakfast happened. Bannock left out on the table for a snack whenever, perhaps to entice us kids to the table, which was used for visiting, as opposed to just meals. There was no inappropriate time to eat bannock. It was comforting.

Until it wasn't. Bannock had been a treat I learned to make myself before this relationship changed, and I had to make it. During thankfully brief phases of my life, it was the cheapest and most filling food I could assemble. I'd pack a few pieces for a long day at work or school. Times when I'd count pennies for TTC fare and put them into no-name zip-lock bags that never really closed right. I would adjust my timing past the fare booth for when other people weren't around to see me empty out the bag. Bannock was there in good times and bad.

I realized that working at health food stores was a thing I could do for a paycheque and to minimize hunger. I began to develop a basic understanding of key components of nutrition and holistic health, or at least what supplements I might be needing when I couldn't afford the food there. I worked at several, and a couple naturopathic offices. Gradually, hippies and naturopaths helped me learn what was going on nutritionally and make the connection between my diet and mental health – something of an ongoing process.

Apparently, I'm allergic to wheat. Not celiac – I don't get physically sick (yet) – but when I eat wheat or sugar, my anxiety becomes crippling. I get all hyper and it's fun for a bit, but then my heart starts racing. I become shaky and it all spirals. I get 'hangry' and panic at the thought of even being hungry. I get vertigo, have a hard time sleeping, and then I become depressed. Eating 'normal' food was making me hungry and anxious all the time. Once this pattern became clear, bannock was no longer my friend.

Bannock was never really a friend, though. It was born of starvation staples issued to First Nations people by government Indian agents. It was made from a recipe of commodities used to keep our ancestors barely alive while they were forced into concentration camps – the reservation system – so our land could be stolen. Its legacy became synonymous with poverty and sicknesses like diabetes. A comfort food that was the opposite of our culture. For me in particular, it caused or contributed to inflammation, anxiety, depression, acne, fatigue, poor gut health – including poor absorption of nutrients – and even a thyroid disorder.

Wheat has become a huge part of our diets – the standard Western diet. It's in pretty much everything. When I share that I don't eat wheat, people are often baffled. 'If you don't eat that, what *do* you eat?' I used to be such a bread person, and I never thought I could give it up. The funny thing is that when you do, the cravings go away. Now it's more about just finding food I can eat. It's a definite challenge when travelling or trying to eat at restaurants. And it's not cheap. I never would have been able to eat this way as a youth. It can also feel isolating or anti-social to watch people eat pizza or Indian tacos and not be able to have any. These are team foods and staples at events.

I miss the social aspect of bannock, and the ritual of mutual gorging. The shared delight in digging in, bingeing, and then sitting in a mutual bannock-induced coma. With gluten-free and keto foods becoming normalized, more and more folks are realizing their bodies don't do well with wheat. More options – at least gluten-free options – are becoming available. Hopefully, one day in my lifetime, I'll be able to eat an Indian taco I can digest at a powwow.

Bannock brings back so many good memories and a feeling of comfort. Which is why I've recently begun making it a part of my life again, albeit in a very different way. While I live alone during the COVID-19 pandemic, this bannock preparation and consumption is solely for me. Yet that's not the biggest change about this ritual. The biggest change is probably that my bannock's ingredients are so far from the standard that it's almost unrecognizable.

In 2019 I moved to Rosedale (still east side!). I love being downtown and able to walk to work (when there was a physical office to walk to). The thing about Rosedale is it's basically a two-tier society. You have these ridiculous mansions and folks cruising around in Lamborghinis. Then you have tents. Everywhere. Not just in the actual valley (where one of my family members lived for a while), but also popping up in parkettes and random little spots all over the area. COVID-19 really is busting the seams of the middle-class dream, and I've got a front-row seat.

Whole Wigwam by Sarena Johnson, Severn Creek Park.

My grocery situation has become a microcosm of this world. One block east of my home is a 'No Thrills.' One block west is a 'Whole Paycheque.' In the first six months of living in Rosedale, I unconsciously avoided No Frills. There are reasons. I can't bear to buy factory-farmed meat or non-organic, Monsanto vegetables. But ethical consumption comes with a cost. Poor folks can't afford to be ethical. Medium folks like me have a choice, and I prioritize ethical consumption over other things – like, I don't know, the hopes of ever having a mortgage in Toronto. (But it's not really ethical consumption if your money's going to Jeff Bezos, is it?) Being downtown, my options are good. But despite the amount of choice, even smack dab in the middle of Toronto, there are still limits to the balance between ethics, health, and cost.

These days, my bannock starts with me walking to Whole Foods. I go to the Yorkville[1] one since it's the closest. Apparently Toronto has turned me into a 'Bougie Native.' So bougie bannock circa 2020 consists of Bob's Red Mill Paleo Baking Flour. This is a mix of almond flour, arrowroot starch, coconut flour, and tapioca starch. (I've experimented with combinations of flours, but the premix has a better consistency.) I add a few free-range organic eggs, some organic 35 per cent whipping cream, a pinch of Himalayan or Celtic salt, and a sprinkle of non-aluminum baking

Whole Wigwam by Sarena Johnson. No more stolen sisters mask by @samnotsamantha (Sam Howden).

powder. Then I fry it in organic virgin coconut oil. When it's done, I smear the bannock with grass-fed butter. I haven't tried baking yet since it can already be crumbly when fried, a common issue with gluten-free baking since gluten acts like glue, and the ingredients are so expensive that I don't want to waste a single crumb. Pro tip: the crumbs are amazing on salad!

The low price point has become a pain point. For me, bannock's gone from a staple to a privilege. But I'm grateful to have started to learn about the best foods for my body and I'm excited to keep learning about how these choices relate to wellness. This isn't Indian Act bannock. It's gone from a starvation food to a luxury, but it still provides me with the comfort and memories of those previous iterations.

I feel like my ancestors would be happy that I have the opportunity to eat this well and I like to think it feeds them, too. Writing this essay launched a conversation about traditional corn-and-bean meal bread and food politics, as well as the Lunaape white-corn wheel bread recipes in my family. There are lots of things to experiment with as I keep striving for bread that I can eat and hopefully share sometime soon.

THE NISHDISH JOURNEY

JOHL WHITEDUCK RINGUETTE

NishDish began as a catering business in 2005 and opened a storefront restaurant in 2017. Due to the 2020 coronavirus pandemic, NishDish is in transition to become a marketeria, while expanding its catering services. The NishDish GoFundMe campaign is accessible at www.gofundme.com/f/nishdish-marketeria-amp-catering.

I was born several kilometres north of North Bay. My mother, Molly Whiteduck, on her maternal side is from Nipissing First Nation. My father is a hunter, trapper, and fisher who also ran his own business, Ringuette's Well Drilling for water.

I have five siblings. My mom liked taking us out to berry picks and maple tapping and was a resourceful cook. My older brother taught me to trap and clean rabbits. But there was no time when my family discussed 'traditional food.' These were just things we did in our everyday life.

My mother knew she was Ojibwe because her mother's relatives came from Nipissing. But that story evolves later, because we find out that my mother's father, Lawrence Whiteduck, who was killed in World War II, is Algonquin, and his mother's people came from Gitigan Zibi originally. In the 1880s, a group of Whiteducks left there and went to the Golden Lake area and some later moved to North Bay.

So the Whiteduck family, they're all Algonquin people. We didn't even actually understand this until I was an adult. My mother always knew we were Ojibwe, but the realization that she was also Algonquin came later and that both Nations are Anishnawbe. We share the same dialect, but to know the different nations and where you come from is very important.

We knew that our great-grandmother was dislocated from Nipissing reserve due to government policy. Her name was Catherine Couchie. I knew her from when I was a child until she passed. She married a Native man, but he didn't have status because he was an orphan. All women during that period who didn't marry status Native men were asked to leave the reserve due to government policy. In 1985, the government passed new legislation, Bill C-31, to allow Native women to apply to get their Native status back or rightfully returned.

These policies changed the journey so many of us Native people faced without our mothers' and their mothers' connection to their home communities. So my mother's mother didn't get raised on the reserve – they lived just outside of it. We had to leave North Bay due to family turmoil and moved to Southern Ontario. In 1986, I followed my sisters to Toronto, when I was seventeen and had finished Grade 13.

I tried to find my way around, coming from a remote part of the world to a very large metropolis. In one sense, it's so incredible and amazing and diverse! But in another, it's completely overwhelming. Where do I find a foothold in this giant city? Where is our Native community?

During my childhood, my dad had two separate hunt camps. One was our family's, which he built on his own. The other was built by a group of his relatives. On weekends, we were constantly travelling to these camps. We would cook at the hunt camps, outside. In the winter, we would be indoors. He also taught us to ice-fish, which is super difficult. I feel like that was my first introduction to food and becoming interested in food preparation and creating food. In a sense, it's one childhood memory that's really wonderful and majestic. It was also my first introduction to fire and learning how to respect the fire.

I got my first cooking job when I was fifteen, in a hotel in North Bay, through my aunt. I started taking different roles in the food industry. Once I moved permanently to Toronto, I became a cater-waiter and began doing more food prep for various catering companies. I navigated in and out the food industry from age fifteen, with several years in the film industry, pursuing a career in filmmaking, right up until I got work in social services in 2000.

In terms of finding the Indigenous community, it took about ten years before I discovered there's a series of social services and community networks like the Native Canadian Centre of Toronto, and this fantastic agency I didn't know anything about called Anishnawbe Health Toronto.

At AHT, I met a traditional teacher, and this was all new to me. No one had ever talked to me about the significance of smudging or showed me how to practise it. I discovered why you smudge with the medicines and what the plants are for. I got access to a traditional teacher who's an Elder in our community to this day. Her name is Wanda Whitebird, and pretty much anyone who's been here for some time knows exactly who Wanda is, because she's touched so many of our lives. She's introduced so many of us to the culture and has given us this great start into finding and reclaiming our identity as Indigenous people.

Wanda's role was to prepare you for anything else you wanted to discover in the culture: what your clan is, what your spirit colours are, what your spirit name is, the purpose of smudging. All this I learned through Wanda.

I got to a point on my journey with Wanda when she said, 'Johl, you're asking all the right questions. Now you need to meet a medicine person.' And she introduced me to Mark Thompson, who became my teacher for many years.

Mark was an incredibly gifted medicine person. When he was required to offer his healing here in Toronto, he would arrange to haul loads all the way from Winnipeg because he was a truck driver. This enabled him to bring his services as medicine man to AHT. Mark is the person I worked with right up until he passed in 2009.

It was Mark who told me I was going to open NishDish and that food was my true gift. I could help bring back the traditional Anishnawbe diet, and this would become one of the ways for our people to heal and to reclaim and restore the circle we have always followed. In the circle of the community, everyone's welcome and we all have gifts to provide, and we learn our roles and responsibilities. Mark gave me my clan, my colours, and my spirit name, which is Paupau Bizhiw, Spotted Lynx. Ahneen, kwe kwe! Ndizhinikaaz Paupau Bizhiw! Dodem zhaangweshi! That's a traditional introduction that all of us do in our way.

I worked at Aboriginal Legal Services of Toronto for the better part of a decade. A lot of that time was spent in Gladue Court, a specialty court at Old City Hall. Gladue Court is an Aboriginal peoples' court. When you get there, you've got to plead and they connect you with Aboriginal Legal Services or other Aboriginal social services to help you on your journey to hopefully not wind up back in custody.

The work I did for many years was to put together what's called the Gladue Aftercare plan. I would bring it to the courts, and they'd review it with the help of duty counsel and the Crown, and come up with an agreement to allow people to start working on this crucial aftercare plan for healing from the impact of the intergenerational trauma of the residential school legacy. That work is what really formed my identity within the Indigenous community, because I had to go to all the Indigenous agencies and get to know their services and their workers in order to advocate for the clients, who are so vulnerable and really in need of assistance within a complex system.

I needed a lot of spiritual guidance from Mark Thompson to deal with the unspeakable history and treatment of Indigenous people. Unspeakable not just because it's so awful and so gruesome, but also because we need words and spiritual help to deal with it all. At this time Mark tells me I have another gift — to bring back Anishnawbe food. I followed his instructions and registered the catering business in May 2005. He said it would be a real struggle to find the food and start the process, but one day soon I'd be very successful. That was the beginning of finding out that I'm going to be on this journey for the rest of my life: Indigenous food sovereignty.

In 2005, you couldn't find wild game anywhere. There was one provider located in Mississauga and he didn't do deliveries. There was another provider, a farm called Universal Game that doesn't exist anymore. They were in Coldwater, northwest of Orillia. There was a lot of driving out to Coldwater to pick up game meat for different catering gigs. It's on this journey that I found out I'll never be able to use wild game until we can change the government policy prohibiting it from being served to the public. A whole bunch of other things come with that, like trying to find wild rice. It's almost impossible to find a large-volume source of Indigenous wild rice. I can find mechanically produced or separated wild rice, but getting our traditional Indigenous rice from our people – that's hard.

Fifteen years later, I've found one producer in Canada, and he's six hours north of Winnipeg. To be clear, there is wild rice locally, but there isn't enough. NishDish just goes through tons of it, and I need to purchase it regularly. If I took it from the nearby communities I know are growing it, there wouldn't be anything left for them.

From the Anishinawbe creation story, and one of the reasons we got here, we know that Nanabozho led us to the wild-rice waters during a time of starvation. We began to follow those paths of wild rice, which is one of the reasons we're known as the wild-rice people. That brings you to the larger and more in-depth understanding that our people have to take care of the water because the rice can't exist without the water. It's one of the reasons the water ceremony is so vital.

All these things I learned through food, and they keep bringing me back to teachings I had to discover through knowledge keepers, about how we are going to get a sustainable system and reclaim our food. Most people aren't aware of what Indigenous food systems are, because basically that knowledge was wiped out.

A lot of Canadians aren't even aware that Indigenous people weren't allowed to have gatherings of more than two people at a time. The ceremonies were all outlawed and, of course, the government was slowly trying to destroy the language through the residential school system. When you're looking at all this, you realize that language is connected to everything. I still don't know my language to this day.

We're trying to create language programs through the Toronto District School Board. Their Urban Indigenous Education Centre is supporting all the Indigenous place-making. Several collectives have formed out of NishDish, because it's such a great community gathering place.

We were trying to revitalize this former group that had been looking to create an Indigenous district many years ago, when, on September 23, 2013, I got hit by a TTC bus on my bicycle. That completely changed the path I was on. I wasn't even in the lane of the bus that came over and sideswiped me. Now, it seems like this accident is not an important part of the project, but it's actually a key part. I lost a great deal of my health and mobility. I couldn't operate the business, so I had to call on friends, family, and community to help me hang on to it.

A couple of groups of people stepped up to assist me in my healing process. I began a lawsuit against the TTC, which I'm still in, seven years later. If it wasn't for the dedication of our community, and people like family and friends, but also the knowledge keepers, there just wouldn't be any way to say that NishDish would have carried on. I could not have continued the path I was on without the assistance of Elders Diane Longboat and Cindy White, who were working at CAMH, where we used to bring food.

Grandma Pauline Shirt and Troy Greene were such important Elders in giving me their healing, too. My son had to move home to assist me when I was super-immobile. It was a real struggle. I had already been looking for a storefront space before I got hit, but then I couldn't carry

Medicine for the People (Red Urban Nation Artists Collective, Bickford Centre).

on physically and I couldn't carry on financially. Not being able to work devastated me, and, to this day, I've still not recovered physically.

I had to connect with a friend of mine to co-sign the lease for the new place (at Bloor and Clinton), because at that point I'd lost all my financial privileges. And that's how I got NishDish opened.

We launched NishDish at the end of April 2017. When we kicked open the doors, there were some eight hundred people standing outside. We had twenty seats if you really crammed in. We couldn't fit everyone into the restaurant, so we had all these people to feed. It was an incredible time, just seeing all these people who'd come to participate in celebrating our grand opening.

The CBC came down to cover it and they told us we were breaking restaurant history as the largest grand opening they had ever covered in Toronto. It was mind-blowing to have so many people there. I remember trying to speak in the microphone and feeling overwhelmed, grateful, and just so excited.

I didn't quite grasp the reality of the work we were doing and what its impact was. In the last few years, I've been asked to do a number of things, including co-hosting a special episode of *Master Chef Canada*. I got asked to help put together an Indigenous chef table of my peers. This was an incredible honour for me, to represent my people and our traditional food to a million and a half viewers. The episode was called 'Gifts from the Earth,' which featured our Indigenous white corn. It was such an exciting time to talk about the 'three sisters,' agro-ecology, and how planting them revitalized the soil. Those were the practices of the Indigenous people – that you take care of the land. It's a reciprocal relationship – one that got altered when settlers came here and brought monoculture. Now, all these years later, we see the outcome.

It was through this gathering place at NishDish that we focused on the green corridor, which lies above an ancestral tributary currently called Garrison Creek. It's one of the lost rivers we used to connect to Lake Ontario and do all our trading. The city developed overtop of it.

There's a series of projects that came out of NishDish, because we now have this little educational hub to gather at and start saying, 'Here's the space to create and curate art and exhibitions.' We had a number of Indigenous artists exhibit their work on the walls of NishDish during the three years we were open, until COVID came and temporarily closed us down.

Food security is a huge part of the work, based on the fact that the food isn't anywhere to be found. NishDish is not like any other restaurant. People have to understand that the food we made was the original diet of the original people on the land, and these food lines no longer exist, so they have to be completely restored. For example, this means replanting wild-rice beds on local lakes, which takes many years; replanting and revitalizing the pawpaw tree, our Indigenous fruit tree; replanting and learning how to grow the three sisters locally; and so many others. What is the process for getting all this food? We don't just talk about how you grow corn according to Indigenous agro-ecology and how that's done through ceremony – we have to relearn and recreate the food lines completely. That's probably the most important part.

Mark Thompson gave me some guiding principles to work with at NishDish, and we do our best to maintain those principles to this day. One of them was to smudge the food, work with the medicines, and create spirit plates that have to go on the land, just as we would for any ceremony or feast.

Yes, it's a little restaurant, trying to get everybody – Indigenous people and non-Indigenous people – to turn our consciousness to our relationship to food, our relationship to land, our relationship to plants, and what it takes to have an understanding of that balance.

NishDish is a lot more than a restaurant. We could never do one-off orders, like takeout, because there's no way to make that financially feasible. All of our money to support the restaurant is done through large-order catering. That was the way to keep NishDish thriving. We had many, many clients before we opened the restaurant, and the restaurant helped quadruple our catering.

In terms of igniting the consciousness of Indigenous food sovereignty, that's the work NishDish is trying to do. We have four local gardens that were created out of NishDish. I founded a not-for-profit called Ojibiikaan. Its offices are out of CSI Annex, and there are currently five staff who teach little ones about the land through the Little Roots program, Ojiibikens.

With all this diversity so many people are obsessed with, and all the different types of food we have access to, a lot of people want to know why the heck there aren't any Indigenous restaurants. Why isn't this a real thing? Why is there no Indigenous district? How come nobody's doing this?

You've got to go right back into history and talk about the really hard things, about the policies put into place to actually starve Indigenous people to death. That was openly discussed by our first forefather, Prime Minister John A. Macdonald. He made the promise that they're doing everything in their power to starve those Indians out. That was discussed openly in Parliament.

They did it by holding back the rations they had promised after they forced so many nations into reserves and then outlawed hunting, trapping, fishing, and getting food from the land in our traditional way.

When people starved, the government said, 'Look, we've got these rations for you – flour, sugar, salt, and lard.' When you start looking at that, you realize the impact and how that impact still exists. In a very large way, the impact hasn't gone away. The Indigenous food isn't here for all kinds of reasons. When people want to talk about food, they don't necessarily want to talk about the horror stories of food, but this is part of our history. As many nations, we have a role in reclaiming that food and getting the current government to understand its role. Part of that is through the Truth and Reconciliation Commission.

The journey we have as a little restaurant is much larger than just trying to get the food on a plate. We're trying to educate people about the history. We're trying to educate our own people. We're trying to unlock where the food went to, why it was taken, and how we are going to get it back. And there's a lot of healing to be done, because the ceremonies were erased, and ceremony is always the key to anything we're doing in our community. The spirit plates I talked about earlier, they are a specific reference to how important food is to our community. By thinking through the symbolism of these plates, we're reconnecting with our ancestors and feeding those spirits to honour them.

There are a lot of different pieces, but they're all part of what we're talking about in terms of reclaiming Indigenous identity through Indigenous food sovereignty and understanding lost knowledge through language.

One of the foods we talk about is bannock – it's a big one. All of our community loves bannock. There's nothing better than the smell of bannock, which is something NishDish loves to serve. But the history of bannock is really tough and hard to learn. The first thing I start with is that wheat wasn't ever a plant that was here. So it's a new introduction to our diets; it wasn't something we were digesting for thousands and thousands of years. This plant was brought here in the 1880s.

We now try to serve bannock that is gluten-free, which makes it four times as expensive to serve. Indigenous people cannot digest wheat – it causes havoc with our gut flora and creates all kinds of ailments.

Elder Grandma Pauline Shirt Blessing the Water in Ceremony.

Government policy eradicated millions and millions of buffalo to clear out Indigenous people and get rid of their way of life on the Plains. The buffalo once even travelled as far east as Ontario. Once the herds were destroyed from the Plains, the settlers were able to take it over for farmland and introduce their monoculture, especially wheat.

We've started realizing the significance of the medicine from the trees, and how important it is to access game meat because the protein strains are much higher. The meat is way leaner than all of the other red meats we have access to, like beef or pork, and so it's cooked differently. A lot of the recipes we've picked up come from different community members who remember how the food was done. We study them just like we were taught to study our clan. What did the buffalo eat and what did it provide? What was its relationship to our people? We do a bunch of different things to create dishes with deer or elk, which I really love. But elk is also very expensive and very hard to access, and, of course, farmed.

We have a contingency plan for the future of NishDish that you've probably seen as a GoFundMe campaign to reopen NishDish as a First Nations marketeria and then expand all of our food lines so you can take them home and just recreate them yourself. For example, we marinate the game in vinaigrette, like balsamic or olive oil, although those aren't Indigenous. We did similar things in the past, but those vinegars aren't available to us. One of my goals is to try and recreate the Indigenous vinegar we used to use. That's a whole journey on its own.

Harvesting wild rice takes an incredible amount of time, and the process is beautiful. The thing NishDish constantly talks about is ceremony. We're reclaiming the ceremonial knowledge of food and sharing that with our community. It was always such a joy at NishDish that many different community members would come in and say, 'Hey, I know how to say this word.' And, 'Hey, that Anishinaabemowin on the board isn't quite correct. You should really be trying to say it this way.' It really became an interactive learning process for all of us, and just such an exciting time. I really hope that all the different projects we birthed out of NishDish will sustain themselves in the community and continue to grow and gather our community.

In the Mink clan, my clan (which is part of Marten clan), in a contemporary society, our Elder Jim Dumont teaches that the role is to be an economic developer. My role is to help develop our economy, and I'm doing that with my life's work. We want to strengthen the food lines, make wild rice accessible again, and bring back pawpaw trees, which used to be here by the millions. There are a handful left in the city, and now we're regrowing them to revitalize that species and help our diets and feed all the pollinators.

These projects that help our environment and the ecology we depend upon at the same time create opportunities for work in our communities. Everyone's welcome to learn these practices. Even in the face of COVID, this programming is still going on and we're still engaging the public and helping people connect and renew or recreate their relationship with the earth and the plants. Every person has a gift to share and a responsibility to participate in the sustainability of their community, and as each person joins the circle, we actively make a healthier place for all the children who are here now to do the same for generations to come.

Gathering Place Trail, Gathering Structure, Humber College, Toronto.
Architect: Indigenous Design Studio at Brook McIlroy Inc. Artist: David Thomas.

JIM DUMONT ONAUBINISAY
(WALKS ABOVE THE GROUND) ON
IDENTITY AND SPIRITUALITY IN THE CITY

ERICA COMMANDA AND REBEKA TABOBONDUNG

As Chief of the Eastern Doorway of the Three Fires Midewiwin Lodge, what inspired you to dedicate your life to learning about, practising, and sharing the traditional philosophies and spiritual beliefs of the Anishinaabe?

I didn't grow up with these things – with the teachings, the culture, and the language. When I moved to Toronto, it was to continue school. I went to work on my master's degree in 1967. At that time, there was no visible change happening, at least that most people could see. There was a sense of wanting to know what our ways were. At that time, *Indian* was the word. We were searching for what being Indian meant and I became part of that movement, that questioning and searching.

There were little pockets everywhere of this growing sense of urgency to get to know who we were. We called it searching for your Indian identities. I let my hair grow long and began to pursue that. At the time, I was looking for a place in the world where I could be with Native people. In school, once I went past Grade 10, there weren't many Native people. My life experience was filled with the erasure of Native people from my daily life and struggling to fit into the white world.

I volunteered at the Indian Friendship Centre that was on Beverley Street at the time. It was my way of being in contact with Native people. I planned and invited young Native people to go on a bus trip across the country, to visit various reserves and events. I did that for two summers in a row. After I got out of school and graduated, I became a Native youth worker at the Centre and started a newspaper called the Toronto *Native Times*. There was an office and a program dedicated to Native youth.

The first bus trip across the country was in 1969. After visiting a number of Indian reserves, we arrived at the Crow Agency, Montana, where the first Indian Ecumenical Conference was being held. There I learned through Ernest Tootoosis about a movement that was led by Chief Robert Smallboy.

That's where I got my start. I smoked a pipe for the first time. I went into a sweat lodge for the first time. I did those things I was seeking to do. The Elder, Joe Mackinaw, gave me his pipe and told me to take it home with me and look for teachings amongst my people. 'We're Cree and you are Ojibwe. You say you want to find your identity, you want to find yourself. You have to do that amongst your own people,' he told me. I came home after that.

I stayed in Toronto for a couple more years. After that, I found my way into Ojibway ceremonies for the first time. These ceremonies were held in 1974 in Irons, Michigan. It was there where I heard the Ojibway prophecies for the first time. I was following the prophecy that one day young people would be searching for their original Anishinaabe way of life. They would begin to ask questions and travel all over, searching for what was left behind somewhere along the trail. Based on that prophecy, I found my way into the whole ceremonial involvement. It was what I had been looking for all my young adult life.

I had never heard of our own creation story. But when I did, I heard the story of my life, the kind of person that I was as Anishinaabe. I never heard anything about our history, the great migration of our people, and about what it meant to Anishinaabe identity and our sacred ways. I had never heard a story that was about me.

Where did you grow up and how did you end up living and working in Toronto?

I grew up in Shawanaga First Nation [north of Parry Sound]. Not on the reserve – my mom married out. We grew up just across the river, on the western/northern boundary, until I was nineteen years old. When I went to university in Sudbury, it was my first time away from home. Then I went to Toronto to pursue a Master's of Divinity degree.

My whole identity was wrapped up in this search and I became part of the prophecies. The Prophecy of the Seventh Fire, a prophecy about the time that we are in now – that young people would wake up and begin to ask questions, travel all over searching, and they would be looking for something. Maybe not even something they could clearly define, but they were looking for what was left, scattered along the trail. That's what it says in the prophecy. Things like our language, culture, stories, arts, music, and our creation story.

After I left Toronto, I lived in Wikwemikong for three years. There were fewer people on the reserve searching for these things than there were in the city. In cities, you became more conscious of what you had lost and what was missing. On the reserve, there seemed to be a complacency or a resistance to thinking outside the box. When I was in Wikwemikong, I stood out like a sore thumb. But at the same time, some young people were interested in what I was talking about.

What was your involvement with the development of Anishinaabeyaadiziwin Miikana, the installation at the Barrett Centre for Technology Innovation at Humber North Campus, which represents the Seven Fires of Creation that correlate with the Seven Stages of Life, as told within the story of the Anishinaabe Life Path? (see page 272)

I'll answer that in terms of my involvement. The details of that installation and the work behind it has to be credited to Shelley Charles, who was the Elder at the time at Humber College. She was more than an Elder who would open meetings and prayers – she was a counsellor for Native students. She made her job mean something more. As a result of her involvement there, establishing Indigenous knowledge programming and building centres, she made the Indigenous presence more known in the college. It was her work that started all those things. She became involved in architecture to design an installation at multiple levels, including students, designers, staff, and Elders. The installation and the details of how that was done and came to be would best be directly from her.

My involvement was to provide the Indigenous knowledge background for the installation, which informed the design elements; the seven teachings, the seven grandfather principles, the seven stages of life, seven major clans of the Anishinaabe, the seven stopping places of the migration from Wabanaking to Lake Superior, and the seven prophecies talk about the history of our people.

The installation is a significant achievement in not only highlighting Indigenous teachings but creating a unique learning opportunity to share

Indigenous knowledge and culture in a contemporary educational environment. Unfortunately, there isn't anybody at Humber College now who knows the whole background, the process, the teachings and Indigenous knowledge that all of the installations are talking about. The staff are not equipped to explain and make the utmost use of it. It's something I think needs to be said.

Why is it important that the Indigenous and non-Indigenous students have an understanding of the knowledge and teachings embedded in the installation?

The installation helped to provide an opportunity to share our collective history and teachings informed from an Indigenous voice.

It is important to understand the historical times that Indigenous people have come through; the sixties and seventies ushered in an era of challenging the status quo and finding our voice, challenging the way Native people were treated and the colonization of people in the world. In the United States, they had Wounded Knee and the American Indian Movement. In Canada, we had the Red Power movement.

This was the era during which Native Studies programs were created in schools and universities. Native Studies began in Canada at Trent University in Peterborough. The next one was created at the University of Sudbury.

When I helped create the Native Studies program at the University of Sudbury, I tried to get a message out to other efforts in Native Studies that we had to build it and design it from a place of Indigenous knowledge and Indigenous knowing. We had to do Native Studies from a place inside the culture. Up to that time, everything was done from outside the culture. Anthropologists, historians, and everybody who became involved in talking about Native people were doing it from outside the culture. They were on the outside looking into Native communities through an anthropological lens. They would then write up something about it and get credited for it.

I was continually advocating and making a place for Indigenous knowledge, culture, and creative expression in the institutes of higher education and learning. It was always my insistence that we do this from a place that was centred in our own culture, our own history, our own ways of life. When I created various programs of study in universities and colleges (and later in Indigenous institutes of learning) and developed a curriculum for them, I put together a core program of study based in the Indigenous world view, history, philosophy, psychology, and our way of life – our family, our community, culture, and spirituality. It is especially important that those who teach about Indigenous culture, tradition, and world view be Indigenous people – knowledge holders and Elders with a solid foundation in the teachings, along with vast experiential learning and practice.

For Indigenous students, it was an opportunity to learn about the Indigenous way of life, the Indigenous foundations of learning, and the distinct history and contributions of the people. For non-Indigenous students, it was an awakening to the fact that while we live in a world with hundreds of years of oppression of Indigenous people, their culture, and their way of life, there are unique values, ways of seeing the world and its interconnectedness to the wholeness of creation.

We need an Indigenous foundation for everything we do. We need to be knowledgeable about the Indigenous spirit, culture, and spiritual ways. As for non-Indigenous students, tomorrow they are going to be future political leaders who may influence change in Canada, so their involvement and inclusion at this time of learning is significant. The prophecy says, 'For us as Indigenous people, we have to find our way back to our original way of life.' For non-Indigenous people, they have to find the spiritual path that is in harmony with the Earth and the natural world.

Why is Toronto important to Indigenous people? What is an Anishinaabe understanding of the significance of Toronto?

Toronto in its earliest use was applied to Lake Simcoe, not Lake Ontario. For Anishinaabe people, it was the centre of activity, a place on higher ground. There was a spiritual meeting place for the people, which is what Spadina Road means – Ishpadinaa. It's the higher ground, the high hill.

Historically, it was an important place of connection between the Upper Great Lakes and the Lower Great Lakes. The portage trail goes from the mouth of the Humber River to the Lake Simcoe area. Lake Simcoe provided access to Central Georgian Bay, which is the access to the Upper Great Lakes. It was a well-travelled route, still significant today. Toronto was a significant meeting place for people of different cultures. Today it's a central meeting place for all kinds of Indigenous activity.

Over the years, what are the biggest changes you've seen within the Indigenous community of Toronto and what are your hopes for the future generations?

I haven't been to Toronto very much in the last number of years, so I can't speak with authority on all the goings-on in Toronto. One of the greatest changes I see is the sense of community, meaning there isn't one 'place' in Toronto. The Friendship Centre, which became the Native Canadian Centre, was a real hub of activity, socially and culturally, in Toronto. That is not the case anymore; while it is more diverse and spread out, the communities themselves have seen a significant growth in cultural development and Indigeneity. The various centres of social activity have changed somehow in Toronto; it doesn't seem to be as inclusive, open, and accepting of people coming into the city. I noticed a greater degree of involvement and community engagement in the arts and music generally.

What should all people in Toronto understand about the Seventh Fire prophecy and teachings?

We are in a time of change. It's a time when the voices of young people will become significant in creating the change that is coming, and the change that is already here. It's always in the spirit of hope. It creates hope. Something is happening in the world that is significant for Indigenous people. Indigenous people are going to take their place on the historical and international stage. This is happening amongst the Anishinaabe people, but it's also happening globally.

Indigenous people have become involved in their way of thinking and doing things. One of the things that has become abundantly clear is that we are related to the environment. We are a part of a great family of this Earth. As a human member of this family of creation, we have a responsibility to take care of our mother, who is the Earth. To take care of creation, which includes all of the surrounding plant world, the medicines, the tree life, and the animal world.

We have to be the conscience and the voice for the natural world, including the water. This is happening everywhere. We were talking about oil, gas, the pipelines, cutting down trees, the rapid extinction of significant animals in our world and how fast that is happening long before the environmental movement. We have become aware of it. Indigenous people are the voice of all of those things. It's significant for us, for the preservation of our life, but also significant for the world. All that goes back to what the prophecies say about this time we are in – the time of the Seventh Fire we have to work together toward creating change in a meaningful way that is in keeping with the way that life is on the Earth.

NOTES

RISING LIKE A CLOUD: NEW HISTORIES OF 'OLD' TORONTO

1. In the index of the 1966 edition of Henry Scadding's *Toronto of Old*, there are few mentions of Indigenous people. But the following do appear: 'Mohawk,' 'Mississauga,' 'Onondaga,' and 'Anondaga.' Not as nations or communities with any humanity, but as schooners or warships named after these feared groups. Did the adoption of the savage Indian mascot used by the Redskins and Braves, or the U.S. military's Apache helicopter and Tomahawk missile, emerge in mid-1700s British North America?

SOURCES

Armstrong, Frederick H., ed. *Toronto of Old by Henry Scadding*. Toronto: Dundurn Press, 1966.

Arthur, Eric. *Toronto: No Mean City*. Toronto: University of Toronto Press, 1964.

Baily, Margaret. 'Writing on the Wall: The Blueprint to Building our History Can Be Read in the Changing Face of Our Edifices.' In *Toronto 150: The Celebration of Friends Commemorative Album*. Toronto Sesquicentennial Committee, 1984.

Bonnell, Jennifer. *Reclaiming the Don: An Environmental History of Toronto's Don River Valley*. Toronto: University of Toronto Press, 2012.

Firth, Edith. *The Town of York (1793–1815): A Collection of Documents of Early Toronto*. Toronto: University of Toronto Press, 1962.

Ford, Lisa. *Settler Sovereignty: Jurisdiction and Indigenous People in America and Australia, 1788–1836*. Cambridge: Harvard University Press, 2010.

Freeman, Victoria. 'Toronto Has No History! Indigeneity, Settler Colonialism and Historical Memory in Canada's Largest City.' *Urban History Review* 38, no. 2 (Spring 2010): 21–35.

Glazebrook, G. P. deT. *The Story of Toronto*. University of Toronto Press, 1971.

Innes, Mary Quayle, ed. *Mrs. Simcoe's Diary*. Toronto: Dundurn Press, 2007.

Kilbourn, William. *Toronto Remembered: A Celebration of the City*. Stoddart, 1984.

Kyte, E. C., ed. *Old Toronto: A Selection of Excerpts from 'Landmarks of Toronto' by John Ross Robertson*. Toronto: MacMillan, 1954.

Levine, Allan. *Toronto: A Biography of the City*. Madeira Park: Douglas & McIntyre, 2014.

Mackay, Claire, and Johnny Wales. *The Toronto Story*. Toronto: Annick Press, 1990.

O'Brien, Brendan. *Speedy Justice: The Tragic Last Voyage of His Majesty's Vessel Speedy*. Toronto: University of Toronto Press, 1992.

Scadding, Henry. *Toronto of Old Collections and Recollections Illustrative of the Early Settlement and Social Life of the Capital of Ontario*. Toronto: Adam, Stevenson & Co., 1873.

West, Bruce. *Toronto* (the Romance of Canadian Cities series). Toronto: Doubleday, 1979.

REMEMBER LIKE WE DO

1. Robert A. Williams, Jr. *Linking Arms Together: American Indian Treaty Visions of Law and Peace, 1600–1800*. Routledge, 1999.

2. Propositions made by the Sachims of the Five Nations to the Commissioners for the Indian affairs, Albany, June 30, 1700.

3. Indian Speeches to General Prescott. Michigan Historical Collections, 1796.

4. Robert S. Allen, 'Renewing the Chain of Friendship,' in *His Majesty's Indian Allies: British Indian Policy in the Defence of Canada 1774–1815*, (Toronto: Dundurn Press, 1992), 95.

5, *Constitution of the Iroquois Nations: The Great Binding Law, Gayanashagowa*, University of Kansas,

WILLIAMS TREATIES

1. Doug Williams, *Michi Saagiig Nishnaabeg: This Is Our Territory*. (Winnipeg: ARP Books, 2018), 159.

2. Ibid.

3. Manitowabi Final Report, p. 50.

4. Ibid., p. 61.

5. Ibid., p. 367.

6. This view is reflected in recent judicial decisions that have emphasized the responsibility of government to protect the rights of Indians arising from the special trust relationship created by history, treaties, and legislation. See Guerin v. The Queen, [1984] 2 S.C.R. 335; 55 N.R. 161; 13 D.L.R. (4th) 321. See R. v. Sparrow (1999).

7. On October 29, 2012, in *Alderville Indian Band et al. v. Her Majesty the Queen et al.*, Canada and Ontario took the position at trial that harvesting rights associated with pre-Confederation treaties signed by the Williams Treaties First Nations were not intended to be surrendered in 1923, particularly the Treaty 20 (1818) area, which was the subject of judicial scrutiny in Taylor and Williams, 1981.

8. The National Indian Brotherhood would become the Assembly of First Nations.

9. Union of B.C. Chiefs.

10. Williams, p. 148.

11. Manitowabi Final Report, p. 195.

12. Wanda Nanibush, 'In the Garden of Signs: Aboriginal Art Criticism.' *Urban Shaman Retrospective*. Winnipeg: Urban Shaman Gallery, 2009.

THE TWO LIVES OF DOCTOR O
SOURCES

'Body of Dr. Oronhyatekha Is Lying in State To-day.' *Toronto Daily Star*, March 6, 1907, p. 1.

Comeau-Vasilopoulos, Gayle M. 'Oronhyatekha.' *Dictionary of Canadian Biography*. www.biographi.ca/en/bio/oronhyatekha_13E.html

'Dr. Oronhyatekha Funeral to Be Held on Thursday.' *Toronto Daily Star*, March 4, 1907, p. 1.

'Dr. Oronhyatekha Replies to Aattacks.' *Globe and Mail*, June 19, 1903, p. 4.
'Dr. Oronhyatekha: An Interview.' *Globe and Mail*, June 24, 1893, p. 16.
'Her Kindred Mourned.' *Globe and Mail*, June 1, 1901, p. 7.
'Honor the Dead Chief.' *Globe and Mail*, March 6, 1907, p. 5.
'Indian as Orator.' *Globe and Mail*, Feb. 27, 1896, p. 2.
Jamieson, Keith, and Michelle Hamilton. *Dr. Oronhyatekha: Security, Justice and Equality*. Toronto: Dundurn Press, 2016.
'Last Sad Rites at Home.' *Globe and Mail*, March 9, 1907, p. 2.
'New Era in the History of Independent Forestry.' *Evening Star*, Aug. 28, 1897, p. 3.
Oronhyatekha. *History of the Independent Order of Foresters*. Toronto: Hunter, Rose & Company, 1895.
Temple-Bayard, Mary. 'Dr. Oronhyatekha.' *Globe and Mail*, June 13, 1896, p. 7.
'What the IOF Is Doing.' *Globe and Mail*, Sept. 7, 1907, p. 17.

THE DANCE OF CABBAGETOWN CONES TO SHIIBAASHKA'IGAN CONES

1. Anishinaabemowin/Ojibway language term for grandmother.

2. Anishinaabemowin/Ojibway language term for sacred medicine offering of tobacco.

3. Anishinaabemowin/Ojibway language term for the 'good life principles.'

4. Anishinaabemowin/Ojibway language term for grandfather.

5. An Anishinaabemowin/Ojibway concept that infers the attributes of an all-encompassing good life.

6. Anishinaabemowin/Ojibway language term meaning 'good.'

7. Anishinaabemowin/Ojibway language term for a cave, a burrow.

8. Through federal legislation, the Indian Act (1867) ruled that if a status Indian woman married a non-status, including any non-Indian, the woman would loss all her Treaty and Indians status rights. This sanction did not apply to status Indian men. Several women, including Jeannette Corbierre, challenged this patriarchal rule and had it reversed. Bill C-31 reinstated their Indian rights in 1985.

ROBERT MARKLE: THE POWER OF THE MARK/AT THE HINGE OF LIGHT AND DARK

1. 'The Landing of the Mohawks of the Bay of Quinte.' mbq-tmt.org/history/.

2. J. A. Wainwright, *Blazing Figures: A Life of Robert Markle*. (Waterloo: Wilfrid Laurier University Press, 2010), 15.

3. Ibid., p. 24.

4. Diane Pugen, telephone conversation with the author, August 12, 2020.

5. Les Automatistes were Paul-Émile Borduas, Marcel Barbeau, Roger Fauteux, Claude Gauvreau, Jean-Paul Riopelle, Pierre Gauvreau, Fernand Leduc, Jean-Paul Mousseau, Marcelle Ferron, and Françoise Sullivan.

6. Painters 11: Jack Bush, Oscar Cahén, Hortense Gordon, Thomas Hodgson, Alexandra Luke, J. W. G. (Jock) Macdonald, Ray Mead, Kazuo Nakamura, William Ronald, Harold Town, and Walter Yarwood.

7. Irving Layton, Leonard Cohen, Al Purdy, and Gwendolyn MacEwan all read at Isaacs Gallery.

8. Stephanie Philips, 'The Kahnawake Mohawks and the St Lawrence Seaway' (MA Thesis, 2000), 12.

9. Wainwright, pp. 76–79.

10. canadaehx.com/2020/08/22/the-kanesatake-resistance/

11. vitacollections.ca/sixnationsarchive/details.asp?ID=3175838

12. Wainwright, pp. 64–66.

13. *Art's Sake* opened with thirteen instructors, among them Dennis Burton, Robert Markle, Graham Caughtry, Gord Rayner, and Diane Pugen.

14. Wainwright, pp. 134–35

15. Paul Young, *Artists' Review* 11, no. 17, May 23, 1979 (cited in Wainwright, p. 183).

16. John Bentley Mays. *Globe and Mail*, June 21, 1980 (cited in Wainwright, pp. 184–85).

17. Wainwright, pp. 201–02.

18. A series of constitutional amendments designed to placate the province of Quebec.

KAPAPAMAHCHAKWEW: WANDERING SPIRIT SCHOOL AND THE VISION OF NIMKIIQUAY

1. Sharon Berg, *The Name Unspoken: Wandering Spirit Survival School* (Big Pond Rumours Press, 2019), 200.

2. Ibid., p. 194.

3. Ibid., p. 20.

4. Berg, Sharon. Personal communication, July 13 and 16, 2020.

5. This greatly abbreviated history is a composite of information from Sharon Berg's book (2019) and personal communication (July 13, 2020); *Dictionary of Canadian Biography* ('Kapapamahchakwew'), and my interview with Pauline Shirt on May 5, 2020.

6. Berg, *The Name Unspoken*, p. 113.

7. Ibid., p. 21.

8. *The Canadian Encyclopedia*, 'Native People's Caravan,' retrieved from thecanadianencyclopedia.ca/en/article/native-people-s-caravan#:~:text=The%20Native%20People's%20Caravan%20was,by%20Indigenous%20peoples%20in%20Canada.

9. For further details, see Vern Harper's *Following the Red Path: The Native People's Caravan*, 1974 (N.C. Press Limited, 1979), a first-person account of the Native People's Caravan.

10. As part of his vision for a 'just society,' in 1969 Prime Minister Pierre Trudeau and then Minister of Indian Affairs Jean Chrétien unveiled the White Paper, which would abolish the Indian Act and extinguish distinct Indigenous and treaty rights. Indigenous leaders swiftly rejected it as a denial of treaty rights and an attempt at cultural assimilation, inspiring nationwide organizing, activism, and legal action.

11. Berg, *The Name Unspoken*, p. 189.

12. Four Seasons' curriculum was developed to be in sync with the activities and ceremonies that take place during each season.

13. Pauline applied to the Ontario Ministry of Education.

14. Watch Albert Marshall's talk *Etuaptmumk Two-Eyed Seeing* (February 20, 2020) at www.youtube.com/watch?v=pJcjfinUckc.

VERNA JOHNSON, NOKOMIS

SOURCES

Alamenciak, Tim. 'Remembering "Grandma": Verna Johnston Smoothed the Transition to Toronto for Countless Native Kids.' *Toronto Star*, Jan. 18, 2015. www.thestar.com/news/gta/2015/01/18/remembering-grandma-verna-johnston-smoothed-the-transition-to-toronto-for-countless-native-kids.html

Enright, Nancy. 'Indian Foods Mix with Ojibwa Tales of Old at Festival.' *Globe and Mail*, April 28, 1982.

Howard-Bobiwash, Heather. 'Women's Class Strategies as Activism in Native Community Building in Toronto, 1950–1975.' *American Indian Quarterly* 27, nos. 3 & 4, (Summer/Fall 2003): pp. 566–82.

Katz, Sidney. 'Grandmother Helps Indian Youngsters Adapt to City Living.' *Toronto Star*, Oct. 10, 1969.

Keeshig, Jocelyn. 'Verna Patronella Johnston Interview.' Indian Film History Project. University of Regina, 1982. ourspace.uregina.ca/handle/ 10294/1859

Mason, Elizabeth. 'Verna Johnston Interview.' First Story Toronto. Native Canadian Centre of Toronto, 1982. firststoryblog.files.wordpress.com/ 2013/ 11/elizabeth-mason-interview-with-vj.pdf

Vanderburgh, R. M. *I Am Nokomis, Too: The Biography of Verna Patronella Johnston.* Don Mills: General Publishing Co., 1977.

'Verna Patronella Johnston.' First Story Toronto. Native Canadian Centre of Toronto, 2013. firststoryblog.wordpress.com/2013/11/17/verna-patronella-johnston/

MILLIE REDMOND: THE FLAME

SOURCES

Toronto Public Library Interview, Evelyn Sit at Council Fire, June 23, 1983.

'Council Fire: Building a Native community in Toronto.' *International Review of Mission*, vol. 71, issue 283 (July 1982).

Hewitt, Priscilla. 'Thoroughly Modest Millie.' *Canadian Woman Studies*, vol. 10, nos. 2–3 (1989).

DR. JANET SMYLIE AND 'OUR HEALTH COUNTS TORONTO'

1. www.welllivinghouse.com/wp-content/uploads/2017/02/PrelimFindingsOHC_May2016_June7.pdf and www.welllivinghouse.com/wp-content/uploads/ 2018/02/Demographics-OHC-Toronto.pdf

SOURCES

'Her Aboriginal Health Research Recognized,' *Queen's University Gazette*, 2012. www.queensu.ca/gazette/alumnireview/stories/her-aboriginal-health-research-recognized

St.Michael's Hospital, 'New Report Finds "Critical and Alarming Gap" in High Quality, Comprehensive and Inclusive Data for Urban Indigenous Populations in Canada, Feb. 18, 2018. www.stmichaelshospital.com/media/detail.php? source=hospital_news/2018/0228

Toronto Birth Centre (n.d.).torontobirthcentre.ca/

St. Michael's Hospital Research, 'Janet Smylie' (n.d.).stmichaelshospitalresearch. ca/researchers/janet-smylie/

Well Living House, *Our Health Counts Toronto: Access To Healthcare* (2018). www.well-livinghouse.com/wp-content/uploads/2019/02/Access-to-Health-Care-OHC-Toronto.pdf

Well Living House, *Our Health Counts Toronto: Adult Demographics* (2018). www.well-livinghouse.com/wp-content/uploads/2019/10/OHC-TO-Adult-Demo-graphics-.pdf

Well Living House, 'Our Health Counts Toronto: What We Do' (n.d). www.well-livinghouse.com/what-we-do/projects/our-health-counts-toronto/

THE GREAT INDIAN BUS TOUR OF TORONTO

1. The same mannequins used in those displays are repurposed in the current gallery through an Indigenous curatorial lens.

NOW THAT WE KNOW

1. Egerton Ryerson, 'Statistics Respecting Indian Schools' (Department of Indian Affairs, 1847), pp. 73–77.

2. Edwin Austen Hardy, *Centennial Story: The Board of Education for the City of Tkaronto 1850–1950*, ed. Honora M. Cochrane (Thomson Nelson and Sons Ltd, 1950).

3. Egerton Ryerson, *Annual Report 1847, Chief Superintendent of Schools* (Tkaronto: 1847), p. 6.

4. R. D. Gidney, 'Ryerson, Egerton,' in *Dictionary of Canadian Biography*, vol. 11, University of Tkaronto/Université Laval, 2003–, accessed October 27, 2020. www.biographi.ca/en/bio/ryerson_egerton_11E.html

5. Indian Affairs, *The Canadian Superintendent, 1965: The Education of Indian Children in Canada. A Symposium written by members of Indian Affairs Education Division, with comments by the Indian Peoples* (Tkaronto: Ryerson Press, 1965), pp. 13–14.

6. www.tvo.org/article/the-story-of-ontarios-last-segregated-black-school

7. Alison Prentice, *The School Promoters: Education and Social Class in Mid-Nineteenth Century Upper Canada* (Tkaronto: University of Tkaronto Press, 2004).

NO THRILLS AND BOUGIE BANNOCK

1. Yorkville is bordered on the north by Davenport Road, the oldest Native trail in Tkaronto. It went east to west, from London to Kingston, millennia before those places were called those places. (Paraphrased from Jon Johnson, First Story Toronto, west-end bus tour)

THE CONTRIBUTORS

Monique Aura Bedard (ukwe x they/them) is a neurodiverse Onyota'a:ka x French artmaker x visual storyteller currently based on Dish with One Spoon Territory (Tkaronto). They grew up on Anishinaabe aki, downriver from Aamjiwnaang First Nation. Through their art practice (sewing, beading, painting murals, journalling), they aim to express and share stories about intergenerational healing, neurodiversity, identity, empowerment, and truth. They are inspired by stories, memory, community, and growth, individually and collectively. Their art is their voice, their truth, and an extension of who they are. Aura's hope is that their art reaches others in a way that inspires thoughts and feelings, igniting questions, curiosity, reflection, and self-love.

A member of the Lac Seul First Nation (Anishinaabe), **Rebecca Belmore** is an internationally recognized multidisciplinary artist. Rooted in the political and social realities of Indigenous communities, Belmore's works make evocative connections between bodies, land, and language. Recent solo exhibitions include *Facing the Monumental*, Art Gallery of Ontario (2018), and *Rebecca Belmore: Kwe*, Justina M. Barnicke Gallery (2014). In 1991, *Ayumee-aawach Oomama-mowan: Speaking to Their Mother* was created at the Banff Centre for the Arts, with a national tour in 1992 and subsequent gatherings across Canada in 1996, 2008, and 2014. Belmore received the Governor-General's Award in Visual and Media Arts in 2013.

Susan Blight (Anishinaabe, Couchiching First Nation) is an interdisciplinary artist working with public art, site-specific intervention, photography, film, and social practice. Her solo and collaborative work engages questions of personal and cultural identity and its relationship to space. Susan is co-founder of Ogimaa Mikana, an artist collective working to reclaim and rename the roads and landmarks of Anishinaabeg territory with Anishinaabemowin. In August 2019, Susan joined OCAD University as Delaney Chair in Indigenous Visual Culture and as assistant professor in the Faculty of Liberal Arts & Sciences and School of Interdisciplinary Studies.

Elaine Bomberry is Anishinabe and Cayuga, from Six Nations of the Grand River Territory, in southern Ontario. She has worked as a freelance

Indigenous Performing Arts activist/promoter/manager/TV and radio producer full-time for thirty-four years. She has made her home on the Capilano Rez, on the unceded Squamish Nation territory in North Vancouver, British Columbia, with her husband, Juno award–winner Murray Porter, for the last fifteen years.

Born in Toronto, **Erica Commanda** (Algonquin/Ojibwe) grew up in the community of Pikwakanagan. From there, she moved across Canada, living in Ottawa, Vancouver, and Toronto again, working in the bar/hospitality industry, mastering the art of listening to stories from her regulars while slinging and spilling drinks (at them or to them). Through a series of random decisions and events, she went on a journey to master her own knack for storytelling as an arts reporter for MUSKRAT *Magazine*, interning with Coach House Books for the Indigenous Toronto anthology, and studying broadcasting at Seneca College.

Anishinaabe-izhini-kaaz-o-win Nodj-mowin-Miskogayaashk Gichi-mani-doo-anishinaabe indoodem Mishu-pishu niin Anishinaabe, Shawnee, Lakota, Potawatomi, Ojibway, Algonquin Min-a-waa Mohawk. **Philip Cote**, MFA, Moose Deer Point First Nation, is a Young Spiritual Elder, Indigenous artist, activist, educator, historian, and Ancestral Knowledge Keeper. He is engaged in creating opportunities for artmaking and teaching methodologies through Indigenous symbolism, traditional ceremonies, history, oral stories, and land-based pedagogy. Citing all of his ancestry, he is Shawnee, Lakota, Potawatomi, Ojibway, Algonquin, and Mohawk. Philip is the seventh generation great-grandson of Shawnee Warrior and Leader Tecumseh, and his ancestor Amelia Chechok is the granddaughter of Chechok who was the first signer of the Toronto Purchase of 1805.

Margaret Cozry originates from Ojibwe First Nation on Wasauksing Lake, Parry Sound. She served as a board member for the Native Canadian Centre of Toronto and Wigwamen Inc. Margaret was awarded the Res '90 Merit of Excellence in Business and the First Prize display award at the inaugural Skydome Pow-Wow. She participated in Miziiwe Biik Employment and Training Panel of Entrepreneurs/Urban Aboriginal Entrepreneur Focus Group. Her work took her to Germany and France, among other destinations. All her achievements were accomplished without government funding.

Bonnie Devine is an installation artist, curator, and educator whose art projects have been exhibited nationally and internationally. She is the founding chair of the Indigenous Visual Culture program at OCAD University and a member of the Anishinaabek of Genaabaajing, Serpent River First Nation.

Onaubinisay indizhinikawz Waubezhayshee indodem, Shawanaga indonjibaa. **Jim Dumont** is an internationally renowned Elder, speaker, and traditional knowledge keeper, also known as the Gichi A:ya: the Elder of the Elders in the Eastern Doorway of the Three Fires Midewiwin Lodge. In 2011, Jim was awarded a Doctorate of Sacred Letters, the first of its kind at the University of Sudbury, for his work in establishing the Department of Native Studies and designing and delivering the Indigenous knowledge courses, and in 2015 received a Doctorate of Anishnaabe Philosophy from the 7th Generation Institute and the World Indigenous Nations Higher Education Consortium.

Joe Hester comes from the Cree community of Waskaganish, located on the southeast shore of James Bay in northern Quebec. He first moved to Toronto in 1967 with his parents and began working at Anishnawbe Health ten years later. He is the current executive director of Anishnawbe Health Toronto.

Heather Howard-Bobiwash is an associate professor of anthropology at Michigan State University and has an appointment with the Centre for Indigenous Studies at the University of Toronto. Centred on collaborative and Indigenous community-driven approaches to research, her work promotes the value of Indigenous knowledge frameworks to scholarship and research that are meaningful to community. Heather has twenty-five years of experience in public education, cultural change and technologies, and community-based organizing of projects that serve the dual role of strengthening Indigenous self-determination and furthering public education on Indigenous issues.

Falen Johnson is Mohawk and Tuscarora (Bear Clan) from Six Nations Grand River Territory. Her plays include *Salt Baby*, *Two Indians*, and *Ipperwash*. She co-hosts *The Secret Life of Canada* (CBC Podcasts) with Leah Simone Bowen and *Unreserved* (CBC Radio One).

Jon Johnson is an Assistant Professor, Teaching Stream, at Woodsworth College, University of Toronto. His research is focused on urban land-based Indigenous Knowledge in Toronto and its representation through oral and digital forms of storytelling. He works actively within Toronto's Indigenous community in his capacity as a lead organizer for First Story Toronto, an Indigenous-led community-based organization that researches and shares Toronto's Indigenous presence through popular education initiatives such as storytelling tours of the city and its freely available smart phone application. He is particularly interested in projects that create mutually respectful and beneficial collaborations between Indigenous communities and the university.

Sarena Sekwun Johnson is Lenni Lenape from Moraviantown, Muncey Delaware and Six Nations, Nehiyaw Michif from Round Prairie, and Anishinaabe from Caldwell First Nation. Sarena is a novice archer, writer, artist, and language learner. Born and raised in Scarborough, she has worked in front-line and communications roles in Tkaronto Indigenous organizations since 2004 and currently does Indigenous resurgence work with student services at Ryerson University.

Hayden King is Anishinaabe from Beausoleil First Nation on Gchi'mnissing in Huronia, Ontario, and a member of the Williams Treaty, which covers Toronto east of the Don River. Hayden is also the executive director of Yellowhead Institute and a professor of sociology at Ryerson University.

Nadya Kwandibens is Anishinaabe from Animakee Wa Zhing #37 First Nation in northwestern Ontario. She is an award-winning portrait and events photographer, an ambassador for Canon, and has travelled extensively across Canada for over fourteen years. In 2008, she founded Red Works, a dynamic photography company empowering contemporary Indigenous cultures through photographic series and features. Red Works also provides image-licensing, workshops, and presentations. Nadya's photography has been shown in group and solo exhibitions across Canada and the United States. She currently resides in Toronto.

Louis Lesage is a member of the Huron-Wendat Nation and lives in Wendake. He holds a master's degree and a PhD in biology from Laval University. He worked for the Canadian Wildlife Service as a biologist/

Aboriginal Liaison from 2005 to 2011. At the CWS, he also contributed to the recovery of species at risk of extinction. Louis Lesage also chaired the Joint Committee on Hunting, Fishing and Trapping of the James Bay and Northern Quebec Agreement from 2006 to 2011. He is now director of the Nionwentsïo Board of Directors' Office, Huron-Wendat Nation.

Ange Loft is an interdisciplinary performing artist and initiator from Kahnawake Kanien'kehá:ka Territory, working in Toronto. She is an ardent collaborator, consultant and facilitator working in storyweaving, arts-based research, wearable sculpture, and Haudenosaunee history. Ange is a vocalist with Yamantaka/SonicTitan and is associate artistic director of Jumblies Theatre and Arts, where she directs the Talking Treaties initiative.

Andre Morriseau (Fort William First Nation) is an enthusiastic advocate and ambassador for Indigenous arts, culture, and public affairs. Former secretariat for the National Aboriginal Achievement Foundation (now Indspire) and communications officer for the Chiefs of Ontario (COO). He chaired the James Bartleman Aboriginal Youth Creative Writing Awards Jury (Ontario Arts Council) and the imagineNATIVE Film & Media Arts Festival. Currently, Andre is chair of the Anishnawbe Health Foundation and on the board of TakingITGlobal. He is the former Director, Awards & Communications, for the Canadian Council for Aboriginal Business, and is currently communication manager for the Ontario Native Women's Association.

Miles Morrisseau is a Métis writer, journalist, and multimedia producer from the Métis Homeland in Manitoba. He began his career as a writer/broadcaster for CBC Radio in Winnipeg and produced documentaries on Sunday Morning, CBC Radio's flagship documentary program. As National Native Affairs Broadcaster, Miles covered the Mohawk Gambling War in Akwesasne, the death of the Meech Lake Accord, and had access behind the barricades during the Oka Crisis, entering on one of a handful of boats that smuggled in food and medicine. He served as editor-in-chief of *Nativebeat, the Beat of a Different Drum*, which was chosen best Native American Monthly by the Native American Journalists Association, as well as *Aboriginal Voices Magazine* and *Indian Country Today*. Miles also produced Buffalo Tracks with Evan Adams for APTN and launched Streetz FM, the first radio station by and for Indigenous youth. He has six children and seven grandchildren, and has been with his partner, Shelly Bressette, for over thirty-five years. He lives in the historic Métis community of Grand Rapids, Manitoba, on the last piece of Métis scrip land still in the hands of Métis people.

Daniel David Moses was registered as a Delaware Indian, though he hailed from the Six Nations lands located on the Grand River near Brantford, Ontario. He held a BA, Honours, from York University and an MFA from the University of British Columbia. From 1979, he worked as an independent, Toronto-based artist, at first as a poet and, subsequently, as a playwright, dramaturge, editor, essayist, teacher, and artist-, playwright- or writer-in-residence with institutions as varied as Theatre Passe Muraille, Banff Centre for the Arts, University of British Columbia, University of Western Ontario, University of Windsor, University of Toronto (Scarborough), Sage Hill Writing Experience, McMaster University, and Concordia University. He also served on the boards of the Association for Native Development in the Performing and Visual Arts, Native Earth Performing Arts, and the Playwrights Union of Canada (now the Playwrights Guild of Canada), and co-founded (with Lenore Keeshig-Tobias and Tomson Highway) the short-lived but influential Committee to Re-Establish the Trickster. In 2016, he was inducted as a Fellow to the Royal Society of Canada. He passed away on July 13, 2020.

Wanda Nanibush is an Anishinaabe-kwe image and word warrior, curator, and community organizer from Beausoleil First Nation. Currently Nanibush is the inaugural curator of Indigenous art and co-head of the Indigenous + Canadian Art department at Art Gallery of Ontario. Her current AGO exhibition, *Rebecca Belmore: Facing the Monumental*, is touring internationally. Nanibush has a master's of visual studies from University of Toronto, where she has taught graduate courses. On top of many catalogue essays, Nanibush has published widely on Indigenous art, politics, history, and feminism and sexuality.

Karen Pheasant-Neganigwane is Anishinaabe and an advocate of social change through expressions of dance, text, and teaching. Karen's path to activism and scholarly work started as a youth during the height of the civil rights era of the seventies. The social project of Rochdale College (Toronto), led with 'idealism, artistic spirit and free speech,' provided the embryonic opening for her inquisitive spirit. Through ceremony and mentorship, Karen has spent the past forty years mentored by iconic Indigenous scholars from the Great Lakes of her people to Treaty Three, Treaty Six, and currently in Treaty Seven. Karen's studies are in poli-sci (BA '03), Eng lit (BA '11), and education (MEd '13). She is currently working on her doctorate, on the topic of Indigenous thought and pedagogy.

Tannis Nielsen (Métis/Danish) has twenty years of professional experience in the arts, cultural, and community sectors. She holds a Masters in Visual Studies from the University of Toronto. Her dissertation asserted the need for localized Indigenous contexts to be inserted accurately within the structures of the academy by visually illustrating the negative consequence of colonial trauma on Indigenous culture/land/language, familial relationships, and memory. She currently teaches the Teaching Intensive Stream at OCAD University, while working on a large-scale public art commission for the City of Toronto.

Lila Pine, Mi'gmewi'sgw of mixed ancestry, is bound by the Peace and Friendship Treaty. She divides her time between Mi'gma'gi, where she belongs, and Tkaronto, where she teaches in the RTA School of Media at a downtown university. Her research seeks to develop a way of 'seeing' sound in order to identify distinct qualities in the speaking of different languages with the goal of better understanding how language informs knowledge(s). Recently, Lila launched Moon Talks, a speaking series that brings together Indigenous and Black anti-racism thinkers. She is also collaborating with Buffy Sainte-Marie on a project called Creative Native: Youth Mentorship in the Arts Initiative.

Kerry Potts is Teme-Augama Anishnabai of mixed heritage, with familial roots in Temagami and Prince Edward Island. A professor of liberal studies at Humber College, she has also taught at George Brown College, Seneca College, and OISE/University of Toronto. At Humber, Kerry is a member of the Indigenous Education Council, and created a course entitled Indigenous Perspectives on Music, Film and Media based on her career in the film, media, and performing arts sectors. For over twenty years she has been fortunate to work and volunteer at a number of social service and arts organizations across T'karonto, and is thankful for all of the teachers, in many forms, who have helped shape her experiences and understanding of the world.

Dr. Duke Redbird is an established Indigenous intellectual, poet, painter, broadcaster, filmmaker and keynote speaker. He was instrumental in the implementation of innovative multimedia, technologies and beyond, bringing an Indigenous approach to art education that was rooted in his pioneering work at OCAD University. His art has been exhibited and his poetry has been published and translated in anthologies around the world. Dr. Redbird received his Master of Arts in Interdisciplinary Studies from York University in 1978, and his Doctorate from OCAD University in 2013. His published book of poetry *Loveshine and Red Wine* was the inspiration for a multimedia musical production at a command performance before Queen Elizabeth II.

Johl Whiteduck Ringuette is Anishnawbe and Algonquin, a descendant of Nipissing Nation, and from the Mink Clan. He is the chef and proprietor of NishDish Marketeria & Catering, specializing in Anishnawbe cuisine since 2005. As one of Tkaronto's leading First Nations food sovereigntists, Johl's journey has led him to reclaiming the traditional Anishnawbe diet.

Jason Ryle is Anishinaabe from Lake St. Martin First Nation (Manitoba). He lives in Toronto and was executive director of imagineNATIVE from 2010 to 2020.

Born and raised on the Six Nations of the Grand River until she was eighteen, **Margaret Sault** married and was transferred by Indian Affairs into the Mississaugas of the Credit First Nation, where she lived and raised her family. Margaret has worked with the Mississaugas of the Credit First Nation Council since 1977 and currently serves as the Director of Lands, Membership and Research. She presents frequently to non-Indigenous peoples and has developed educational materials, including booklets and a video, on the history of the Mississaugas of the Credit. Margaret was also part of the negotiating team that resolved four land claims and served for two years (2015–17) as a councillor. In 2009, she completed a Personal Support Worker Certificate from Mohawk College to be able to care for her aging parents, and continues to work part-time as a PSW in Six Nations.

Margaret has three adult sons and is 'gramma' to five grandchildren, the position that is dearest to her heart.

Dr. Janet Smylie is the Director of the Well Living House Action Research Centre for Indigenous Infant, Child, and Family Health and Well-Being, Tier 1 Canada Research Chair in Advancing Generative Health Services for Indigenous Populations in Canada, and Professor at the Dalla Lana School of Public Health, University of Toronto. Her research focuses on addressing Indigenous health inequities in partnership with Indigenous communities, ensuring all Indigenous peoples are counted into health policy and planning wherever they live in ways that make sense to them; addressing anti-Indigenous racism in health services; and advancing community-rooted innovations in health services for Indigenous populations.

Kory Snache is an accomplished educator, filmmaker, cultural programmer, and adventure guide. His family comes from the Sturgeon clan of the Anishnaabeg and his ancestors come from the community of Mnjikaning. His passions have taken him international, working with organizations and communities helping humans consider their impacts and interactions with the natural world. Kory carries forward the traditional understandings of his people to deliver educational and cultural programming with an Indigenous lens.

Drew Hayden Taylor is an award-winning playwright, novelist, journalist, and filmmaker. Born and living on the Curve Lake First Nation, he has done everything from performing stand-up comedy at the Kennedy Center in Washington, D.C., to serving as artistic director of Canada's premiere Indigenous theatre company, Native Earth Performing Arts. The author of thirty-three books, Drew is currently working on a documentary series about Indigenous people for APTN, called *Going Native*.

Stacey Taylor is an Anishinaabekwe of the Michi saagiig. She has been a terrestrial archaeologist with Parks Canada for almost twenty years, working in national parks and national historic sites in Ontario, Nova Scotia, Quebec, and Northwest Territories. Though focused on Indigenous archaeological sites within Ontario, Stacey has conducted archaeology in Italy and Greece. She is learning Anishinaabemowin, her Indigenous language. An avid world traveller, Stacey enjoys cycling and hiking in her spare time.

Ronald F. Williamson is founder of Archaeological Services Inc. He is an adjunct professor in anthropology at the University of Toronto and Western University, chair of the Board of Directors of the Museum of Ontario Archaeology at Western, and vice-chair of the Shared Path Consultation Initiative. He has published extensively on both Indigenous and early colonial Great Lakes history.

PROJECT MANAGER

Journalist **John Lorinc** is the Toronto Non-Fiction Editor for Coach House Books. His parents fled Hungary and anti-Semitism, settling in Toronto in late 1956. John contributes regularly to local and national media, including *Spacing*, the *Globe and Mail*, the *Toronto Star*, and *The Walrus*. He was the 2019–20 Atkinson Fellow in Public Policy, focusing on smart cities. John is the author of three books, and has co-edited five previous anthologies, including *The Ward* and *Any Other Way*, both part of Coach House's ongoing uTOpia series.

THE EDITORS

Denise Bolduc creates, curates, and produces innovative platforms inspiring creative experiences, transformation, and exchange. Throughout her expansive career of close to thirty years in arts and culture, Denise has committed to elevating Indigenous voices with countless celebrated artists, creative thinkers, and leading cultural institutions across Turtle Island and globally. Denise is Ojibwe-Anishnaabe and French from the Lake Superior–Robinson Huron Treaty Territory, and is a member of the Batchewana First Nation, with deep familial roots in Ketegaunseebee/Garden River First Nation.

Mnawaate Gordon-Corbiere is Grouse clan and a member of M'Chigeeng First Nation. She is Ojibwe and Cree. Born in Toronto and raised in M'Chigeeng, in 2019 she obtained her BA, majoring in history and English, from the University of Toronto. While completing her degree, she worked with the Great Lakes Research Alliance for the Study of Aboriginal Arts and Cultures to migrate its new database. Upon graduating, Mnawaate worked with Heritage Toronto as the agency's Indigenous Content Coordinator. This project marks her first time working as a co-editor and contributor to an anthology.

Media and story creator **Rebeka Tabobondung** is the founder and editor-in-chief of MUSKRAT *Magazine*, a leading online Indigenous arts and culture magazine. Rebeka is also a filmmaker, writer, poet, and Indigenous knowledge researcher. In 2015, Rebeka co-founded the Gchi Dewin Indigenous Storytellers Festival in Wasauksing First Nation, along the beautiful shores of Georgian Bay, where she is also a member. Since 2017, she has been working as a creator, researcher, and writer with award-winning Montreal-based Rezolution Pictures. Rebeka is the co-owner of the award-winning whole communications company Maaiingan Productions. In 2019, she and her partner acquired ReZ 91.3 FM, a designated Native community radio station.

Widely recognized as the authority on Native music, **Brian Wright-McLeod** (Dakota/Anishnabe) is a Toronto-based author, artist, producer, archivist, and educator. His radio work resulted in *The Encyclopedia of Native Music* and the companion three-CD *Soundtrack of a People,* which were the basis for the Smithsonian Institute's Native music exhibit *Up Where We Belong* and the documentary film *Rumble,* which earned three 2018 Canadian Screen Awards and a 2020 Emmy nomination. Brian has lectured internationally, worked as a music consultant for film, television, and recording projects. He served on the Juno Awards Indigenous music committee and helped establish the Native American Music category for the Grammy Awards. He teaches Indigenous music and media at Centennial College, George Brown College, and York University. New projects include an essay collection on pedagogy with Routledge Press; a documentation project on *Renegade Radio* with University of California, Berkeley; a book version of *Rumble;* and the completion of his graphic novel series, *Red Power.*

ACKNOWLEDGEMENTS

Denise Bolduc: Gchi miigwech to the land, water, air, and animals for the teachings, stories, and gifts you offer. Gchi miigwech to my ancestors, family, partner, friends, mentors, and teachers who have guided me on this life-path. My deepest respect and appreciation to the team at Coach House, editorial colleagues, the storytellers, Tomson Highway, Wayne Booker, Jay Pitter, and my dear friend, the late Gregory Younging.

Mnawaate Gordon-Corbiere: Thanks to my friends, family, and teachers.

Rebeka Tabobondung: To all Indigenous Peoples who have lived in Toronto, you've blessed the land with your spirit and presence. And to the storytellers who've welcomed Indigenous presence and done the beautiful work of unearthing, remembering, creating, and sharing their stories with us. Chi-Miigwetch (Big Thanks!) to my partner David Shilling for introducing me to the city and its many hidden familial stories, and to our son, Zeegwon Shilling-Tabobondung, who inspired me to unearth and share them.

Brian Wright-McLeod: To Mother Earth; the Great Spirit; the ancestors, my entire family: brothers, sisters, my son and future generations. Those who helped guide me through this journey – Tomson Highway, Jay Mason, Art Solomon, the Dreavers, Leonard Crow Dog, Joe Chasing Horse, Agnes Patak, Paul De Main of *News from Indian Country*, CKLN 88.1 FM, and everyone who touched my life at different times.

John Lorinc: I am enormously grateful to have had the opportunity to collaborate on this project with four such collegial and engaged co-editors, and also to have met and worked with this book's amazing contributors, who taught me a great deal about the city I love.

The entire editorial/project team would also like to acknowledge and thank Lee Maracle, Cherie Dimaline, Elaine Bomberry, and Hayden King for their advice and contributions throughout; Barb Curley, Eric Ladelpha and the members of Daniel David Moses' extended family;

Keith Barker, artistic director at Native Earth Performing Arts; Elder Carolyn King, C.M., former Chief, Mississaugas of the Credit First Nation; Amy Furness and Tracy Mallon-Jensen of the Art Gallery of Ontario; Kaitlin Wainright and Heritage Toronto; and the fabulous Coach House Books crew for their hard work and commitment to seeing this book through to fruition: Crystal Sikma, James Lindsay, Stuart Ross, Emily Hamilton, Tali Voron, Rick/Simon, John De Jesus, Nick Hilton, Stan Bevington, and Alana Wilcox.

IMAGE CREDITS

p. 18. Map of the Toronto Carrying Place, public domain, from Wikipedia; p. 19. Map of Lac de Taronto, public domain, University of Toronto Map and Data Library, NMC 6409; p. 27. Photograph of Dish with One Spoon wampum belt, public domain; pp. 31, 34–35. X by Rebecca Belmore, photographs courtesy of Rebecca Belmore; p. 39. Signatories of the Toronto Purchase, public domain; p. 40. Map of the Toronto Purchase, public domain; p. 42. Toronto Purchase, public domain; p. 45. Projectile point, photograph courtesy of ASI; p. 46. Carving, photograph courtesy of Museum of Ontario Archaeology; p. 48. Ossuary map, courtesy of ASI; p. 53. Pipe illustration, courtesy of ASI; pp. 56–57. Archaeologists, photograph courtesy Stacey Taylor; p. 65. *The Original Family* by Philip Cote, photograph by Bryan Taguba; p. 66. *Resurge: First Timeline* by Philip Cote, photograph by Nelly Torossian; pp. 68–69. *The History of the Land* by Philip Cote, photograph by Bryan Taguba; p. 71. *Ojibway Dreamer* by Philip Cote, photograph by Nelly Torossian; p. 78. Photograph of Tannis Nielsen by Tia Cavanagh, courtesy of Tannis Nielsen; pp. 80, 81. Photographs of the Simcoe Street Mural, courtesy of Tannis Nielsen; p. 85. Photoraph of Oronhyatekha, used with permission of the Woodland Cultural Centre; p. 89. Temple Building, Library and Archives Canada/Canadian Intellectual Property Office fonds/ao28963; p. 90. Sherwood's Castle, public domain, from Wikipedia; p. 91. Oronhyatekha, used with permission of the Deseronto Archives; p. 94. Family photograph, courtesy of Karen Pheasant-Neganigwane; pp. 101, 102. Family photographs courtesy of Elaine Bomberry; p. 112. Photograph of Robert Markle teaching, courtesy of Diane Pugen; p. 113. Robert Markle, *Denim jacket*, used with permission of the Art Gallery of Ontario. Gift of Marlene Markle, 2004. LA.RMF.S17.F1.1. © Estate of Robert Markle, Photo: AGO; p. 115. Robert Markle, *Lovers II*, used with permission of the Art Gallery of Ontario. Purchased with funds donated by AGO Members, 2001. 2001/11. © Estate of Robert Markle, Photo: AGO; p. 117. Photograph of Robert Markle, courtesy of Diane Pugen; p. 123. Photograph of *Dry Lips* cast by Michael Cooper; p. 125. Photograph of Tomson Highway by Sean Howard; p. 135. *Cottagers and Indians* photograph by Cylla von Tiedemann, courtesy of Tarragon Theatre; p. 140. Photograph of Daniel David Moses by Eric Ladelpha; p. 149. Photograph of scene from *Two Indians*, courtesy of Falen Johnson; pp. 155, 157. Photographs of Margaret Cozry, courtesy of Margaret Cozry; p. 159. Scan of prize ribbon, courtesy of Margaret Cozry; pp. 165–168. Photographs of the Ogimaa Mikana Project, courtesy of Hayden King and Susan Blight; p. 177.

Photograph of Pauline Shirt (Nimkiiquay) by Nadya Kwandibens, Red Works Photography; pp. 191–192. Graphs from 'Our Health Counts,' courtesy of Janet Smylie; p. 199, 200. *Renegade Radio* images, courtesy Brian Wright-McLeod; p. 200. Courtesy Brian Wright-McLeod; p. 208. Photograph of Andre Morriseau, courtesy of Andre Morriseau; p. 212. *Ontario Indian* cover, courtesy Brian Wright-McLeod Archive; p. 213. *Poetry Toronto* cover, courtesy Brian Wright-McLeod Archive; p. 215. *The Phoenix* cover, courtesy Brian Wright-McLeod Archive; p. 216. Honour Mother Earth Day ad, courtesy Brian Wright-McLeod Archive; p. 217. *The Phoenix* cover, courtesy Brian Wright-McLeod Archive; p. 219, 220. Demonstrations, photographs by Henry Martinuk, courtesy of Henry Martinuk; p. 223. Artist photograph, used with permission of Nadya Kwandibens; pp. 224, 225, 226. Images from *Concrete Indians* by Nadya Kwandibens, used with permission of Nadya Kwandibens; p. 231. The Great Indian Bus Tour of Toronto postcard, courtesy of First Story Toronto; p. 255. Image courtesy of Lila Pine; p. 260, 261. *Whole Wigwam* by Sarena Johnson, photograph by David Draper; p. 267. *Medicine for the People* by Red Urban Nation Artists Collective, photograph courtesy of Johl Whiteduck Ringuette; p. 270. *Elder Grandma Pauline Shirt Blessing the Water in Ceremony* by Red Urban Nation Artists Collective, photograph courtesy of Johl Whiteduck Ringuette; p. 272. Gathering Place Trail, Gathering Structure, photographs by Tom Ridout.

Typeset in Albertina and Hero Neue.

Printed at the Coach House on bpNichol Lane in Toronto, Ontario, on Lynx Cream paper. This book was printed with vegetable-based ink on a 1973 Heidelberg KORD offset litho press. Its pages were folded on a Baumfolder, gathered by hand, bound on a Sulby Auto-Minabinda, and trimmed on a Polar single-knife cutter.

Coach House is located on the traditional territory of many nations, including the Mississaugas of the Credit, the Anishnaabeg, the Haudenosaunee, the Chippewa, and the Wendat peoples, and is now home to many diverse First Nations, Métis, and Inuit people. Toronto is covered by Treaty 13 signed with the Mississaugas of the Credit, and the Williams Treaties signed with multiple Mississaugas and Chippewa bands. We are grateful to live and work on this land.

Seen through the press by John Lorinc
Cover and section title page art by mo (monique aura bedard)
Cover and interior design by Crystal Sikma

Coach House Books
80 bpNichol Lane
Toronto ON M5S 3J4
Canada

416 979 2217
800 367 6360

mail@chbooks.com
www.chbooks.com